MW00618844

EFFECTIVE NEGOTIATION
AND CONFLICT RESOLUTION
IN TODAY'S ENVIRONMENT

A READER

FIRST EDITION

TIMOTHY GRAINEY

Arizona State University

cognella® | ACADEMIC PUBLISHING

Bassim Hamadeh, CEO and Publisher
Kassie Graves, Director of Acquisitions and Sales
Jamie Giganti, Senior Managing Editor
Jess Estrella, Senior Graphic Designer
Susana Christie, Developmental Editor
Natalie Lakosil, Licensing Manager
Abbey Hastings, Associate Production Editor

Copyright © 2018 by Cognella, Inc. All rights reserved. No part of this publication may be reprinted, reproduced, transmitted, or utilized in any form or by any electronic, mechanical, or other means, now known or hereafter invented, including photo-copying, microfilming, and recording, or in any information retrieval system without the written permission of Cognella, Inc. For inquiries regarding permissions, translations, foreign rights, audio rights, and any other forms of reproduction, please contact the Cognella Licensing Department at rights@cognella.com.

Trademark Notice: Product or corporate names may be trademarks or registered trademarks, and are used only for identification and explanation without intent to infringe.

Cover image copyright © 2016 by Arianna Grainey. Reprinted with permission.

Printed in the United States of America

ISBN: 978-1-5165-1341-3 (pb) / 978-1-5165-1342-0 (br)

CONTENTS

INTRODUCTION

The purpose of this book is to provide the reader with theoretical approaches and practical suggestions—along with real life examples—that explore how to use effective strategies for negotiations and conflict resolution. The goal is for the reader to learn the benefits of being flexible in negotiations and the importance of planning and research ahead of these situations.

The book is divided into four units. Unit 1 presents seven chapters analyzing such key concepts as developing a bottom line, goal, and most desired objective; negotiating with multiple variables; and setting traps for the other party. Unit 2's five chapters explore negotiations in cross-cultural situations, highlighting the dangers of stereotyping, styles of reasoning, and other key concepts. Unit 3 has three chapters specifically focused on applied business and organizational negotiations, stressing the importance of salary negotiations for first-time and more experienced workers. Unit 4 concludes with five applied chapters on conflict resolution, including direct and indirect confrontations and salvaging bad situations.

The chapters present a variety of examples and settings, including applications within the automotive industry, environmental negotiations, and international business settings and concluding with Chapter 20's case study of hostage-taking negotiations—certainly the most stressful situation anyone could encounter. Though the book surveys a number of different examples and issues, the focus is to leave the reader with a coherent and fully applicable understanding of how to plan a negotiation, manage it, and conclude it with both sides satisfied and willing to work together in the future.

UNIT 1 OVERVIEW

BASICS OF NEGOTIATIONS

The goal of this unit is to provide the reader with the necessary basics to become a more astute negotiator. Readers will learn that a negotiation is a process and how to guide it to a successful conclusion, not just for their benefit, but to maximize *the gains for both parties*. This unit *combines* fundamental concepts, found in Chapters 1 and 2 with practical application through the case studies in Chapters 3 and 4. These cases feature a car purchase negotiation—a situation that many people dread—in Chapter 3 along with a land use negotiation with environmental implications in Chapter 4.

We focus on overcoming obstacles while allowing the negotiation to continue, including reviewing traps that professional negotiators use, such as a false "time urgency," "limited budget," or a "fait accompli" for an item that has not been discussed. These and other traps are used to pigeonhole your counterpart to an agreement that is more advantageous to you. We want to avoid using them but also know how to counter the tactics if they are used on us. Chapter 5 presents the benefits of using professionals to help mediate negotiations.

Some of the key concepts in this unit include:

- The benefits of a Win-Win Approach
- The power of multi-issue negotiations, which allow the sides to move beyond straight price bargaining
- The common steps in presenting and countering offers
- Stemming high-pressure negotiation situations

- The importance of research and planning for a negotiation
- Developing a bottom line, goal, and most desired objective during the planning process
- Closing a deal and ensuring that it is final
- Overcoming roadblocks in negotiations
- When to use non-partisan intermediaries, a facilitator, mediator, or arbitrator, and the unique pressures of the role
- Reviewing the traps of professional negotiators and how to counter them
- Things to avoid doing during a negotiation

In Chapter 1, Tim Grainey discusses using techniques including thorough preparation, developing a bottom line, setting a goal and most desired objective, and adding other issues besides price to assist you in developing a collaborative negotiation that is productive for you and the other side in the process. You will also see why viewing any negotiation as a long-term relationship is a benefit to both sides.

Chapter 1

Becoming a Better Negotiator

by Tim Grainey

This chapter presents some suggestions for negotiators to increase the effectiveness of the process for *both parties*, rather than thinking only about how much your side stands to gain. We should approach a negotiation understanding that we may find ourselves engaged repeatedly in this process, possibly even over the space of years. Maximizing the outcome for both sides then becomes a priority, wherein the other side will trust you more and actually look forward to working with you.

It is important for all parties to approach the event with an attitude of "Win-Win" rather than "Win-Lose." The "Win-Lose" strategy (or "more for me") tends to prioritize *compromising*, in which each side makes sacrifices to reach a solution. Compromises tend to leave both sides dissatisfied, as they both give up something, usually splitting the difference. If you have a dispute over a bill and believe that you owe $1,000 while your supplier wants $2,000, in many cases, the result is a compromise in which the difference is split in half, and you have to pay $1,500. You are unhappy because you paid $500 more than you wanted, and your supplier is annoyed for receiving $500 less than they wanted.

I was involved in a negotiation with a Fortune 500 company for a large project worth several hundred thousand dollars. There was some disagreement over the final amount that our company was owed, which amounted to $80,000. After months of negotiations—during which our costs were rising as the amount owed was in a foreign currency, which was declining in value versus the U.S. dollar at the time—with senior financial people, and 20 minutes of buildup, my client suggested that we "split the difference." My impulsive reaction was, "Really? That's the best you can come up with after months of internal review?" which wasn't well received, but I did make my point. The compromise, which we had to accept, amounted to a loss of $40,000 and ended the dispute, but it was unsatisfying, because the parties did not challenge themselves to consider different approaches. It was an opportunity-lost, instead settling for a quick and easy solution.

A better approach than compromising is *collaborating*. Collaborators approach each negotiation by making a conscious effort to understand the other side's point of view and work with them to resolve the problem by taking the time to develop creative and unique solutions that benefit both sides.

I once had a situation with a client, which had awarded us a large customer satisfaction telephone interview project worth just under $500,000 a year on a 3-year contract. The client had provided information on what their previous supplier had done. On the basis of that information, we assumed we would average three completed telephone interviews an hour. Once we started, the sample—which came from the client's stores—was problematic, and we were receiving less than one completed telephone interview an hour. My boss was apoplectic; he wanted to shut down the project and cancel the contract since we would have substantial losses over the 3-year period at that productivity rate. I spoke with the client and explained the situation. The client's initial reaction was, "Can we wait and address it under the next contract?" I did not disclose what my boss's knee-jerk reaction was; however, I emphasized that the issue was something that we needed to address quickly. After a few meetings and analyzing data, my client suggested that we add a small surcharge to stores that provided incomplete customer records (bad phone numbers, email addresses, etc.). This provided us with additional revenue while incentivizing the retailers to send accurate and complete data. This client-suggested change resulted in our completion rate increasing to 4.6 an hour within a few months, well over our original three-completes-an-hour target. The client came up with a different solution that was hugely effective.

My boss was happy, which was rare, but I ended his mirth shortly by giving my client a small percentage refund on the 1.6 completes an hour that we achieved above original projections. It worked out to about $12,000 over the course of the multi-year contract, and when my boss discovered what I had done, he started braying like a mad donkey. I explained my rationale to his boss, and he replied, "I get it. You want to reward the client for working with us to fix the problem." Exactly right! I wanted a long-term relationship with the client, and their company and felt it was a small price to pay. The financial director of the company said that, in more than 20 years of business, no company had ever volunteered to share a profit windfall with them. The goal for any negotiation should be: *Think in terms of both partners being satisfied and building a trusting and strong relationships.*

EXAMPLE 1—HARDCORE NEGOTIATING AT A GEM SHOW

Every year, the Tucson Gem Show brings buyers and sellers from all over the world. One time, I saw an American customer trying to buy a ring from a vendor from Mumbai, India. The seller's original asking price for the ring was $420. The American buyer offered $300. Typically, we would see resolution somewhere in the $350–$380 range after three to four rounds of offers/counteroffers. The buyer, however, was belligerent and used some vulgar, aggressive language with the seller; he continued to offer $300 and wouldn't budge. The seller dropped his price to $395, $380, and then $360, at which point he explained that he could go no lower than $360. The buyer started to walk away, at which point the seller further lowered his price to $350. The buyer then took out three $100 bills from his pocket and, holding the bills in his hand, demanded, "Take it or leave it." The seller said he couldn't go that low, the buyer walked away again, but the seller called him back and accepted the $300 offer.

I talked with the seller afterwards and said that I thought the buyer was quite rude. The seller said, "I've still made a little profit, and it was near the end of the show, and that's why I took his money. It wasn't any fun though, and I won't deal with him again." He further said that he felt like "the guy was holding a gun to my head."

We want to be assertive in our negotiations but the buyer crossed a line and became aggressive. To be a productive negotiator, we want both sides to feel good about the deal; we want both sides to win. The Tucson ring buyer didn't collaborate, didn't compromise, and approached the negotiation as an aggressive situation; he wanted to win at the expense of the seller (who was really a nice guy). He did win, but he poisoned the well with the seller for any future negotiations.

Some specific recommendations for negotiations include:

THE PLANNING STAGE

- **Do your homework—identify your goals and your partner's goals.** This sometimes takes an extensive amount of research to develop your strategy and anticipate the other side's approach. Take the time to think about different scenarios (even via a spreadsheet of initial offers and potential counteroffers) but don't make assumptions regarding what the other party will or won't do . . . or pre-negotiate yourself away from your intended goals.

- **Think big and ask for what you want.** Some people do not feel comfortable with negotiations and give away ground early with tentative offers that undercut their position. These people want to avoid any conflict and close out the negotiations as soon as possible. In doing so, they do untold damage to their position. If it's important to you, bring it up. It's also acceptable to ask the other side about their interests and objectives.

- **Single-issue negotiations are more difficult.** Think of what else you can bring to the table to make it multiple-issue. Emphasize value besides price—think of other elements you can use besides money. Multiple issue negotiations are more difficult to turn into a compromise offer, because there are more discussion items involved than just money. Other value propositions could be financing and payment terms, add-ons, even bundling separate negotiations, staffing, and timing. Timing is one that I always negotiate with, perhaps accepting a lower payment amount if I am allowed an additional week or two to complete the project. One thing that you should never negotiate with is quality. One supplier told me that they could lower their price to be competitive with another bidder, "If we took some shortcuts on the quality of the deliverables." The idea that a company will charge you less while — yes also providing lower quality is never a strong bargaining position—very few people would agree to such a proposal.

In multi-bid business situations, a lower competitive offer sometimes brings price reductions (I only specify a range for the percentage difference and not the actual amount of the lowest bid. I also do not reveal the names of the other bidding companies). I've seen drops of up to 50% due to the pressure that a competitive offer places on a seller.

NEGOTIATION PROCESS

- **Present realistic goals and then justify them**. Let's analyze a new vehicle purchase situation. A customer will present a low offer for a vehicle only to have the dealership salesperson laugh hysterically or give a dismissive look of shock; the customer quickly loses their resolve and agrees that their offer is unrealistic. As long as you have a reason for your initial offer, the sales representative may still react dramatically, but you put them on the defensive. Justifications could include: "I saw the price at another dealer or via the internet," or "It's what a friend paid for a similar vehicle," etc.

  For example, when negotiating for a particular vehicle that you want, if your goal is to not pay more than $275 a month—which would be your **Bottom Line**—you must identify two other figures: **Your Goal** (a realistic estimation of what you would like to pay) and **Most Desired Objective** (the best case scenario or ideal payment amount). With this information, you can develop your first offer. When a customer walks into the dealership, a salesperson typically asks "How much are you willing to pay?" (the Bottom Line). When a customer provides that number, that is the price where the negotiation starts, and they end up paying more than they wanted to. We want to start with our initial offer near or even below the Most Desired Objective point; we then have a better chance of reaching our goals.

In the example below, we see a vehicle that, from the sticker price, works out to a monthly payment of $270 a month. Our bottom line is $275—we don't want to pay more than that—and the sticker price is very close to that figure. We set a goal to pay $245 a month and our Most Desired Objective is $200.

Table 1.1

MOST DESIRED		BOTTOM
Objective	Goal	Line
$200	$245	$275

When the dealer asks what I want to pay, my first offer would be $180, well below the Most Desired Objective, in order to put pressure on the dealer to come in well under the sticker price. I present a justification for that low of an offer, stating that I saw a recent advertisement at another dealer for that price.

FIRST ROUND OF OFFERS SUMMARY

- Sticker Price—$270

- Customer Offer—$180

- The gap or difference between the offers is a number that I track and is currently at $90.

The next round of offers is where we typically see the largest movement on both sides. Let's say that the dealer reduces their price from $270 to $255, while we move up from $180 to $205. Keep in mind that the buyer in many situations needs to move at a higher percentage than the seller.

Concessions are largest on first offers, and then become smaller on the subsequent rounds.

SECOND ROUND OF OFFERS SUMMARY

- Dealer Offer—$255
- Customer Offer—$205
- The gap is now $50—a significant decrease from $90 at the start of the negotiation.

The third round of offers will see smaller declines from the dealer, in this scenario they reduce to $250, while the customer moves up to $218.

THIRD ROUND OF OFFERS SUMMARY

- Dealer Offer—$250
- Customer Offer—$218
- The gap is now $38 and has narrowed considerably from the original $90 difference.

The negotiation will typically end after a fourth (or possibly fifth) round, with very little movement, particularly from the selling side. We will assume that the dealer's final offer is $248 a month while the customer moved up to $224.

FOURTH AND FINAL ROUND OF OFFERS SUMMARY

- Dealer Offer—$248
- Customer Offer—$224
- The gap is now $24

With the gap at $24, it is really the customer's choice if they will accept the dealer's offer of $248 a month. Let's analyze what has taken place if the customer purchases the vehicle at that price. He/she is slightly above their goal of $245, but at this point, the most important number is the Bottom Line, and the customer is $22 below that figure. In any negotiation, if I come in even a dollar under the Bottom Line, I consider it a success. The customer in this automotive purchase example should be very pleased.

The above scenario left out a lot of other possible factors that can enter into a dealership sales situation (trade-in of a used vehicle, purchasing a new vehicle from the previous model year, leasing the vehicle, financing terms and arrangements, aftermarket offers such as maintenance offers, insurance, etc.). As we discussed above, we want to work with more than a straight monetary scenario in negotiations, which gives us more leverage and keeps the negotiation from sliding into a compromise solution. In a car buying situations, it is easy to bring other issues into the negotiation, but you must keep in mind your overall Most Desired Objective, Goal, and Bottom Line throughout the process.

It is important to realize that in a dealership, clocks seem to move backwards. Dealers purposefully slow down the process in order to put more pressure on buyers. Don't expect anything to happen quickly, and if you remain calm, that benefits you. A senior executive of an automotive company once told me that people who come into a dealership with no intent to buy and drive home with a new car pay substantially more than those customers who have shopped online, done their research and come in prepared. I always use a calculator and will re-engineer their figures to make sure that they are no hidden fees; car dealer staff doesn't like it but they can't prevent you from double-checking their numbers.

- **The multiple-level offer/counteroffer process described above is not applicable in all other cultures** but is popular in Latin America and West Asia. In East Asia, negotiations tend to take much longer, with all issues discussed, rather than concentrating on the more important issues. The Japanese are known for being very thorough and patient negotiators—many times in group settings—and don't feel the pressure of a clock or deadline the way that North Americans or Northern Europeans do. Japanese negotiators have said that Americans try to do too much too quickly—particularly on business trips—and end up with a less advantageous deal than if they had taken more time. Africans and Southeast Asians like to establish a personal relationship with someone before they begin to negotiate and start a business relationship. In North America, we hold the view that the buyer can always say no during a negotiation and end it early, before finalizing a deal. However, when a buyer starts a negotiation but then doesn't finish it in other regions, it can be perceived as an insult to the seller, particularly in West Asia (Middle East) and Latin America.

Another part of the world where you don't want to start a negotiation if you don't intend on making the purchase is in Russia. Western Europeans, who are similar to North Americans in that they do not negotiate prices as frequently as people in other regions, find that Russians negotiate everything in business, shopping, and personal situations, forcing them to be on their guard all the time. Russian sellers typically balk at initial attempts to negotiate, but if the buyer persists, then the seller will make an offer that is a sizeable deduction from the original asking price (usually in the 20%–40% discount range). There are then no further discussions or offers/counteroffers, and the buyer must accept the offer. It's done without the emotions that we see in other regions, particularly on the part of the seller, and the friendly banter that we see in the Middle East or in Latin America is typically absent.

On a family trip a few years ago, we landed in St. Petersburg, Russia, from Stockholm, Sweden, and I tried to negotiate the price for a cab ride from the airport to downtown down from the initial offer in Rubles that was the equivalent of US $125. It was late in the afternoon, and we seemed to be the only people at the taxi stand. There were quite a few taxi drivers and "officials" there. At first, "the boss" refused my request to drop his price to $30, (near the $45 I had a paid a few years before). I explained that I had been in the city previously and that $125 was too much for the 30- to 40-minute trip. It took a few minutes, but he cut the price down to $55, less than half the original offer price. My wife thought it was the most terrifying and intimidating scene she had ever seen. Our driver was young and drove like Mario Andretti, but I was pleased with the price. Over the next few days, we ran into tourists from France, England, and Italy, who all complained about the cost of their taxi from the airport ($120–$150). They were astonished when I told them how little we had paid.

Throughout Russia, negotiations fit the same pattern of initial reticence, and then a substantial price reduction with no further negotiations. It doesn't necessarily affect my determination as to what my initial offer is versus a negotiation in Latin America or in the United States (you still start with a low offer that you can justify), but it does change things in terms of evaluating whether I received a good deal or not. Negotiations in Russia also take less time than in other regions.

Other tips to keep in mind include:

- **Listening is key throughout the process, even if you think you have heard it all before.** On average, we speak at 125 words per minute. We can listen at 600–800 words per minute. We think at 2,000 words per minutes. Avoid multi-tasking during negotiations. Listening is hard work, but it pays off in the end.

- **One question that people frequently ask is who should make the first offer.** You should try to have the other side make the first offer but always be prepared to present one that is well thought-out with justifications, so that you do not "leave money on the table" with a higher-than-necessary position. If you do your homework, it nullifies the advantage of either side making the first offer.

- **Never accept their first offer.** It causes too much doubt from the other side as to whether they made too good of an offer for you. I have, in a few cases, negotiated against myself (slightly) on a very favorable first offer to my side, so that I don't accept that initial offer—obviously you try not to hurt yourself too much—but by doing a few rounds of offers, I send the message that the first offer was not "unbelievably good." You can always justify a more rapid negotiation solution through citing authority ("My boss or company wants to conclude this deal quickly before the end of the month for tax reasons," etc.).

- **Everything is negotiable.** It has become popular of late to say, "That point is non-negotiable." What that can do is close a door, and I don't want to end the negotiation prematurely. There may be issues that I am unwilling to barter with, but I don't present that information to the other side. I want to be seen as reasonable and open to any ideas. Another word to avoid is "no." A better word to use is "*if*" as in "I could present that idea internally *if* there are some changes or modifications" (and then specify them). Rather than saying "no," use procedures or laws ("Company policy won't allow us to do that"), authority ("My boss won't approve this"), independent standards (market value, competing offers) or other reasons (past agreements, precedence) as an excuse for not accepting their offer, then develop and present your own counteroffer.

- **Keep the negotiation moving.** A negotiation can be a long process but part of the planning is to identify concessions that you can provide that are not as important to you but keep the negotiation process alive. Build in "thinking" time before accepting an offer. Even the simple process of pausing for a sustained period (30 seconds or more) can put pressure on the other side—the ambiguity of silence creates a feeling of unbalance to the recipients. Remember—"speed kills" in negotiations.

- **Don't get emotional, even if the other side does.** This approach is for the movies. Sometimes people have bad days, and its okay to postpone the call or meeting in order to preserve the relationship. A client in a meeting during a negotiation once said to me, "All sales people were prostitutes." I did not react to the name calling—even though I would have been justified—but continued to discuss the content of the issue on the table. Afterwards, multiple clients apologized, and they removed the hostile client from the negotiation team. Reacting to insults ultimately makes you look as poorly as the instigator. Always take the "high road."

EXAMPLE 2—HIGH-PRESSURE SELLING

A former student of mine has been working in Las Vegas for some years. Las Vegas is the prototype setting for "high-pressure sales" (discount tickets, time shares, night clubs, etc.) He runs his own stylist salon but earns a significant portion of his revenue from selling organic creams for skin care. He worked for another firm selling similar products before starting his own company.

Recently I shadowed him while he was pitching his products to some passing customers. He was very personable and started the conversation by asking questions about where they are from, what they do, and how they like Las Vegas. He then focused on a customer's wrinkles by applying some sample creams and presenting "before and after" pictures from past customers. (I said that, in Phoenix, many lawn care services show "examples" of their work, but they just use pictures of what competitors have done). He said that he would expect that some of his competitors do that, but all of his photos were from past customers—it makes it easier to tell stories of what they were suffering from (frostbite etc.).

He then described the two stages of his skin care process. He was very positive throughout and joked about his accent—he is from the Balkans region of Europe. Then he showed how the two stages are usually about $5,400, but both could be offered for $600. He directly asked customers if they would pay cash or use a credit card.. By this time, he knew what their occupation was (he loves small business owners who tend to spend more while teachers tend to be frugal). He tries to prevent sticker shock and unrealistic expectations from "People who think this should cost $40."

If there is resistance, he usually will throw in an 18 months' supply of a free moisturizer. He can then add a second moistener, so it would be 3 years' worth of products for "free." If necessary, he has a couple of other side items that he can throw in (usually for free or for an additional $15–$20) to help influence the customer. He said that he should be able to close the whole sale within 5–10 minutes. I told him that after his first or second offer—I would ask him to leave us alone if I were with my wife—so we could discuss the purchase while putting more pressure on him through our ambiguous response. He said that not many people use that approach, but if they did, he knows he's in trouble. He would try to sweeten the offer with more free ancillary products in order to save any chance of closing the deal.

At one point, he said that he only offers the deal that day. That's a problem for me; my rule of thumb is that if the offer is for just one day (unless it's a dated coupon or something similar) then I assume that I don't need it. He admitted that it was a high-pressure move, but that if customers do walk out, they're not going to spend $400–$600 for his products at a later time.

Unless someone takes the $600 offer, he usually will sell the products between $390 and $550. It was also interesting to hear him say that each time a customer thinks that they are receiving a spontaneous special deal or price break, but he knows exactly the steps that he will take in terms of price reductions and throwing in additional products. He knows to the penny what his costs and profits are at each level. He will not go below $390—it's not worth it to him—plus it sets a precedence and cheapens the brand.

He was very professional, and overall, his interactions with his customers were very pleasant, even entertaining in a city that was built on the leisure and recreation trade; he is what I would call a master salesperson, though it was not apparent to his customers. He is always in control and rarely surprised by how his customers react. He can always counter objections or concerns calmly and deftly.

For dealing with high-pressure sales situations:

- Know ahead of time what the product or service typically costs.
- Take your time—that puts more pressure on the seller.
- Take a break to discuss it with your friends/family without the sales person.
- Strike an agreement because it is a product or service that you want, not one that the sales person decides you need.

SUMMARY

It is important to focus on developing solutions in negotiations that benefit both sides. Using techniques, such as slowing down the process, thorough preparation, developing a bottom line, goal, and most desired objective, and adding other issues to the discussion besides price will assist you in developing a collaborate negotiation that is productive for you and the other side, as well.

In Chapter 2, Philippe Korda discusses handling the negotiation en bloc versus item-by-item. Korda also presents advice for determining if the other party feels that they have made a good deal.

Chapter 2

How to Guide Negotiations to a Successful Conclusion

by Philippe Korda

Carl RITCHIE: For a seller, it's painful to agree to a deal on poor terms.

Margaret PEAKE: But the worst thing of all is not to be able to agree to a deal at all.

THE BOARDROOM, 2 YEARS EARLIER

Margaret Peake sighs, shakes her head, and says, "You need to be flexible with your pricing, Mr. Ritchie. You're not even in contention." Discussions continue over pricing. Carl Ritchie defends his offer and then proposes an 8% discount, but the buyer wants 15%. Ritchie explains that he will be able to go no further than 12%. Margaret Peake accepts this. Yet just when Carl Ritchie is hoping to complete the purchase order, his counterpart intervenes again: "You see, Mr. Ritchie, the problem mainly concerns your payment terms. You're offering us 30 days from invoicing, whereas

Philippe Korda, "How to Guide Negotiations to a Successful Conclusion," *The Five Golden Rules of Negotiation*, pp. 53-63. Copyright © 2011 by Business Expert Press. Reprinted with permission.

our standard purchasing terms are 30 days end of month 10th of following month. So if you won't accept those terms, I'm afraid we might not be able to do business."

Discussions continue over payment terms. Carl Ritchie defends his firm's commercial policy robustly. Yet he feels that if he does not back down, all his work will go to waste. He agrees to 30 days end of month. "I've saved 10 days," he thinks to himself. Now Carl Ritchie is more relaxed. The deal is now within his grasp.

But the buyer leans over to him: "Finally, there's something that I wanted to discuss with you—but I'm sure it won't be any problem for you. I noticed from your tender that you intended to invoice us for the installation of the equipment. Yet most of your competitors agree to cover those costs, particularly for an order as large as mine. Was that your intention, too?" Carl Ritchie sighs and closes his eyes for a moment. "I mustn't give her an excuse to scupper the sale now," he thinks. So, in response, he mumbles, "Yes, if you like."

He is just about to suggest that they sign the contract, when Margaret Peake asks innocently, "Of course, your offer comes with a free supply of consumables for the first 6 months, doesn't it?"

Carl Ritchie is taken aback and starts to feel hot under the collar. "Absolutely not! And as you are fully aware, the consumables are the subject of a separate tender that you have already received."

The buyer hunches back in her chair and shrugs helplessly. "Oh, Mr. Ritchie, that's exactly as I feared, but I'm sure that you'll be able to sort out a little thing like that."

This was going too far. Carl Ritchie repressed his frustration and coldly retorted, "I'll put the question to my line management, but I'd be astonished if we were able to make any such offer. We have already given a lot of ground for you."

The buyer gestures toward her telephone: "Go ahead, Mr. Ritchie, put the question to your line management."

But Carl has no intention of giving in to her pressure. He gets to his feet and suggests that he should call the buyer back the next day. He takes his leave with unconcealed frustration at seeing his sale delayed. Margaret Peake spends a couple of minutes sorting through her paperwork. She then picks out a file and makes a telephone call: "Hello, Mr. Martin? I have a problem, Mr. Martin, because your competitor, Mr. Ritchie, has been making some very tempting proposals. I'm afraid you'll have to revise your tender."

IN THE RESTAURANT

Carl RITCHIE: I often wonder how I could have given so much ground on price and terms, only to end up missing out on that deal.

Margaret PEAKE: It must have been infuriating for you, I have to admit.

Carl RITCHIE: Whenever I made a concession, I had the impression that I was getting that little bit closer to the finish line.

Margaret PEAKE: You could have crossed that finish line, you know.

Carl RITCHIE: How?

Margaret PEAKE: Imagine if you had simply asked, "Apart from pricing, are we in full agreement about everything else, Mrs. Peake?"

Carl RITCHIE: And if you had said that we were?

Margaret PEAKE: You could have added, "Right, if we reach agreement on this issue, can I count on your order right now?"

Carl RITCHIE: You would have signed?

Margaret PEAKE (*smiling*): Would you like a little more salad?

Carl RITCHIE (*stunned*): It all seems so obvious to me now!

GOLDEN RULE NO. 5: ENSURE YOU LEAD THE NEGOTIATION TOWARD ITS CONCLUSION

When concluding negotiations, you must ask yourself two key questions.

WHEN IS IT IN MY INTEREST TO AGREE TO A DEAL?

It is not necessarily desirable to conclude negotiations quickly. For example, if you believe that the other party really does need to close a deal within strict time limits, and if you are their best option, it is in your interest to play for time.

In practice, the more urgent the situation becomes for the other party, the more he will be obliged to reduce his demands in order to reach an agreement. Using "delayed response" is therefore a good way of using up time. You can find others: ordering trials, setting up committees, inviting the other party to visit your premises before concluding negotiations, and so on.

In contrast, if you are under an absolute obligation to do a deal within a short period of time, and if you are in a weak position, then clearly you need to conclude quickly, but check the following points first:

- Is your "deadline" negotiable in-house?

- What is the objective risk if you defer the deal by 2 days, 2 weeks, or 2 months?

In short, while the desire to conclude is understandable, patience is also essential. In any case, you must have a clear idea of the date by which it is in your interest to conclude.

Should I Negotiate "En Bloc" or "Item by Item"?

Item-by-item negotiating, also known as the "salami slicing" method, can bring many benefits:

- It gives both negotiators the feeling that they are making "progress" whenever a partial agreement is reached on an issue.

- When the opposing party is in a weak position, it can allow you to erode his position little by little, without the negotiations breaking down.

- It gains you time vis-à-vis a negotiator who is in a very dominant position. "Throwing him crumbs" throughout the negotiations can help you to hang on to the essentials.

However, this salami slicing method has two disadvantages compared with negotiating "en bloc." It sometimes impedes any innovative, wide-ranging solution. Furthermore, it can carry the constant risk of a stalemate caused by the other party's additional demands (such as those made by Carl Ritchie's counterpart).

In practice, it is often in the buyer's interest to deploy the salami slicing technique and in the seller's interest to negotiate "en bloc," at least in order to reach an agreement in principle on the key issues.

PRINCIPLES FOR IMPLEMENTING GOLDEN RULE NO. 5

DEPLOY PRECLOSURE TECHNIQUES

In particular, this involves conditional commitment questions: "If we reach an agreement on this issue, can I count on your final agreement today?" Such techniques allow you

1. to ensure that there will be no other points of disagreement to negotiate over,
2. to ensure that you are dealing with someone who is able to make a decision (unless this crucial issue has been confirmed in advance),
3. to "seal" the deal.

In practice, your counterpart is placed in a tricky situation in which, if she answers no or maybe to the question posed, she loses almost any chance of achieving a satisfactory outcome; if she answers yes, she is obliged to agree to a deal.

So how do you deploy these preclosure techniques? A word of advice: Proceed in two stages.

1. *Start with a "detection question."* This is the "magic" question: "Apart from that one issue, are we in full agreement about everything else?" This question puts the other party in a tricky position. If he answers no, you can drive him into a corner, refusing to make the slightest concession until such time as the picture is clearer: "What are the other issues that you want to look at?"

A skilled negotiator generally tries to dodge the question, for example, by claiming, "If we are not agreed on this issue, it is not even worth pursuing these discussions." He thereby obliges the other party to give ground without giving anything in return, only to then add insult to injury by demanding a few more concessions that are less costly. Believing he has done the important bit, the first party may make the mistake of continuing to give ground out of fear that the contract will be jeopardized "over nothing." Naturally, from the outset, you should refuse to back down on one issue while others remain unclear.

Lastly, if your counterpart responds in the affirmative, stating that he is "in agreement on everything else" and that it is only this final issue (generally the price) that is causing the problem, it is in the seller's interest to press home the advantage: "So, to sum up, let's make sure that we are agreed on the following points . . ."

It is true that such reformulation can cause jitters. Will the other party take advantage of this to raise other points of disagreement? Will this cause the agreement to break down at the last minute? You need to be specific, avoiding any gray areas that the other party will use to his advantage, sooner or later. Furthermore, if your counterpart is keen on getting his way on the final issue under negotiation, he will studiously avoid raising extra demands that you might use in order to rebuff him on the key issue. So you need to have the boldness to confirm and to clarify.

2   *Then pose the "commitment question."* This question allows you to seal the deal: "So, if we can reach an agreement on that final issue, can I count on you making a commitment right now?"

The net is tightening on the buyer: He now has just two potential responses. He can claim that he needs time or can remain vague about his intentions, which amounts to the same thing. You must then ask why.

If your counterpart needs to consult other people, you know full well, and have known for a long time, who those people are. If you have no access to these people, at least you can get a "commitment" from the buyer: "If you were the only one making the decision, what would you do?" If the response is favorable, you should have no hesitation in helping him convince his colleagues or his line management.

If he needs "time to think," a good response would be, "Me, too. I need to have further discussions with my line management, so I won't be able to give you my final offer for a few days."

Your counterpart may be prepared to agree to the deal, at which point it will be difficult for him to retreat from that commitment. You then need to negotiate compensation and make the final concession that allows you to clinch the deal.

WITH YOUR COUNTERPART, LIST THE VARIOUS POINTS AT ISSUE

The number of issues subject to negotiation may range from one (the price) to several dozen, not to mention more complex negotiations such as the sale of nuclear power stations or takeovers of companies or entire groups. In all circumstances, it is desirable to *define the scope of the negotiations* so as to limit them and avoid the other party continually extending his list of demands, as well as to allow you to gain an overview of the areas of agreement and disagreement. Thus it becomes possible to propose overall solutions "en bloc" or, if necessary, negotiate item by item so that subjects on which an agreement has been reached can be removed from the list.

Take care! The terminology employed can be important. It is better to refer to "items still to be discussed" rather than to "items still to be negotiated," as you do not want to give the impression that you are willing to give ground on all those items.

TAKE THE INITIATIVE TO SEAL THE DEAL

The concept of concluding negotiations varies depending on whether it is a "single transaction" or "sales negotiations." For a "single transaction," it is advisable for the seller to trigger the conclusion. In practice, it is a case of overcoming the customer's hesitations and avoiding a competitor being given an opportunity to seal a deal before you do. For sales negotiations, the seller must also take the initiative, but for different reasons. Indeed, buyers can only really take the initiative if they are convinced that they have exhausted all the seller's potential concessions. Thus it is in their interest to wait for the seller to propose a final deal.

Four hints When Concluding a Deal

- *Never appear to be completely satisfied.* Your counterpart will wonder if she has "been had" or think that she can make much greater demands.

- *Keep "a trick up your sleeve":* There is no certainty that the other party will agree to conclude. On the contrary, your desire to conclude will be *implicitly suspect*, as the assumption will be that you are satisfied with the outcome achieved. Thus it is possible that the other party will make (at least) one further demand before agreeing to settle.

- *Do not expect enthusiastic agreement from your opponent.* If only for the sake of appearances, a negotiator will generally display dissatisfaction with the outcome achieved. By expressing frustration and disappointment, each party is hoping to obtain a further concession or to give the opposing party the feeling that he owes a "moral debt" when future negotiations come around. You must therefore distinguish between a firm refusal to settle and a token protest.

- *Proposing is better than imposing.* If you try to reduce your negotiating partner's options or to impose a solution, he will often seek every possible means of getting out of this bind. If he has the impression that you are trying to pressure him against his will, he will devote his energies to defending his lines and pressuring you in return.

Presenting justifications, suggesting alternatives, and proposing without imposing are the best means of presenting a final deal.

You must remember a simple maxim: Your counterpart must be content with her negotiating. However bitter the exchanges and whatever is at stake, you need to ensure that the other party leaves the negotiations with a feeling that she "made a good deal."

If I am the buyer, what might give me this feeling?

- Having paid less than the list price
- Having paid less than expected
- Other people telling me that I have made a good deal
- The conviction that I have succeeded in getting "the best possible deal"
- The feeling that I have obtained a product that someone else wanted
- The impression that my decision proves my ability (or my taste, my resources, my boldness, my humor, etc.)
- Certainty that I will not regret my decision in the future (purchase offering security)
- Having paid less than I would have done elsewhere for a similar product
- Having paid less than others do

If I am the seller, what might give me this feeling?

- Having sold at a higher price than that demanded by the buyer
- Having sold at a higher price than expected
- Other people telling me that I have made a good deal
- The conviction that I have succeeded in doing a deal that my competitors were really keen to do
- The impression that the outcome proves my ability
- Certainty that I will not regret my decision in the future
- Having sold at a higher price than I would have gotten from other customers for a similar product
- Having sold at a higher price than others would have gotten (e.g., my competitors)

Clearly it is in your interest to give the other party reasons to be satisfied, but those reasons need not be costly for you.

HOW DO YOU APPLY GOLDEN RULE NO. 5 WHEN THINGS GET DIFFICULT?

For you, the most difficult circumstances are those in which the decision is taken in your absence: for example, if you are a seller and your purchasing committee sees various suppliers and then makes a decision alone. Another example is where you are the buyer and the seller presents the draft contract to a committee that makes a collective decision.

In both cases, it is very difficult for you to steer the negotiations to a conclusion. What should you do?

In face-to-face negotiations, I suggest the following:

GET YOUR COUNTERPART PERSONALLY INVOLVED

- Develop interpersonal communications: Talk about "you and me" rather than "our companies."
- Obtain a moral commitment from your counterpart. Too often, he is able to take refuge in group decisions, thus avoiding making a personal commitment. A few simple questions can greatly reinforce your position.

Buyer: Right, now I'll have to wait until the committee meeting before giving you our response.

Seller: But on a personal level, Mr. Monks, how do you feel about our offer?

Buyer: It seems very attractive, but I'm not the only one making the decision.

Seller: But as far as you are concerned, you are convinced that our offer is "very attractive"?

Buyer: Absolutely!

Seller: Which elements of our offer did you find particularly attractive?

Buyer: It's clear that your monitoring process would give us greater security …

- Give your negotiating partner the means to present and support your offer. Data packs, slides, electronic files, and informational material may help him to win the backing of the committee.

SEPARATE AGREEMENT IN PRINCIPLE AND NEGOTIATION OF SECONDARY ISSUES

It is sometimes possible to exercise control over the conclusion of complex negotiations by refusing to negotiate over "secondary" issues until such time as an agreement has been reached on the core issues. This is a means of accessing the other party's senior decision makers so as to negotiate an "agreement in principle" (e.g., regarding the product and the price). You can then deal with the various secondary issues at a subsequent meeting. However, you need to take care not to abuse the balance of power, which sometimes becomes highly favorable after the other party has given his agreement in principle.

REMEMBER THAT DECISION-MAKING METHODS ARE NEGOTIABLE

Except in the case of procedures relating to certain public tenders, all the in-house procedures that organizations follow in order to make sales and purchasing decisions are themselves the result of negotiations. There is a principle that says everything created through negotiation can be changed through negotiation. It is up to you to demonstrate that yours is a "special case" that deserves special treatment.

KEY POINTS TO MEMORIZE

- "Apart from that issue, are we in full agreement about everything else?"

- Do not offer price concessions until everything else has been clearly accepted.

- "So, if we reach an agreement on this issue, will you be able to sign up immediately?"

SENSIBLE QUESTIONS TO ASK YOURSELF

- When is it in my interest to seal the deal?

- Who makes the final decision?

Michael Luthy, et al., in Chapter 3 illustrates how to work with multiple variables beyond costs in an automotive negotiation, which dovetails with the example automotive purchase negotiation presented in Chapter 1.

Chapter 3

Developing a Strategic Negotiation Plan: Toyota Highlander

by Michael R. Luthy, Mike H. Ryan,
Bettye R. Desselle, and John T. Byrd

CASE DESCRIPTION

The primary subject matter of this case concerns the evaluation of gathered information to develop a negotiation plan prior to a consumer's purchase of a sport utility vehicle. Secondary issues examined include the sales process and the increasing role of the Internet in consumers' information search activities. The case has a difficulty level of one (appropriate for freshman level courses) although it may be used through level five (appropriate for first year graduate level) depending on the amount and complexity of background reading assigned. The case is designed to be taught in as little as one class hour, but may be expanded to as many as three class hours depending on the

Michael Luthy, et al., "Developing a Strategic Negotiation Plan: Toyota Highlander," *Journal of the International Academy for Case Studies*, vol. 13, no. 3, pp. 53-56. Copyright © 2007 by Allied Academies. Reprinted with permission by Allied Academies and www.thecasecentre.org.

amount of theoretical material discussed by the instructor, if role-play negotiations are carried out, and whether any out-of-class preparations are assigned. The case is expected to require from zero to approximately four hours of outside preparation by students.

CASE SYNOPSIS

Introducing students to the topic of sales negotiation is always challenging. While it is typically a significant part of business-to-business purchases and many higher-ticket priced consumer goods, negative word-of-mouth and uncomfortable personal experiences leave many students apprehensive. Presenting the topic in the context of purchasing an automobile, or in this case study, negotiating the purchase of two sport utility vehicles, students will draw on their own experiences, those of their friends and family members, and any assigned readings. The overall goals of the case are to defuse the anxiety many students associate with negotiation, underscore the importance of analysis and planning prior to face-to-face encounters, and better prepare students for future business and personal purchase situations where negotiation is a factor. Specifically, in this case students examine collected price and non-price information, and develop a negotiation plan. Through this task the instructor may explore various fundamental aspects of negotiation (e.g., agenda analysis, concession strategies) and the distributive bargaining model (e.g., aspiration targets, reservation points, buyer and seller surplus).

INTRODUCTION

As Michelle Tipton read through the brochure for what seemed the tenth time she found herself nodding in agreement. "The new Highlander. An unexpected bit of comfort in the rugged world of the SUV. Breaking new ground is nothing new to Toyota, but this time around, we've built a vehicle that boldly redefines everything you've come to expect from a sport utility vehicle. Highlander gives you uncommon comfort and unparalleled smoothness in an unmistakable form. It's designed for those drivers who crave the versatility and space of an SUV, but aren't willing to sacrifice a refined, comfortable ride. With exceptionally smooth handling, clean, unique styling and a spacious interior, Highlander is the civilized ride you've been looking for." (Toyota Internet Website and Highlander brochure).

After months of investigating, Michelle knew that this was the vehicle she wanted. Sifting through piles of Car and Driver, Auto Week, and Consumer Reports magazines, visiting websites for Acura, Subaru, BMW, and Honda brands among others, convinced her that this was the vehicle for her. Now the question was how to get the best deal from one of the local Toyota dealerships in the Louisville metropolitan area. Located in the city were Toyota of Louisville and Oxmoor Toyota. Just across the river in Southern Indiana was Green Tree Toyota. Because of negative comments and stories she had heard about Oxmoor Toyota, Michelle decided to limit her dealership choice to either Toyota of Louisville or Green Tree Toyota.

An unexpected twist in Michelle's deliberations came when one of her colleagues at work, Ashley Lacey, dropped by her office one day and told her that she and her husband Robert were also looking for a new sport utility vehicle for their family, which included their nine year-old daughter Alex and one good size Labrador retriever. After talking for a while concerning what Michelle had discovered in her research, and about a week after she loaned Ashley all of the information she had collected on various models, Ashley came back and told her that she and Robert were convinced the Highlander was the vehicle that was right for them.

Further discussions between the two parties discovered that with the exception of the choice of exterior color, they both wanted virtually identical models and accessories. Both Michelle and the Lacey family wanted the 6-cylinder, four wheel drive model, with a significant number of options. In Michelle's case she would be able to purchase the vehicle outright, trading in her low mileage 1992 Honda Accord LX. With the Lacey's however, they would be keeping their current car and financing the purchase beyond a $5,000 down payment.

Both Ms. Tipton and the Lacey's knew that if they went to the dealerships together with the intent of buying two vehicles as a package deal, it would be a different, or at least unusual, situation that the salespeople didn't see too often. They hoped that it would allow them to get a better overall price.

Through various online sources, Michelle has been able to find not only the Manufacturer's Suggested Retail Price (MSRP), which typically served as the high end or full price benchmark for consumers, but also wholesale prices. These wholesale prices represent the amount the car dealership paid for the vehicle, excluding any givebacks or other incentives provided by the manufacturer. Michelle's further investigation indicated that there were no other incentives provided to the dealerships for sales of the Highlander model. As she sat at the kitchen table with the Lacey's and with the financial information spread out before them, they knew they had a number of decisions to make and questions to answer in putting together their negotiation plan before they approached the dealerships.

Exhibit 1		
Used car information for 1992 Honda Accord LX		
Source	Trade-in to dealer	Retail price sold by dealer
Kelley Blue Book	$4,575	$7,600
Edmunds	$4,977	$6,708
Consumer Reports	$4,775	$7,365

Exhibit 2				
Toyota Highlander—Base Vehicle Costs and Options				
MSRP	Wholesale	Model and Engineering Options	Michelle Tipton	Lacey Family
$24,390	$21,761	4 door sport utility with base engine	No	No
25,790	23,007	4 door, 4 wheel drive sport utility with base engine	Yes	Yes
1,580	1,407	3.0 Liter, 6 cylinder 220 hp	Yes	Yes
650	559	Vehicle skid control	Yes	Yes
MSRP	Wholesale	Exterior Options	Michelle Tipton	Lacey Family
$699	$455	Fender Flares	No	No
310	248	Glass, deep tinted	No	No
102	61	Hood protector	Yes	Yes

Exhibit 2				
Toyota Highlander—Base Vehicle Costs and Options				
MSRP	Wholesale	Model and Engineering Options	Michelle Tipton	Lacey Family
220	176	Luggage rack	Yes	Yes
80	64	Mud guards	Yes	Yes
625	405	Running boards	No	Yes
334	200	Rear spoiler	Yes	Yes
900	720	Power sunroof	Yes	Yes
MSRP	Wholesale	Interior, Security, Safety, and Miscellaneous Options	Michelle Tipton	Lacey Family
$379	$235	Molded wood dash	No	No
90	58	All weather floor mats	Yes	Yes
$147	$88	Glass breakage sensor	No	No
309	185	VIP security system	No	No
250	215	Side impact air bags	Yes	Yes
40	32	Daytime running lights	Yes	Yes
30	24	Outside heated mirrors	Yes	Yes
400	352	Heated seats	Yes	Yes
200	150	Premium sound package with CD changer	Yes	Yes
520	416	16" aluminum wheels	Yes	Yes

QUESTIONS TO ANSWER

1. What should Michelle and the Laceys' negotiation strategy be? (e.g. how much information to share concerning where they are in the buying process, that there is a vehicle trade-in, that they are looking at other

dealerships as well, that they have wholesale price information from Internet sources, whether and how much deception is ethical/allowable, etc.)

2   What do you expect the behavior of the sales people to be when Michelle and the Laceys visit the Toyota dealerships?

3   Develop a negotiation plan (i.e. characteristics of opening offer, reservation price, tactics, tradeoffs they should make, how to react if the seller brings up issues before you are ready to discuss them, e.g. whether you have a trade in vehicle, etc.). What would your Plan B be if your original plan becomes untenable?

4   What do you believe the salespersons' negotiation plan will be? How can you determine what their plan is?

Chapter 4, by Nicholas Dorochoff, analyzes roadblocks in a land use negotiation with Native Americans.

Chapter 4

Responding to Roadblocks

by Nicholas Dorochoff

THE PORT ANGELES GRAVING DOCK PROJECT

In 1997, the Washington State Transportation Commission reviewed a plan to replace the eastern half of the Hood Canal Bridge, built in 1961. (The western section of the pontoon bridge had been reconstructed in 1979 after a storm caused the anchors to fail and the pontoons to sink.) Funding for pre-construction activities was approved in 1999, and the project was scheduled for completion by 2007.[1] As the project moved forward, efforts were made in 2000 to engage various tribes in a discussion about the adverse effects that could occur during reconstruction of the eastern portion of the bridge or that could ensue from construction of the temporary ferry terminals needed to manage traffic while the bridge was out of service. However, the state's decision to build a graving yard for the construction of the new pontoons and their selection of the site of a former mill at Port Angeles resulted in a compelling example of a roadblock to negotiations, specifically with regard to the participation of the Lower Elwha Klallam tribe in the consultation.

Nicholas Dorochoff, "Selection from 'Responding to Roadblocks'," *Negotiation Basics for Cultural Resource Managers*, pp. 107-117, 122-123. Copyright © 2010 by Taylor & Francis Group. Reprinted with permission.

The case is complex. The legislative review of the project and the report prepared by the Washington State Department of Transportation (WSDOT) and the Washington State Transportation Committee, taken together, provide cautionary tales on a number of cultural resource management issues. It's important to note, however, that the community of Port Angeles enthusiastically supported the project, as did the Lower Elwha Klallam tribe—once they were engaged in consultation.

The report issued by the WSDOT and the Washington State Transportation Commission indicates that consultation with the Lower Elwha Klallam tribe during project planning was inadequate and that the initial cultural resource survey was flawed. Once construction began in late 2003, midden and fragmentary human remains were discovered, and consultation with the business committee of the tribe began in earnest. Subsequent excavation determined that the graving yard's area of potential affects (or APE) included portions of the village of Tse-whit-sen, which held particular importance to the Lower Elwha Klallam. In addition, fragmentary burial remains recovered early in the project were apparently discovered beneath concrete foundations of buildings previously constructed on the site, suggesting that burials disturbed by construction in the early part of the twentieth century had not been recovered, but simply reburied.

The reassessment, completed in October 2003, identified four areas deemed likely to yield additional archaeological remains, but no evidence of significant numbers of burials. An assumption held by all as negotiations moved forward was that the APE included portions of the village, associated artifacts, and a limited number of intact and fragmentary burials. Archaeology consultants performing the work assumed the discovery of an additional twenty-five intact burials in order to estimate recovery costs. Evidence suggested that the village cemetery was somewhere nearby, but not within the APE.

As early as October 2003, tribal representatives indicated their desire, as part of the mitigation, to acquire the portion of the village site outside the project's boundaries, a parcel of not less than ten acres. The tribe also requested funding for continued archeological work and the reinterment of recovered human remains at the adjacent site to be secured for that purpose.

The MOA incorporated by reference the site treatment plan and a separate mitigation agreement entered into solely by WSDOT and the tribe. Finalized in March 2004, the mitigation agreement included payment of $3.47 million for the tribe's archaeological recovery, curation and reburial efforts, and securing the property necessary for those activities. Neither the WSDOT report nor the legislative audit specifically comment on the nature of the agreement to assist in acquiring the property, but the WSDOT report does indicate that the agency later offered to assist in negotiations for the purchase of property near the graving yard site.[2]

While negotiations regarding the agreements took place, and with the tribe's approval, construction continued outside of the APE. Drainage work on the northern edge of the site had been in progress since November; in March, fragmentary human remains were uncovered there. Soon after the agreements were signed, the first of several hundred intact burials was discovered. It was eventually revealed that the graving yard site encompassed not only parts of the ancestral village, but an extensive tribal cemetery which lay outside the four areas previously identified as having archeological significance.

By the end of May, after fifty intact burials had been recovered, the tribal chairman wrote a letter to WSDOT and the SHPO expressing a desire to expand recovery efforts while allowing construction work to continue. It was in this letter that the tribe first stated its desire to recover all burials from the site, even those beyond the bounds of excavation.

In June, in a meeting attended by agency representatives, the tribal business council, and other members of the tribe, it became apparent that the council's decision to allow construction to continue while recovery efforts were underway was not fully supported by all members of the tribe. However, the tribe's business council continued to authorize the continuation of work and seemed encouraged by WSDOT's offers to expand recovery to include the areas where the intact burials had been discovered. By this time, 100 intact burials had been recovered, along with remains of a long house and other features which indicated that the portion of the village within the APE was largely intact.

The discovery of intact burials continued at a rate of between thirty and fifty per month. In August 2004, the tribe first formally stated its position that the MOA assured the recovery of all burials within the project site, even those beyond the APE. While discussion continued over the meaning of various provisions in the MOA, it became clear that the construction site encompassed one of the richest archaeological sites of its kind. But the Lower Elwha Klallam tribe's position through all of this continued to be that the project could move forward as long as their request was honored for recovery of all burials, which they maintained was stipulated in the MOA. Given the tribe's previous cooperation and enthusiastic support of the project, as well as their continued willingness to allow work to go forward, it is reasonable to assume that the apparent change in their position was driven by necessity rather than choice.

Dispute resolution regarding the meaning of the MOA continued, with each side maintaining its position. Media coverage cited in the reports indicates that the situation became increasingly emotionally charged. In the face of the tribe's continued insistence that all burials be recovered, the agencies made offers of additional (though not complete) recovery of remains—essentially attempts to develop concessions in the hope that the tribe's primary position would somehow change as a result. Practical considerations, such as the difficulties in dewatering the area and the effects of compaction on any remains beneath the APE, became the focus of agency investigation—attempts to explain the agencies' position and educate the tribe on the difficulty of meeting its demand. But none of these efforts affected the tribe's insistence that the MOA required the recovery of all burials. In November, the tribe's lawyers asked that consultation with the Advisory Council be initiated, but before the council could respond, in December 2004, the Lower Elwha Klallam tribe formally requested that the graving docks project be abandoned.

The Port Angeles case includes many of the hallmarks of failed negotiations: inadequate investigation and preparation, insufficient engagement of the consulting parties, and faulty (or, at best, incomplete) communication. Both communications issues and outcomes issues seem to be at play here, and both the WSDOT report and the legislative audit indicate a primary problem in the negotiations was the agencies' incomplete understanding of the impacts of cultural and spiritual values on the tribe's negotiating positions. In addition, these negotiations moved forward against the backdrop of the recovery of a seemingly endless number of burials—a situation that must have been equally shocking and disturbing for all involved. The primary roadblock to negotiations during 2004, and the issue that ultimately halted the project, was the tribe's insistence that the MOA required the recovery of all burials.

The legislative audit is incomplete, as the tribe refused to cooperate after filing suit in the case, so interviews with tribal members did not go forward as planned.[3] Had the auditors completed their interviews with members of the Lower Elwha Klallam tribe, perhaps they would have discovered specific assumptions, goals, or values that would help explain the tribe's apparent change in position—which is clearly an issue related to the outcomes of the project. A thorough consideration of the tribe's assertion that the MOA required the recovery of all burials cannot be adequately assessed within the scope of analysis presented here. A brief review of select facts in the case, however, does reveal that problems related to both communications and outcomes seem to have been compounded by the parties' assumptions and underlying goals regarding the project, which in turn affected the parties' selection of strategies in addressing the roadblock.

UNRECOGNIZED ASSUMPTIONS AND GOALS

In November 2003, nine months after the first intact burial was recovered, tribal chairperson Frances Charles published a personal statement in a number of publications which included the following:

> *We thought we had an agreement, but again it was broken because agencies felt that this land next to us here was not a place to have an Indian cemetery, because it did not fit the scope of their "economics" for an industrial land base. What was implied to us earlier [was] that we would negotiate and we would purchase the land for the burial process and for the curation of the artifacts, and for the development of a cultural center to continue to educate the surrounding county and the visitors who come into Port Angeles area.*[4]

Charles mentions the tribe's goal to acquire adjacent land for a cultural center and a burial ground for recovered remains. In a November 2004 story in the *Seattle Times*, the secretary of the WSDOT is quoted as follows: "But the tribe doesn't want to lay people below concrete. That's a new card: They do not want to separate the community."[5] The WSDOT report underscores this point: "For the Tribe, however, the critical question was that the ancestral community not be pulled apart. A new burial for all human remains would be necessary to preserve that physical proximity of the souls."[6]

One of the tribe's goals in mitigating adverse affects was to secure the remaining site of the Tse-whit-sen village for ongoing archeological work, curation, and reburial purposes. The WSDOT report indicates that the tribe's efforts to obtain this property failed.[7] Early in 2004, the tribe sought part of an eighteen-acre parcel which presumably encompassed at least part of the village. The tribe refused WSDOT's offer to assist in negotiations for six acres of this parcel; negotiations did not complete, evidently because of the tribe's concern that six acres was not sufficient for their purposes.

Later in the summer, the Port offered to sell six acres of nearby land, but the tribe expressed no interest. Around the same time, the tribe unsuccessfully attempted to purchase four acres west of the site, land closer to the discovered burials than the parcel they previously attempted to acquire. In October, the tribe sought to reopen negotiations for a portion of the eighteen-acre parcel to the east of the site, but discovered it was no longer for sale. It was during this time that the tribe invoked the dispute resolution clause of the MOA, which ultimately led to abandoning the project entirely.

The legislative audit and WSDOT report do not specifically point to the Lower Elwha Klallam tribe's inability to acquire suitable property for reburial as a critical factor in their demand that all burials be recovered. Although the prospect of dividing the community of the dead was seen as troubling to the tribe, perhaps its significance was not fully appreciated by WSDOT and other parties to the consultation. This is suggested in the WSDOT report; immediately following the statement cited above regarding the tribe's need to maintain the physical proximity of all the dead, the report goes on to discuss the problems associated with dewatering to retrieve burials from beneath the water line, and compaction and other sources of potential disturbance to any ancestors left behind. That section ends with the assertion that these findings "might understandably have left the Tribe with little satisfaction in its conclusion that vibratory installation of sheet pile walls would have little effect on nearby archaeological resources or burials."And of course, it certainly would not have satisfied the tribe, if the real issue concerning the tribe was the location, rather than the treatment of the ancestors' remains.

In October, the second failed attempt to purchase property that presumably included the remaining portions of the village coincided with the Lower Elwha Klallam tribe's decision to invoke the dispute resolution clause. The connection between this particular mitigation goal and the tribe's position that all burials be recovered is speculative; the fact that possible connections were not investigated, however, suggests that the identification of the tribe's assumptions and underlying goals was incomplete. Such lack of understanding is fostered by unclear or incomplete communications, which were cited by both reports as contributing to the failure of negotiations. In addition, inaccurate assumptions regarding both communications and outcomes as the parties negotiated the agreement ultimately contributed to the impasse.

COMMUNICATIONS ISSUES

The findings of the legislative audit regarding communications among the parties to the Port Angeles dispute illustrate the importance of clear, accurate communications to successful negotiations, and how the lack of such communication can foster misunderstandings that lead to roadblocks.

The legislative audit questioned "whether a truly positive relationship and open communication" had been established between the agencies and the tribe.[8] Faulty communication typically includes gaps between what parties say and what they mean, as well as between what parties say and how their counterparts interpret what they are saying. In all communications, each party has to rely on assumptions regarding meaning. The goal of clear communication is to minimize that reliance on assumptions.

The legislative audit suggests that the lack of formal documentation of meetings contributed to misunderstandings among the parties.[9] This assertion is supported by the WSDOT report, which cites a number of instances in which reports to the media by tribal leaders conflicted with the agency's understanding of previous communications. In the absence of detailed documentation of face-to-face communications formally reviewed and approved by the parties involved, it is difficult, if not impossible, to assess the true outcome of a given verbal exchange. Follow-up correspondence among the parties by mail or e-mail does not suffice, as it describes only one party's understanding of meeting outcomes and attendant obligations. The result is essentially a series of monologues, which do little to produce a shared understanding of the results of these sessions.

In the absence of a shared understanding, the two parties were left to guess at or make assumptions about what their counterparts truly meant. This situation may have contributed to the agency's decision to offer concessions— such as expanding the recovery area during the summer of 2004—without appreciating that the tribe's insistence that no burials be left behind represented their bottom-line position.

After all, the agency had already gone far beyond the obligations typically understood as legally required by Section 106 in offering a considerable amount of money for the tribe's use in recovery, curation, and reburial of remains and the purchase of property for that purpose. And the tribe continued to maintain that work could move forward while recovery activities continued—indicating that they shared the ultimate goal of seeing to the timely completion of the project. Wouldn't additional concessions related to specific portions of the construction site outside the APE be enough to satisfy the Lower Elwha Klallam?

Most negotiators are willing to accept any concession offered, but unless those concessions address the counterpart's primary concerns, they are ultimately useless in moving the negotiation forward. In this case, WSDOT's concessions and attempts to educate the tribe on the difficulty of meeting their demand gave the impression of movement on the issue without directly addressing the tribe's position that all burials be recovered.

OUTCOMES ISSUES

In the Port Angeles case, outcomes issues played a significant role. In this regard, a number of primary assumptions that formed the basis of the agreements failed:

- *the vast majority of recoveries would be artifacts, rather than burials,*
- *the majority of burials likely to be recovered would be fragmentary, rather than intact, and*
- *intact burials to be recovered would be few, rather than many.*

The inaccuracy of these assumptions prompted widely divergent responses from the parties involved. The agencies maintained that they were not legally required to renegotiate the agreements signed in March simply because these assumptions proved untrue. Only changes to the project's scope could reopen negotiation on points stipulated in the MOA and related agreements. The focus of outcomes issues for the agency was the timely completion of the project. For the Lower Elwha Klallam tribe, however, the discovery of the burial ground was material to the conduct of recoveries under the existing agreement. The most important outcome for them, once the construction site revealed the presence of an extensive burial ground, was the appropriate treatment of the ancestors' remains. They further maintained that if review and comment on the situation by the Federal Highway Administration resulted in a finding that the MOA did not require recovery of all burials, then the agreement needed to be renegotiated to address that consideration.[10] For the tribe, the number and condition of the burials recovered directly affected their position regarding the treatment of the remains.

The tribe's developing position on this point could have been affected by assumptions they held going into the negotiations the year before. The legislative audit suggests that tribal representatives may have believed that they truly could not stop the project from moving forward.[11] Given this as an underlying assumption, it would make sense that the tribe would pursue an accommodating strategy from the start: accepting limited concessions over time and slowly building up to their decision to halt the project, rather than stating their position forcefully up front. This is consistent with the manner in which they communicated the desire to recover all burials, which was first put forth in written correspondence in May 2004 as a desire, repeated in the tribal meeting with agency representatives in June, followed by formal insistence on that point when asking for a temporary halt to the work in August. Negotiators who perceive themselves to be in a position of weakness will typically take such an approach: testing the waters with low-key requests and accepting any concessions offered while determining how far their counterparts are willing to go in meeting their needs. That the agencies continued to offer limited concessions may have contributed to the tribe's belief that their primary objective was attainable while allowing the project to move forward.

A thorough analysis of failure of negotiations in the Port Angeles case requires considerably more effort and space than is available here. But this brief review of some facets of the case suggests the extent to which lack of verified assumptions and goals, communications issues, and outcomes issues all contributed to the failure of negotiations. As with any roadblock, determining the extent that communications issues contribute to the impasse is as important as correctly identifying whether your counterpart is capable of adjusting his position or is merely posturing. Openly addressing all parties' goals and assumptions is equally important in overcoming roadblocks, as they directly affect the parties' basic positions and negotiating strategy.

CONCLUSION

Roadblocks are best addressed by first considering gaps in communication. Making sure all parties to a negotiation truly understand one another's positions is typically the first step in addressing failure of the problem-solving cycle. If communication is not the problem, the next step is to assess whether the lack of movement of your counterpart's position is due to necessity or choice. If necessity is driving the lack of movement, the only options are to walk away, to make concessions, or to address underlying goals in a way that will allow the negotiation to move forward. If, on the other hand, your counterpart is choosing to stand firm, it is crucial to determine whether strategy, personality, or ignorance is driving that decision.

If the roadblock is strategic, refocusing attention on the parties' goals or the substance of the agreement being negotiated can sometimes make a difference. Issues of personality are addressed primarily by the manner in which information is conveyed, depending on your counterpart's primary motivation (affiliation, achievement, or power/influence motivation). Finally, identifying ignorance as a driver of stalled negotiations can be either easy or difficult to address, depending on the nature of the information your counterpart is lacking and the extent to which the negotiations have failed.

In some negotiation texts, general principles regarding roadblocks are reflected in lists of specific situations and their remedies. Books of this type that are most helpful in terms of the negotiation contexts discussed here are included in the bibliography. But because no negotiator can foresee all potential problems, simply understanding the basic causes of roadblocks can help to overcome them.

The best way to deal with roadblocks, however, is to prevent them from happening in the first place. Careful preparation prior to the start of negotiations, efforts to fully engage the consulting parties during the connection phase, and careful communication throughout the negotiation can minimize their occurrence. The sooner these issues are addressed, the more likely negotiators will meet success in overcoming roadblocks.

NOTES

1   Douglas B. MacDonald and Dan O'Neal, The Hood Canal Bridge Rehabilitation Project and Graving Dock Program (Olympia, WA: Washington State Department of Transportation and Washington State Transportation Commission), 1–3.The specifics regarding this project are drawn from this source, as well as JLARC's previously cited "Review of the Port Angeles Graving Dock Project."

2   MacDonald and O'Neal, 131.

3   JLARC, ii.

4   Frances Charles, "I Wish This Upon No Other Nation," cited in MacDonald, 185.

5   "Ancient Village Torn Apart by Bridge Project," cited in MacDonald and O'Neal, 167.

6   MacDonald and O'Neal, 161.

7   MacDonald and O'Neal, 131.

8   JLARC, 108.

9   JLARC, 108.

10   MacDonald and O'Neal, 174.

11   JLARC, 104.

In Chapter 5, Lawrence Susskind and Jeffrey Cruikshank continue with the environmental negotiation theme by stressing the importance of considering introducing mediators, intermediaries, and other outside forms of assistance.

Chapter 5

Mediation and Other Forms of Assisted Negotiation

by Lawrence Susskind and Jeffrey Cruikshank

In an ideal world distributional disputes would be settled by the parties themselves, as the *Jordan Lane* case. But, because the participants in multiparty, many-issue disputes are usually unable to deal with their differences on their own, assisted negotiation is often necessary.

Assisted negotiation is the complement to unassisted negotiation. Many public disputes—in fact, the great majority of the distributional disputes to which we have alluded—do not meet the preconditions ... for successful unassisted negotiation. Most public disputes are highly complex, for example, and the affected groups are hard to identify and difficult to represent. Disputing parties often have great difficulty initiating and pursuing discussions. Emotional, psychological, or financial stakes may be so high that the disputants are unable to sustain the collaborative aspects of unassisted negotiation. Finally, power imbalances may preclude direct and unassisted dealings among disputants.

Consider, for example, the problems posed by relatively the simple task of initiating a dialogue—or, as we have labeled the first step in the prenegotiation phase, "getting started." We have already discussed some of the psychological traps that

Lawrence Susskind and Jeffrey Cruikshank, "Mediation and Other Forms of Assisted Negotiation," *Breaking the Impasse*, pp. 136-185. Copyright © 1989 by Perseus Books Group. Reprinted with permission.

come into play as disputing parties consider whether or not to pursue negotiations. Like some couples involved in marital squabbles, each partner refuses to make the first conciliatory gesture. "You started this," each says, "so you solve it." In other words, public postures alone may preclude unassisted negotiation. If that is the case, then the disputing par ties have only two choices: they can resort to the conventional legislative, administrative, or judicial means of resolving distributional disputes, or they can seek the help of a nonpartisan intermediary—a facilitator, mediator, or arbitrator—and engage in assisted negotiation.

"Getting started" is relatively easy, when compared with some of the subsequent phases of negotiation. Suffice it to say that when complexities arise, a neutral intermediary is often the only solution.

ENTRY

There are numerous ways that intermediaries can arrive on the scene. As suggested earlier, an unassisted negotiation can easily get bogged down; and as the frustration level rises, one of the disputing parties may suggest the need for a "neutral." Alternatively, a neutral may present himself or herself to the various stakeholders and indicate a willingness to provide assistance. Finally, a disinterested observer may advise the disputing par ties seek outside assistance.

This last approach is particularly fruitful when the various parties are "frozen" into uncompromising public postures. In such cases, all parties may in fact want to initiate negotiations, but fear the consequences of appearing weak. ("If I seem eager to negotiate, the others will attempt to gain more by hardening their positions.") This may be partially true, but the overriding reality is that these parties are unlikely to resolve their dispute without help. Therefore, the neutral may have to be introduced into the dispute by a nonparticipant.

A second problem of entry has to do with perceptions of control. In many cases, one or more disputants is convinced that employing an intermediary will amount to surrendering control over the outcome. This is a common misperception, which arises out of the publicity that often accompanies binding arbitration, a process in which an arbitrator listens to each sides arguments and arrives at a judgment by which the parties have agreed to be bound. In contrast, there are several types of assisted negotiation which are not binding, and which proceed only with the continuing assent of the negotiating parties. In other words, all parties must be satisfied with the settlement reached through such a consensual process, or there is no settlement. Because the stakeholders retain veto power over the final outcome, they retain a vital measure of control.

Government agencies and officials are particularly sensitive to issues of control. "I have a legal mandate," such officials frequently tell us. "It would be inappropriate and perhaps illegal for me to accept terms dictated by someone else." The answer, of course, is that in the types of consensual negotiations described in this book, no one dictates terms, or has terms dictated to them. Government agencies are constantly entering into negotiations that produce legally binding agreements—for example, labor contracts. Given that fact, nothing prevents government officials from engaging in nonbinding negotiations, assuming, of course, that they are attentive to "sunshine" laws and other due process considerations.

Two other issues of entry—the neutrality and competence of the proposed helper—often present themselves early in the negotiating process. How can all sides be certain that the go-between is unbiased, and will be equally helpful to all the parties? Wouldn't it be easy for a seemingly disinterested helper to favor one side over the others while disguising his or her stance as neutral? Even if all sides can be sure that the intermediary is impartial, can they be sure of his or her competence? What if the neutral botches the job, causing everything to take far longer and cost far more than would otherwise have been the case?

The question of neutrality is actually not difficult to resolve. Once again, "veto power" is the key. Any party to a dispute can disqualify a proposed helper who seems biased. Obviously, the background and affiliation of the intermediary are fundamental considerations. It is much easier for a helper to be accepted by all the parties, for example, if he or she has had no direct affiliation with any of the stakeholders. Also, the record and reputation of the proposed helper should be reviewed and approved by all the participants. If the helper begins work before all anticipated participants have joined the negotiations, it should be with a clear understanding that the helper may still be disqualified by a late participant with a complaint about bias.

These same four criteria—background, affiliation, record, and reputation—are equally useful in assessing a potential intermediary's competence. [...]

Different helpers have distinct styles. Some define their role very narrowly; others are willing to take on a broader set of roles. Some expect the disputants to handle many of the details of the negotiation; others are willing to carry more of the burden.[1] It makes sense to ask a potential helper to submit a proposed contract enumerating his or her concerns and commitments. It is not uncommon for disputants to collect written information about and interview half a dozen potential helpers before settling on one. A written agreement spelling out the disputants' expectations regarding the helpers role and obligations can avoid misunderstandings later.

ROLES AND FUNCTIONS OF AN INTERMEDIARY

The easiest way to think about the functions that a helper plays in a public dispute is to refer again to the three phases of the consensus-building process ... There are several tasks that the helper can complete at each step. [See Table 5.1.]

Getting started, as we have already emphasized, may well depend on the assistance of a nonpartisan convenor. The helper, however he or she entered the process, will probably have to spend a substantial amount of time meeting with potential stakeholders to convince them that a negotiated approach can work. Because the notion of joint problem solving is alien to most parties in public disputes, helpers often find it necessary to describe situations in which consensual approaches produced better outcomes than conventional approaches. This means that the intermediary needs to be well versed in the actual practice, and not just the theory, of dispute resolution.

The neutral can allow all parties to maintain the appearance of "toughness" while still supporting the search for integrative outcomes. This is accomplished by allowing the parties to communicate cooperative messages through the helper while maintaining a less cooperative "public" stance in meetings of the full group. To the extent that the helper can alert the parties ahead of time to the fact that an uncompromising statement is about to be made, but that the statement does not really represent that stakeholders "bottom line," the helper can head off

Table 5.1 Tasks of the Mediator

PHASES	TASKS
PRE-NEGOTIATION	
Getting started	Meeting with potential stakeholders to assess their interests and describe the consensus building process; handling logistics and convening initial meetings; assisting groups in initial calculation of BATNAs
Representation	Caucusing with stakeholders to help choose spokespeople or team leaders; working with initial stakeholders to identify missing groups or strategies for representing diffuse interests
Drafting protocols and agenda setting Joint fact-finding	Preparing draft protocols based on past experience and the concerns of the parties; managing the process of agenda setting Helping to draft fact-finding protocols; identifying technical consultants or advisors to the group; raising and administering the funds in a resource pool; serving as a repository for confidential or proprietary information
NEGOTIATION	
Inventing options	Managing the brainstorming process; suggesting potential options for the group to consider; coordinating subcommittees to draft options
Packaging	Caucusing privately with each group to identify and test possible trades; suggesting possible packages for the group to consider
Written agreement	Working with a subcommittee to produce a draft agreement; managing a single-text procedure; preparing a preliminary draft of a single text
Binding the parties	Serving as the holder of the bond; approaching outsiders on behalf of the group; helping to invent new ways to bind the parties to their commitments
Ratification	Helping the participants "sell" the agreement to their constituents; ensuring that all representatives have been in touch with their constituents
IMPLEMENTATION OR POST-NEGOTIATION	
Linking informal agreements and decision making	Working with the parties to invent linkages; approaching elected or appointed officials on formal behalf of the group; identifying the legal constraints on implementation
Monitoring	Serving as the monitor of implementation; convening a monitoring group
Renegotiation	Reassembling the participants if subsequent disagreements emerge; helping to remind the group of its earlier intentions

confrontations. In addition, by suggesting neutral turf for the first meeting, handling all the logistical arrangements, and proposing a provisional set of protocols to guide the initial discussions, the helper can assist the parties in overcoming many of the initial obstacles to successful negotiation.

It may appear that we are describing a "chicken-and-egg" problem: The parties must meet in order to identify a helper who will help them arrange a meeting. This is rarely the case in practice. Typically, a potential helper is contacted by one side (without the concurrence of the others) or by a noninvolved observer. The helper then calls the other parties and (assuming conditions are right) proposes either an initial get-together, at which everyone can talk, or a round of private caucuses between the helper and each stakeholding group. The helper has no guarantee that he or she will be paid, or that negotiations are even likely to happen. This is an "up-front" investment of time that potential helpers must make, comparable to the investment builders make when they prepare a bid for a possible project.

Representation is another prenegotiation task that helpers are often called upon to handle. Before a professional mediator or facilitator will invest the time needed to complete a conflict assessment or to help with representation, however, he or she will probably require a contract. Such a contract might cover only the first few steps in the proposed negotiation process. It might be written initially with just the key stakeholders, and amended later as more groups are added, and as the stakeholders decide to commit to a full-fledged negotiation. The preliminary contract gives the helper an indication of the seriousness of the group's commitment to the process.

Intermediaries can advise potential stakeholders about strategies for selecting spokespersons. They can also assist all the participants in undertaking a preliminary analysis of their alternatives to negotiation. They can make it clear to groups anxious about perceived imbalances of power that everyone will have a chance to be heard, and that available information will be shared.

As a spokesperson for and manager of the process, the helper is the only one in a position to promise the parties that the rules of the game will be enforced. The helper can also serve as a link to the media. In fact, it is often advisable for the helper to be the only person who talks to the press during an ongoing negotiation. This minimizes the temptation some groups may feel to negotiate through the press.

The neutral can play a critical role in bringing recalcitrant parties to the bargaining table. For example, by offering assurances that the rules of the game will be strictly enforced, the helper may be able to sign on less powerful groups.

Conversely, the neutral may bring subtle pressure to bear on more powerful parties, by convincing them that sit ting on the sidelines could entail a high price. If used heavy-handedly, of course, such tactics usually backfire. But if used skillfully, they may overcome what would otherwise be insurmountable barriers to consensus building.

Development of protocols and agenda setting are tasks that are best managed by a neutral—first through private discussions with each party, and then in group discussion. The listing of potential agenda topics may seem a simple mechanical task, but in fact there is an art to compressing numerous items into a manageable set of priorities that all parties can accept.

Experienced intermediaries can also save disputants a great deal of time by drafting preliminary protocols. Blending elements from past dispute situations, the helper can provide a draft that the group can use as a starting point. At the very least, illustrations of the ways in which other groups have handled similar problems are reassuring. The helper can also include the draft agenda and the agreed-upon protocols as conditions of his or her contract. This not only commits the neutral to procedures the participants want, but it also reassures mistrustful parties that the protocols will not be ignored.

Joint fact-finding may require various kinds of assistance from a neutral. For example, the group may rely on a helper to come up with names of potential expert advisors that all stakeholders can accept. The intermediary may serve as the "banker" for studies that are jointly commissioned—holding and allocating funds contributed by each of the stakeholders. In situations involving confidential or proprietary information, the helper may be asked to summarize data in ways that protect one party's legitimate need for privacy, without concealing useful data. A variation on this role arises when negotiators must share business information, but such sharing may constitute a violation of antitrust laws. The neutral, in such a circumstance, can serve as a repository for information, using summaries of findings without mentioning particular companies.

A neutral may also be asked to assist in raising money to establish a resource pool—that is, a "kitty" of money which the group as a whole can draw upon. At one point, for example, the EPA created a resource pool to ensure the availability of funds to the participants in that agency's "negotiated rulemakings."[2] The participants were meeting, at EPA's request, to help draft regulations to implement a portion of the Clean Air Act. The funds in the resource pool were available to any of the twenty-five participating groups who needed reimbursement for travel or other expenses incurred during the negotiations. Resources were also available to the group as a whole to commission joint fact-finding studies. The convenor—not an EPA official—held the funds for the group and allocated them in accordance with decisions made by the group as a whole.

Sometimes a *team* of intermediaries is needed. This is particularly useful in complex disputes hinging on scientific questions. In such a case, an expert in process management may want to team up with a neutral who has relevant technical background. Again, the second member of the team would also have to be acceptable to all the stakeholders, even though he or she would advise the process manager rather than the participants.

Even more elaborate teams are sometimes appropriate. In the Harmon County sewage cleanup case, ... the out-of-state mediator appointed by the court teamed up with a local mediator—who had a thorough knowledge of the state's political and legal systems—as well as with several engineering professionals, who developed a computer model the mediators could use to forecast the costs of various settlement proposals.

Inventing options ... requires a process of brain storming and intensive subcommittee work. The neutral can be the one to declare a period of "inventing without committing." He or she can also be the compiler of good ideas. The helper may even put forward options that participants want considered but feel uneasy about suggesting themselves. So, for example, one or another group might approach the helper privately and ask that he or she mention an option without revealing its source.

Inventing options has its perils, though. Intermediaries have to be careful not to become too closely identified with particular options or proposals, for if a participant feels that the helper has become too supportive of a specific proposal, that stakeholder may feel that the helper can no longer be trusted to remain neutral. This does not mean, of course, that intermediaries cannot offer suggestions. Skilled neutrals should know how to present ideas in a dispassionate fashion, thereby reassuring the participants that the intermediary is nonpartisan.

Packaging is the step that generally involves the greatest skill and insight. It is here that helpers can play their most important role. By meeting privately with each participant, an intermediary should be able to discover which items are tradeable. Typically, the helper says to each party in a private caucus, "What's most important to you?" Or, "What can you most readily give up?" Through confidential questioning, an effective intermediary should be able to figure out a set of trades that will bring the participants as close to agreement as they can possibly get. (Of course, this can only occur if the neutral has already demonstrated competence and earned the trust of the parties.)

An intermediary can offer the parties a chance to suggest possible trades without making commitments. In a private conversation, the helper might say, "I know what you've said in the full meetings, but tell me: Would you will be willing to trade X if the others offered you Y and Z?" At this point, the disputant might say, "I won't say it out loud at the meeting, but if I were offered Y and Z, yes, I would trade X." This is crucial information which the helper must find a way of testing with the other parties—without violating a confidence, of course.

A skilled intermediary can, in private meetings with the other participants, explore whether they would be willing to give up Y and Z in exchange for X. This might be phrased, "What if I could get them to give up X? Would you trade Y and Z?" Of course, the neutral already knows that such a trade is possible. He or she must phrase the question, though, in what-if format to protect the confidentiality of the information secured earlier. If the answer is "yes," the helper might call everyone together and offer the following observation: "I have a hunch that if the folks on this side of the room were willing to offer X the others would promise to give Y and Z. Am I correct?"

By proceeding in this fashion, the intermediary has made no promises, and has attributed no commitments to anyone. The end result, if all goes well, is a package that everyone can accept.

Written agreements need to be drafted by someone, and in most cases the neutral is the obvious person to play this role. To the extent that an intermediary can produce a single text and carry it from party to party, he or she can ensure that everyone agrees to the same thing. This is a great advantage in negotiations. Long-time international treaty negotiators use the "single-text" procedure described earlier, which is much more likely to produce agreement than a process in which each party drafts its own version of the final agreement and those versions are later integrated.

In the single text procedure, the helper asks each party to suggest "improvements" in a draft attributed to the intermediary. Because the draft is not "extreme" and refrains from arguing only for what one side or the other wants most, progress is likely to ensue.

Binding the parties involves the invention of enforcement mechanisms. We have already described the device of setting aside funds. In some instances, the intermediary may be the person favored by all sides to "hold the bet." In other instances, the helper may be asked to approach someone who has not been involved in the negotiations, to see whether that individual might play a role in binding the parties. It is usually the case that skilled helpers can assist disputing parties in inventing new ways to bind each other to an agreement.

Ratification requires each participant to go back to his or her constituents and seek approval of the draft agreement. For some participants, this may present difficulties, particularly if their group began the negotiations with utterly unrealistic expectations. The helper may be able to aid such participants in "selling" the agreement to their members, perhaps by pointing out how far all the other stakeholders have come in accepting the draft agreement. The helper may also be able to emphasize truthfully how effective the group's negotiator was. ("You should have seen how far along your spokesperson was able to pull the rest of the group. She was an incredibly effective advocate of your interests.") The group's spokesperson, of course, could not make such claims without seeming to brag. If true, though, the fact of effectiveness is significant, and needs to be pointed out.

The process of *linking the informal agreement and formal decision making* requires interaction with elected or appointed officials, who may not have participated directly in the negotiations (although they should have been apprised of the progress of the negotiations by their staff or appointed observers). Because the neutral is an advocate of the process and not of any particular outcome, it is usually easier for officials to accept a helper's claim regarding the legitimacy of the process than the claims of a stakeholder.

The participants may want the helper to play a role in *monitoring* implementation of the agreement. Although this is not often the case (it is better to have monitoring performed by people on the scene), it is sometimes a possibility. The helper may be asked by the participants to approach outsiders who have not been involved in the negotiations to ask them to play the monitoring role. In many cases, it is easier for the helper to make these contacts, and to be convincing about the legitimacy of the process, than it is for any one of the disputants.

It is likely that the participants will want to specify in the agreement what the helper's role will be if *renegotiation* (or "remediation") is necessary. Who better to reassemble the parties, or to remind them of their previous commitments? Also, the parties are likely to feel that the helper will be a fair referee of what was originally intended, should subsequent disagreements arise. It should be noted, though, that very few helpers will accept a renegotiation role if they have assisted in drafting the original agreement; they prefer to move on to new disputes.

When we describe the roles and functions of intermediaries in distributional disputes, some people mistakenly conclude that helpers in public disputes do roughly what intermediaries in labor disputes or international disputes do. But those familiar with the roles of such intermediaries (or "third parties," as they are often called, as there are usually only two disputing sides in labor negotiations) will recognize immediately from the preceding descriptions that there are very substantial differences between assisted negotiation in distributional disputes and other kinds of assisted negotiation.

In short, neutrals in distributional disputes need to be more activist. They have a much broader array of responsibilities, because the context in which they work is much less structured. They need a different kind of background, different skills, and perhaps a different temperament from their counterparts in labor relations and international relations. Intermediaries in distributional disputes usually need to be quite conversant with the ways in which the public sector operates, because they may spend as much time creating the context in which negotiations take place as they do managing the consensus-building process. They also need more sharply honed communication skills, since they may have to spend significant amounts of time "selling the process" to potential participants and the community at large.

Given the scope of the intermediaries' involvement in most distributional disputes, it is important that they be willing to accept some responsibility for the fairness, efficiency, wisdom, and stability of the outcomes. This is not inconsistent with the concept of neutrality. While those who participate directly must "own" the agreement, the neutral must also assure himself or herself that everything possible has been done to meet the concerns of those who chose not to participate directly as well as the concerns of those who did. Long-term voluntary compliance requires that this test be met. Unless it is, the credibility of the consensus-building effort is likely to erode. In addition, to the extent that consensual dispute resolution processes are likely to be judged against the conventional judicial, administrative, and legislative mechanisms, assisted negotiation must meet the same tests of performance they do.

THREE FORMS OF ASSISTED NEGOTIATION

Within the realm of assisted negotiation, various approaches can be taken. We will consider three: *facilitation, mediation, and nonbinding arbitration.* These techniques, though distinguishable, are not mutually exclusive. In fact, a helper may find it advantageous to move back and forth among them as a negotiation progresses. These approaches are presented separately in the following pages primarily to make clear what each entails.

In general, the stakeholders must make a preliminary decision about the form of assistance they want—if only to help them choose an appropriately skilled neutral. The question they must first answer is, "How much help will we need in order to work together effectively?" Conceived differently, the same question maybe phrased, "How much assistance in managing the negotiation process are we likely to require in order to reach a satisfactory conclusion?" Process is the key word here. Facilitation, mediation, and nonbinding arbitration assign different degrees of procedural responsibility to the helper. In all negotiations, the issues of managerial responsibility is paramount. Ideally, the disputing parties should retain as much control as possible over the dispute resolution process. If they do, they are much more likely to produce an agreement they will support.

Indeed, this was our rationale for focusing first on unassisted negotiation. We maintain that it is best when disputing parties retain full control over both the process and substance of a dispute resolution effort. But when unassisted negotiations fail, or when the problem is obviously too complex for resolution without help, the disputing parties must consider the various forms of assistance available.

As noted, we have chosen to limit our discussion and recommendations to facilitation, mediation, and nonbinding arbitration. We have not included a fourth technique: binding arbitration. One compelling argument against employing binding arbitration in distributional disputes is a legal one. In most cases, public officials are not permitted to delegate their authority to an arbitrator. Therefore, the application of binding arbitration is severely limited. More important, in the context of this book, is our conviction that disputing parties can and should deal with their differences themselves. They are more likely to confront the sources of difficulty and improve long-term relationships if they do. Turning over responsibility for decision making to an outsider rarely resolves under lying conflicts.

FACILITATION

Facilitation is the simplest form of assisted negotiation. The facilitator focuses almost entirely on process, makes sure meeting places and times are agreed upon, sees that meeting space is arranged appropriately, and ensures that notes and minutes of the meetings are kept. He or she sometimes acts as a moderator, usually when many parties are involved.

Even in the moderator's role, however, facilitators rarely volunteer their own ideas. Instead, they monitor the quality of the dialogue and intervene with questions designed to enhance understanding. "Are you really listening to each other?" the facilitator might ask. "I've jotted down what each person has said. Are you sure you've identified what's most important to you? Why don't you say again what you are really concerned about, so that the others can focus on that?"

Comments of this type certainly touch on the substance of the issues being discussed, but the facilitator's emphasis is on communication. He or she uses whatever tools are available to create and foster an environment conducive to joint problem solving. Without pretending to be a therapist, the facilitator also tries to make it easier for the participants to express their emotions.

A facilitator must improvise from meeting to meeting, taking cues from the negotiations themselves. Perhaps the best way to illustrate this improvisational activity—as well as the more general and constant activities of the facilitator—is to return to two of our original cases: RiverEnd and the dioxin dispute.

FACILITATING THE RIVEREND DISPUTE RESOLUTION EFFORT

The RiverEnd negotiations took place over fourteen months, with the participants meeting one evening every two weeks. Meetings were held in a state agency field office in the RiverEnd area. Attendance rarely dropped below twenty-five, and there were almost always observers and reporters present, in part because all meetings were listed in the local newspapers. Participants agreed at the onset that no formal votes would be taken, and that informal procedures would be used in preference to Robert's *Rules of Order*. Facilitator Elliott Lawrence was asked to chair all the meetings, to regulate the pace and topics of conversation, and to assume whatever other responsibilities for managing the process he deemed necessary.

Included in the group of active participants were engineers, landscape architects, and environmental scientists. All had backgrounds and professional credentials equal to or greater than those of the agency personnel or the consultants selected by the state government to assist the group. Neighborhood representatives had extensive firsthand information about such significant factors as flooding patterns, water flow, noise levels, and wildlife habitats. The citizen participants, to their credit, were not intimidated by claims that certain evidence or analytical techniques might be too complex for them to understand. They plowed through the reports, references, and documents produced by the consultants, and spent hours debating the merits of baseline estimates, forecasts, and impact assessments.

The negotiations generally confirmed the adage that the best ideas occur to prepared minds. A consensus could not have emerged before the individuals stakeholders under stood the details of the proposed project, and were unfamiliar with each interest group's priorities. Preparation, therefore, was essential, and the facilitator Lawrence used five techniques to enhance the group's understanding: (1) "charettes," (2) opinion surveys and straw polls, (3) brainstorming sessions, (4) role playing, and (5) collective image building.

Charettes, or intensive problem-solving workshops, were used to explore specifics such as possible alignments of the transit tracks through residential areas. Participants sketched the most desirable alignments and station locations on a large map. Each participant or coalition presented its map and argued for its proposals. The rest of the participants then indicated their concerns and raised questions about possible engineering constraints.

Between meetings, participants were asked by Lawrence to mail back questionnaires designed to clarify underlying conflicts. For instance, a poll with multiple-choice answers detailing the probable advantages and disadvantages of different parking garage sizes narrowed the scope of the debate, and suggested that a broader basis of agreement existed than was indicated by the participants' public positions. Presentation of these survey results eliminated the need for extended debate and sharpened the agenda to every one's satisfaction.

Brainstorming sessions were used to generate additional design options, and also to identify issues about which the participants were confused. For instance, early attempts to generate new roadway and ramp designs indicated that many of the participants were unclear about the constraints posed by grade, slope, and soil characteristics, even though they had already heard general presentations on these subjects. As a result, the facilitator scheduled additional presentations by outside experts acceptable to the entire group.

Role-playing exercises, which encouraged disputants to switch positions, helped to build respect and understanding for opposing points of view. The most ardent developers, for example, were teamed up with the environmentalists to examine the probable environmental impacts of suggested roadway designs. Similarly, environmentalists were asked to look at the same roadway proposals with an eye toward maximizing the return on private investment and increasing tax revenues for Capital City.

Finally, in an effort to focus the participants' thinking about possible open-space improvements, the group examined color slides of parks and parklike elements—such as landscaping along highways, lighting, and pedestrian walkways—from other places in the country. These explorations helped the group crystallize its concerns about esthetics. One of the most interesting outcomes of the collective imaging process was that after viewing slides of other garages (including some superimposed on the proposed RiverEnd site), almost everyone agreed that a 10,000-car garage, the size proposed initially by the state, was utterly inappropriate.

As meeting after meeting clarified concerns and sharpened differences, facilitator Lawrence searched for ways to help the parties put together a package that would be acceptable to everyone. He encouraged the formation of a subcommittee to think about the opportunities created by the regional mass transit facility, rather than just the problems or adverse impacts it was likely to cause. At his suggestion, the group was headed by the most ardent environmentalist, Horst Seybolt, and dubbed itself the "Linear Park group." It envisioned parklike landscaping along the transportation corridor that would connect open space areas, soften the impact of the automobile, and create a pleasant atmosphere for pedestrians. Other environmentalists supported this idea because they thought it would reinforce the hoped-for "human scale" of the new transit facilities, and enhance the visual appearance of the area. It also had some potential to channel federal and state transportation money into a "kitty" that could be used to add recreational and open spaces, improve pedestrian and bicycle paths, and restore the long-vanished park like atmosphere along the roadway.

The Linear Park group, with consulting assistance arranged by Lawrence, prepared and presented detailed proposals to the full group. The development-oriented members of the group agreed that the linear park concept would provide a competitive edge in attracting commercial investment and new customers. Landscaping and land acquisition would complement, rather than impede, construction of the new subway station and garage.

The linear park concept emerged in large part because the environmentalists were unhappy with most of the options put forward by the state and regional agencies. The proposals generated by the state presumed that the primary objective of the project was to create a regional transit stop that would spur economic development; it was clear that effecting environmental improvements was not an important agency objective.

The environmentalists originally felt they had no choice but to argue for the no-build option, which they did. They were immediately accused of impeding progress, of sabotaging the planning effort, and of frustrating the legitimate economic interests of the neighborhoods. This was an uncomfortable position. Moreover, they soon realized that a constructive alternative would give them additional bargaining leverage. Although they threatened more than once to block the entire project in the courts, they ultimately decided instead to use the proposed subway extension to seek environmental improvements. Why? Because they had reached a crucial realization: No outcome resulting from a lengthy court battle was likely to reverse RiverEnd's decline, which after all had resulted from decades of neglect and unplanned development.

RiverEnd, then, can serve as a useful model of facilitation. Through the activities designed and managed by the facilitator, the stakeholders began to see items that could be traded. The emergence of the linear park proposal, through which almost every group could gain at least partially, helped to persuade skeptics that a consensual approach was both possible and promising. By managing meetings to ensure effective communication and by assisting the participants in programming their time, Lawrence created a climate in which joint problem solving was possible. Significantly, he did not offer proposals. He did not meet privately with the parties between meetings. He did not carry confidential messages back and forth among the factions at the bargaining table. He did not help the parties produce a written agreement, or design mechanisms for binding each other to their commitments. Lawrence basically "managed" the group discussions—and, by the time those discussions concluded, all parties felt they had achieved a fairer, more stable, more efficient, and wiser agreement than would otherwise have emerged.

FACILITATING THE DIOXIN NEGOTIATION

You will recall that Dr. Gene McGerny, the facilitator in the dioxin case, was asked by the Academy of Sciences to bring together the scientists and engineers who disagreed about the risks associated with the proposed resource recovery plant at the Federal Navy Yard. Most of the members of the city council (or representatives from their staff) were in the audience; they faced the assembled experts seated at the front of the room. Approximately thirty neighborhood and environmental groups, including many residents of the Brownstone neighborhood, were also in attendance.

Dr. McGerny had worked hard before the meeting to get the city council members to list in writing the issues that most concerned them. The questions he received in response were easily grouped under three headings: the nature of the dioxin risk, the possibility of reducing or eliminating the risk, and the health impacts of dioxin emissions. The first set of questions was most usefully put to environmental scientists; the second to engineers; and the third to medical or public health specialists. Dr. McGerny had taken special care to assemble balanced panels: None of the participants had as yet taken a public stand on the question posed by the city council.

As Dr. McGerny put the first set of questions, one at a time, to the panel of scientists, he tried to avoid any indication that he was taking sides. Each panelist was given all the time he or she needed to answer each question. Panelists had the chance to pose questions to each other, as well as to comment on what the others had said. City council members had the opportunity to ask follow-up questions through Dr. McGerny. Whenever the interaction among the scientists drifted into highly technical exchanges, McGerny interrupted, seeking clarification in "plain English."

By the end of the first panel on the nature and sources of dioxin, it had become clear that there were two very different schools of thought. One side believed strongly that dioxin was the natural and inevitable by-product of incinerating plastic and paper at the same time (a theory popularized by the ubiquitous ecologist, Professor Lassiter, who attended the session). The other side disputed this view, arguing that dioxin and its dangers could be eliminated entirely by proper burning.

By the end of the second panel—which examined the prospects of controlling the dioxin risk, if it indeed arose—conflicting views had again emerged. One group of engineers believed that burning municipal trash at a high enough temperature, and by simultaneously controlling the amount of oxygen present, dioxin emissions could be all but eliminated. Whatever tiny amounts remained could be captured by flue filters or removed by precipitators. But another group of engineers argued that based on the data they had obtained from resource recovery plants operating elsewhere, high temperatures, controlled oxygen flow, and filters and precipitators would still permit the escape of a significant amount of dioxin.

A split also developed among the health experts regarding the nature of the risk to humans posed by dioxin in the air. They disagreed on whether it was reasonable to infer from tests on laboratory rats what the effects of dioxin would be on people. Each side posited different models of events that might lead to unsafe dioxin emissions from the resource recovery plant. One model, for example, depicted a chain of events in which the plant broke down during the summer. Emissions then drifted into homes through open windows, dust settled on the floors and windowsills, and dioxin was ultimately ingested through hand contact.

As the panelists talked, the facilitator highlighted their arguments on large pads of paper displayed at the front of the room. As each page was filled, the facilitator taped it to the wall. Soon paper covered practically every available inch of wall space. Dr. McGerny repeatedly checked with the panelists to be certain that he had recorded the points they thought were most important. This somewhat exhausting process lasted almost eight hours, but as certain patterns began to emerge, it proved to be time well spent.

For example, some of the conflicts arose from reliance on different sets of data, with one side claiming that precedents cited by the other were irrelevant. The engineers could not even agree on whether existing resource recovery plants were similar enough in design to the plant proposed for the Navy Yard to permit comparisons.

A second source of conflict could be traced to the different ways in which the experts framed their questions. For instance, one health-effects expert attempted to answer the question, "Is there any chance that a dangerous amount of dioxin could escape into the environment?" His answer was yes. His scientific adversary, however, was trying to answer a different question, "Is it likely that a dangerous amount of dioxin will escape?" His answer was no. When pressed by the facilitator, the first expert agreed that the chances of getting cancer from a dioxin leak were less that a nonsmoker's chances of getting cancer from living with a smoker. Both experts agreed, on the other hand, that if a large amount of dioxin did manage to escape into the air, the cancer rate in Metropolis might well increase significantly.

The most important source of controversy, however, did not result from these sorts of scientific, engineering, and epidemiological differences. The disagreement hinged, as it turned out, on one sides use of a "worst case" scenario and the other's reliance on a "most likely case." It soon became clear that what had been thought of as a fundamental disagreement regarding the facts—in other words, the basic science of the dispute—was in reality a disagreement over the choice of a method of analysis. (Everyone had agreed, we should note, that the state's proposed dioxin emission standard was reasonable.)

Although the sessions were somewhat heated, the debate proceeded in an orderly fashion. After hearing the presentations, the council had to consider its options. First, however, after some prodding from Dr. McGerny, Professor Lassiter made what appeared to be a significant concession. He agreed to support construction of a pilot resource recovery plant if the city would promise that (1) a careful and regular dioxin monitoring procedure would be adopted; (2) the commercial builder of the plant would sign a contract indicating a willingness to have the plant closed down permanently if it emitted more dioxin than permitted under the state standard; and (3) all liability for accidents or injuries caused by the plant would be covered by either the city or the commercial builder of the plant.

Professor Lassiter, it seems, was assuming that no commercial vendor would agree to build the plant under such unattractive conditions. He was evidently surprised when the Department of Sanitation immediately indicated its readiness to accept these terms. Perhaps that readiness should not have come as such a surprise. After all, from the city's standpoint, a plant ought not to be licensed unless it could meet the agreed-upon state standard. On this point, then, agreement was possible because the contending interests continued to operate with totally different assessments of probable risks. Lassiter, for his part, thought the risk of significant dioxin emissions was high and that no vendor would be willing to live with a double-edged sword of shutdown and liability dangling over its head. The city, on the other hand, was convinced that the technology had been proven effective, and that finding a vendor willing to build a plant that would meet the state standards would be no problem. Therefore, the financial risk was, in their view, small. Although the disputing parties continued to disagree on the nature of the risk, they were—by exploiting their differences—able to agree on how to proceed.

In this case, the facilitator spent little or no time meeting privately with the parties. Instead, McGerny devoted most of his energies to making the meeting work. He was able to clarify the sources and nature of the disagreements, and to make sure everyone understood what was being said. Finally, the facilitator played almost no role in devising the actual terms of an agreement. Instead, Dr. McGerny focused on achieving an agreement in principle.

FACILITATION: A SUMMARY

Because facilitation is the simplest form of assisted negotiation, and because the facilitator restricts himself or herself to procedural questions, it might seem that the facilitators role is insignificant. This is not the case. The facilitator makes possible a negotiating process that would otherwise be impossible. Consider a situation in which each of the disputing parties is unwilling to make the first phone call. ("We don't want to look too anxious; let's wait for them to call us.") Clearly, unassisted negotiation is unlikely to begin in such a situation, let alone succeed. In other cases, one or more of the parties may make it clear that they will not even consider coming to the table, if by so doing they must give up any control over the substance of the negotiation. Again, the facilitator makes otherwise impossible negotiations possible.

Even after negotiations have begun and seem to be proceeding well, the facilitator can play a vital role. What happens, for example, if one of the disputing parties stalks out of the proceedings as a result of a real or imagined slight? Without a facilitator, the negotiations simply stop. With a facilitator, there is a chance that they can resume, perhaps on an improved footing. "Let me talk with the others privately," the facilitator can say to the aggrieved party. "Let me see if I can get them to recognize that from your standpoint they are being unreasonable."

In summary, facilitation is called for when the disputing parties need some assistance, but want that help limited to focusing or moderating their discussions. The facilitator serves at the pleasure of all the negotiating parties. All parties must jointly choose the facilitator, but each group has the right to "fire" that person if they conclude that he or she is biased, incompetent, or otherwise unsatisfactory. The facilitator, a skilled process manager, takes whatever procedural steps are necessary to keep the discussion on a useful course.

MEDIATION

Mediation intensifies the substantive involvement of the neutral without removing control over the outcome from the parties. It also involves the helper in a great deal more confidential interaction with the parties. Just as some disputes are too complex for unassisted negotiation, others are too formidable for facilitation. In such cases, the disputing parties should decide ahead of time that they need more help from an outside neutral.

The parties may begin with facilitation and discover that they are not making much progress, or that the progress they are making is too slow. Or—simply put—the parties may not be good at sitting in a room together. The "hardness" of their public postures may preclude real give and take. If this is the case, they may need someone to relieve them of responsibility for devising and presenting options. "We know we need help," they may conclude, "and that means more than someone to facilitate communication and arrange meetings. We need someone who can meet with each side privately and give us a sense of how far apart we really are."

For those private meetings to succeed, the neutral must be knowledgeable about the issues of concern to the parties. This is one important function of the mediator: carrying private messages among parties. In essence, the mediator plays a transforming role—helping the parties out of a zero-sum mind-set into an integrative bargaining framework. Early in the negotiating process, private caucuses are crucial to understanding the real interests of the parties and the ways they have calculated their BATNAs. To ensure can did exchanges, the mediator must be able to promise confidentiality.

With the inside knowledge that comes from these meetings, the mediator is not in the position to understand what is tradeable and what is not. Moving back and forth among the parties, the mediator is in a position to launch trial balloons. As we mentioned earlier, the mediator may begin meetings with statements like this: "I have a hunch that if Group A offers this and Group B offers that, you will find yourselves much closer together than you imagined."

While taking a large measure of responsibility for the substance of the agreement that emerges, the mediator must remain neutral. In other words, the mediator must submerge his or her sense of what is "best," and focus instead on the disputing parties' own measures of success. For many professional mediators, this is a very difficult role to play. Many of them have extensive knowledge about the substance of the dispute; this means they are likely to have personal feelings about what will work and what will not. Their previous mediation experience, furthermore, may tempt them to "steer" the negotiations toward solutions that have proven successful in the past.

Both of these temptations must be resisted. As for the mediators own conclusions regarding the substance of the negotiated agreement, they can be destructive if expressed in a way that implies partiality. A mediator with a commitment to a particular outcome is akin to a real estate agent—who seems to act as a neutral intermediary, but is in fact an advocate for one side, with a direct financial interest in the sale price. At the same time, the mediator must generate enthusiasm and support for a proposed settlement. If the mediator steers a negotiation in a direction that the parties only halfheartedly support, subsequent implementation of the agreement will be difficult.

There are qualities of a negotiated agreement for which a mediator must be willing to be held accountable. The perceived fairness of the outcome, for example, is as much the mediators responsibility as it is the parties'. If the mediator permits a process that is viewed as unfair at its conclusion, and does not urge the parties to consider other, more appropriate ways of proceeding, he or she will not have done a creditable job. This is very much an interventionist posture, because raising such concerns does not necessarily guarantee that the parties will make adjustments. (If they fail to do so, of course, the mediator must ultimately decide whether or not to remain a part of the negotiations.) The long-term credibility of a mediator depends on ensuring that every possible effort was made to meet the interests of all the parties involved. If a proposed settlement appears exploitative or unworkable, the mediator is obligated to question the validity of such a settlement. He or she should seek to "raise doubts," either by invoking concerns about subsequent implementability or fairness.

Sharing responsibility means that the mediator will raise these concerns. It is not the mediator's role, however, to dictate terms, or to represent specific interests who may be having trouble representing themselves effectively. When conflicts arise—whether between the disputing parties or between the parties and "outside-world" interests—the mediator rarely says, "I'll tell you what you ought to do." Instead, the mediator tends to ask, "Can't we review the procedures we have followed, and come up with something that will get everyone closer to their individual objectives? I'll tell you how I think the outside world will respond to what we have come up with so far; but my job is to help you reach an agreement that is yours."

The circumstances were different and therefore different approaches to mediation were required. Nevertheless, they illustrate clearly the advantages of mediation.

Mediating the Fishing Rights Dispute

Judge Eastman encouraged the disputants to select a mediator from the list of twelve candidates he had identified. (His assumption was that the parties would be more inclined to work with someone they had selected.) The disputants settled on mediator Leslie Burmaster, who was hired with funds provided by the federal and state governments. Each level of government put $100,000 into a "kitty," from which the mediator could be paid by the court (at a specified hourly rate), and through which technical studies could be purchased.

Burmaster spent three months getting to know the parties. The key participants included the director of the state's Department of Natural resources, a lawyer for the state, the deputy undersecretary of the U.S. Department of Interior, and the negotiators for the tribes. Burmaster also spent the first few months assembling a team of technical consultants, whose responsibility it would be to advise the parties about the impact of alternative management policies on the total fish catch. The consultants, including specialists from a range of disciplines, put together detailed models of the lake's ecology.

Before beginning the full negotiations, Burmaster decided to bring the tribes together to negotiate an intertribal allocation plan. She encouraged them to negotiate an agreement that would go into effect whether or not the tribes and the state reached an agreement. From Burmaster s perspective, whether the tribes collectively ended up with 20 percent or 80 percent of the overall catch, they would still have to agree on how to divide their share. Burmaster saw a successful intertribal negotiation as an inducement to the state to bargain seriously. Finally, she knew that the intertribal negotiations could only help the relatively inexperienced tribal negotiators sharpen their bargaining skills.

The tribes met for five days under Burmaster's watchful eye. Burmaster spent most of the time helping the parties understand each other's positions. She talked to them in a way that they could not, or would not, talk to each other. Burmaster made no effort to develop specific proposals; these, she felt, should come from them. In a relatively short period, the tribes were able to reach agreement, allocating certain sections of the lake to each tribe, and indicating specific times of the year when each tribe would be allowed to fish in given areas.

Having settled their internal differences, the tribes then collectively demanded 70 percent of the whitefish catch, leaving the remainder of the whitefish and the blue trout to commercial and sports fisherman. State officials resisted this demand for an overall allocation of the catch; they preferred instead to allocate the right to fish in certain zones of the lake. This might have been a difficult point, except for the fact that the federal government offered substantially more money than expected to cover the costs of managing the fisheries. The state, by prior agreement, was forced to match this increased federal allocation. The combined sums available for fish management assured the tribes that the total catch would increase, and that a rigid allocation of the catch was unnecessary.

In brief, the agreement divided the lake into zones for tribal fishing, nontribal commercial fishing, and game fishing. Several blue trout refuges were established and made off limits to all parties. Federal and state funds were assigned to a biological monitoring system, as well as the new fisheries management program. Mechanisms for implementing the agreement (which was to remain operative for fifteen years, until 2000) were also negotiated. Three joint committees were established: one to monitor the fish, one to decide how to manage the resources, and one to resolve disputes.

Although the drafting of a written agreement took a great deal of time, the final version was completed in a two-day session. Working through the night, the parties had nearly completed a final draft when the process stalled in the predawn hours. Everyone at the table was exhausted and short-tempered. Nevertheless, Burmaster feared that if she allowed the parties to break for even a few hours, the fragile understandings arrived at to that point might well unravel. She took a calculated risk: leading the key parties into a private room, she closed the door and staged a mock tantrum. Burmaster told them curtly that the agreement would almost certainly fall apart if they did not finish quickly. In fact, she said, they had to decide then and there whether they really wanted an agreement; then she stalked out of the room. The ploy worked: The parties quickly agreed on a final draft of the document.

Burmaster made several strategic choices that paid off. She decided to play a less intrusive role in shaping the agenda and formulating specific proposals than she might have. She encouraged the parties to think in terms of a fifteen-year agreement, rather than one that would last "in perpetuity." This took some of the pressure off the parties: If they made a mistake, there would be an opportunity to renegotiate. She also realized that "zoning" the lake was the key to transforming a win-lose situation into an all-gain opportunity.

As noted, she worked first with the tribes to produce an intertribal agreement, which in turn could be used to bring the state to the table. Burmaster decided to work directly with the parties, rather than their lawyers. (The lawyers were later assigned the task of drafting a document consistent with the commitments the parties had made to each other.) In short, she concentrated on enhancing the parties' ability to understand each other. Through her active interventions, the parties were able to reframe issues, share and generate new information, and develop procedures that allowed them to work together in spite of a lack of trust.

Above all, Burmaster focused on getting agreement in principle, assuming that the design of an implementation strategy could be handled afterward. This assumption turned out to be correct—largely because Burmaster was functioning as a special master under the aegis of the court. When one of the tribes unexpectedly reneged at the last minute on the terms of the final agreement, Judge Eastman ruled that the negotiated agreement was the agreement that the court would enforce. All the parties eventually concurred.

MEDIATING THE REGIONAL SEWAGE DISPUTE

Ron Jones and his local assistants, the mediation team, did as Judge Rollenkamp suggested: They searched for a cost allocation formula that all sides could accept. For the first few months, Jones did nothing but meet privately with the stakeholders—thirty-nine municipalities, the Harmon County Regional Sewage Authority, the Randall Company, the state agencies, and various other interests such as the County Homebuilders Association. At each meeting, he asked the same two questions, "What do you think a fair formula would be, and why?"

Jones also consulted with a variety of experts in the area of utility cost allocation. He needed a computer program that the parties could use to forecast the cost implications of alternative formulas.

As the private meeting progressed, the mediation team clarified and added to the list of concerns previously expressed by the parties. From the standpoint of the city of Harmon, the dominant issue was affordability, while the suburban communities and smaller towns were much more concerned about fair cost allocation. The communities in the northern part of the county wanted the sewage system in their district to be designed differently and to operate independently of the main plant in Harmon. This, they argued, would save everyone money. Finally, many of the communities expressed strong distrust of the regional Sewage Authority.

The mediators called in experts to review the detailed design of the sewage system proposed by the Sewage Authority. They sought advice on alternative strategies for financing the system. The more they explored the technical complexity of the dispute, however, the more mired in detail they became. Small but worrisome questions arose by the hundreds. Who, for example, would do a quarterly billing? Who would be responsible for unpaid sewer bills?

The development community, for its part, was worried that the overall capacity of the new regional system might not be sufficient to sustain future growth. Local officials were determined to receive compensation for past investments in local collection systems and treatment plants. Moreover, almost all the local officials wanted some additional role in the management of the new regional system, arguing that the Sewage Authority was not adequately accountable to local concerns.

At a large meeting to which all interested parties were invited, Jones asked for responses to a preliminary "package" of ideas the mediation team had drafted. The proposal had been sent to more than one hundred stakeholders before the meeting.

The all day session produced a number of suggested refinements that were blended into a revised proposal, which Jones submitted to Judge Rollenkamp for review. The judge distributed it for formal comment.

Jones was surprised when negative reactions began pouring into the Judge's office. He thought the proposed agreement had responded to all the issues raised by the parties. As it turned out though, the city of Harmon had decided to press for an even more favor able cost allocation. From Jones' point of view, the adverse reaction arose at least in part because the judge had asked the wrong question. Judge Rollenkamp had asked, "Are you completely happy with this agreement?" Jones would have preferred the judge to ask, "Can you live with this agreement?"

While agreeing that the mediator's package was reasonable, some of the smaller com munities argued that they still preferred not to be included in the regional system at all. Indeed, almost every stakeholding group indicated some change it wanted in the proposed agreement.

The judge thanked Jones, and indicated his satisfaction that the issues in the dispute had been narrowed. He also found all the background material and forecasts Jones and his staff had assembled to be quite useful. Jones was not satisfied, however; he asked for a six-week extension, and one more chance to develop an agreement that all the parties would accept. Judge Rollenkamp agreed.

The mediators began another round of private meetings, hoping to find out what it would take to bring the dissenters on board. They soon realized that there were three possible ways to reach closure: first, reduce the overall cost of the system through redesign; second, reduce the cost to the dissenters by bringing in new state or federal funds; or third, redefine the scope of the sewage clean-up problem so that the funds already in hand would be sufficient. Not wanting to limit his options prematurely, Jones decided to push on all three fronts. First, he pressed the regional authority to consider the merits of smaller treatment plants, instead of one large one. He and his staff met with federal and state officials to see if they would increase their financial contributions, in exchange for the parties dropping all pending litigation, and taking prompt action to clean up the rivers and streams. Finally, he pressed the EPA and the state Department of Environmental Protection to consider reducing the scope of the effort—or at least dividing the project into phases, which would have the effect of spreading the project's cost over a much longer time.

After five weeks of intensive negotiations, Jones proposed another package. This time, the city and the Randall Company promised in advance to support the package. The reason for their switch lay in a revised basis for calculating annual sewage charges. Previously, those charges were to be municipally defined "shares" based on each community's percentage of the total flow into the regional system. Under the new plan, there would be a consistent average household charge for everyone in the entire region. (This reduced Harmons overall charge.) Other towns found tempting amendments in the new package as well. For example, the revised package included a promise of a long-term, no interest loan from the state, a shift in responsibility for billing and collection from the local to the regional level, compensation to municipalities for abandoned treatment facilities, an option for smaller decentralized treatment plants (if they could be built at lower cost to the region), and the creation of a local advisory board that would ensure greater regional accountability to local concerns.

This time the package won practically unanimous approval. In response to his second "poll" of disputing groups, Judge Rollenkamp heard again from several municipalities that they would still prefer to stay out of the system altogether. This time, though, they indicated a new willingness to live with the proposal if the judge decided to impose it. All the other participants agreed to drop their lawsuits and work together to implement the plan.

Jones and his staff, obviously, played a very active role at every stage of the negotiations, generating proposals and working hard to "sell" those proposals to the parties. The mediators assembled a team of consultants across a broad range of disciplines to back up their efforts. They also worked out a sequence of hoped-for agreements. For example, although they focused first on generating an agreement on the basic components of a cost allocation formula, they also knew that each local official would require a precise forecast of what that formula would mean to his or her constituents before any commitments could be made.

Jones spent a great deal of time meeting behind the scenes with senior state officials. The state's promise of a no-interest, long-term loan to assist in the financing of the second stage of the regional sewage system proved to be the key to lowering each community's total cost. Indeed, when some municipal officials heard that the average annual sewerage charge for the new system would be less than $300 per household per year, they simply lost interest in the entire issue. They had been led to believe that such changes might exceed $1,000 a year. The mediators' success resulted in part from their ability to put together a package that was less onerous financially than what the parties had come to expect and dread.

Social Service Block Grant Allocations

When over one hundred participants met to discuss priorities for the allocation of the "public/private partnership" social service funds, they filled a large hall in one of the universities located in the central part of the state. The mediator, Denise Donovan, had met privately with each of the teams and with the team leaders prior to the first full negotiation session.

Donovan had been chosen by a mediator-selection committee that included five of the initial organizers from each of the four teams. She had been one of the three finalists the committee interviewed. Her contract was officially with the state government (for a total of $35,000), but the terms of the contract had been approved by each of the teams.

It took six hours to reach agreement on the major agenda items and on the protocols that would structure the negotiations. Throughout these initial steps, a great deal of skepticism was expressed by some team members, who felt that there was no chance of reaching a consensus.

The state agency team, headed by the assistant commissioner of the Department of Social Services, included staff from the department's various regional offices. This group pressed for new state guidelines that would give funding priority to underserved groups. The private donors team was headed by one of the directors of the United Way; this group made it clear that they wanted more flexible matching requirements for donors. The citizen/consumer team was headed by a professor of public administration who had been active on behalf of minority groups in the state, and whose particular interests she intended to serve. The Association of Social Service Providers team was headed by the elected chair of that statewide organization; on behalf of his constituents, he planned to press hard on the issue of wage parity between privately supported and publicly supported social service workers.

Donovan assembled a staff of assistant mediators, who began to meet regularly with each of the teams. They also served as support staff for subcommittees (consisting of two people from each team) assigned to generate possible responses to each of the agenda items: matching provisions, needs assessment, minority and underserved client groups, monitoring and evaluation of contracts, timing and duration of requests for proposals from new grantees, and overall service priorities.

The teams met monthly for almost a year. There were two points at which the process almost fell apart. First, the social service providers team refused to discuss any changes in priority setting procedures until the other three teams endorsed their position on wage parity. The others were put off by this "take-it-or-leave-it" attitude. At a team leader s meeting organized by Donovan, the four groups managed to work out an understanding. Formally, it was agreed that no one would be asked to commit anything until the full draft of a package was complete. Informally, everyone agreed that the wages for providers in nonprofit agencies were much too low.

The second stumbling block arose when the state team presented its proposed changes in overall spending priorities—that is, naming specific client populations that ought to be the focus for further spending. The providers team insisted that no change in priorities should be permitted if it eliminated grantees who had been eligible in the past. The solution, suggested by Donovan, was to find the best way of spending any *increment* in block grant money that the group as a whole could get from the governor and the legislature. By concentrating on the allocation of an increment, the group was able to avoid a zero-sum situation. Indeed, by presenting a united front on the need for more money they were able to advance their individual as well as their common interests.

Eventually a draft agreement was worked out. Copies were distributed to more than 2,500 groups and individuals throughout the state prior to the final signing. The mediator prepared and distributed more than 10,000 copies of a quarterly newsletter describing the progress of the negotiations.

Almost eighteen months from the time they began, a consensus was reached. In their agreement, the groups spelled out monitoring and implementation procedures designed to ensure appropriate follow-up evaluation. A number of the procedural suggestions that emerged during the course of the negotiations were implemented immediately by Commissioner Dorada. Other reforms, everyone agreed, would take more time. Some real shifts in spending priorities were approved when it became clear that the public/private partnership program would receive a substantial overall increase in state funding. In the commissioner's view, these shifts were important: but more important, she had the consensus she wanted. She considered the negotiations extremely useful.

Mediator Donovan's success illustrates two facts that we feel are significant in an era of diminishing governmental resources. First, despite the apparent zero-sum aspect of fund allocations, it is possible to establish spending priorities through a consensus-building process. Second, such consensus building can take place even among a very large group of participants, none of whom have negotiated before.

NONBINDING ARBITRATION

As we have already explained, binding arbitration has only limited application in public disputes because most public officials cannot legally delegate their authority to an arbitrator. Public officials appear to be equally wary of nonbinding arbitration—a process whereby a private judge or panel listens to the arguments of all sides, and then suggests an appropriate solution that the parties can either accept or reject.

Because nonbinding arbitration is a relatively new and untried approach in distributional disputes, we will introduce it in hypothetical terms. The approach has been tested in complex private disputes, but these are only partially relevant. Based on these applications, it seems clear to us that nonbinding arbitration may well be an acceptable and desirable means of resolving the types of distributional disputes that do not give way to facilitation or mediation.

Imagine that the parties in a public dispute have reached an impasse even after working with the mediator. Perhaps their estimations of their BATNAs, constantly undergoing revision, have led them to question, once again, whether they could do better away from the table. They can agree only on one thing: They need a solution. A great deal of time, money, and energy had been invested in the negotiations to date, and deadlines of one sort or another are looming. What are their alternatives? One alternative, of course, is to admit failure and go to court. Let us assume, however, that the outcome of adjudication is unclear, that the case is likely to be resolved on a winner-takes-all basis, and that neither side wants to risk losing everything.

Instead, the disputants decide to submit to nonbinding arbitration. In so doing, they may adopt any one of a number of strategies. For example, they may jointly choose a private "judge"—perhaps a retired jurist, or someone else with a background the disputants think appropriate—to whom they present their respective arguments, and from whom they seek a judgment. "After you have heard our arguments, tell us how you think the case will come out if we go to court," the disputing parties might say. "We are not necessarily bound by your judgment, but we want to hear it." Alternatively, the disputing parties might assemble a jointly chosen panel of private arbitrators and ask for a majority ruling (again, not binding). Finally, with appropriate assistance, the parties may stage a mock trial, and invite the heads of all the participating groups or organizations (not just their negotiators) to watch. This last technique may be helpful when one or more of the constituent groups insists on demands that its own negotiators know to be unrealistic.

In many cases, stalled negotiations reflect the simple fact that the expectations of one or more parties are unrealistic. Learning what would probably happen in court, and why, can change those expectations. (In other words, nonbinding arbitration can make a BATNA seem less attractive.) Lowered expectations, in turn, allow the disputing parties to go back to the bargaining table—either unassisted, or with facilitation or mediation—and reach a mutually satisfactory accord.

As noted earlier, few distributional disputes have been resolved through nonbinding arbitration thus far. There have been a significant number of nonbinding arbitrations in the private sector, however, and it seems likely that some version of the technique will cross over into the public sector. We will therefore summarize the ways in which the private sector currently employs nonbinding arbitration, particularly through "minitrials."[3]

Since about 1980, minitrials have proven to be a quick, low-cost mechanism for settling disputes between corporations. Because minitrials are voluntary, confidential, and nonbinding, many corporations embrace them with enthusiasm. In general, corporate minitrials have had four objectives:

- Narrowing the dispute to each party's summary of the critical issues
- Promoting a face-to-face dialogue between the heads of the companies involved
- Encouraging more realistic BATNA calculations
- Preventing business disputes from turning into lawyers' disputes by avoiding many of the legalistic distractions of courtroom procedure

The elements of a minitrial generally include (1) a short period of pretrial preparation; (2) a meeting or meetings in which top management representatives—who are authorized to settle on behalf of their companies—meet to hear informal summaries of each party's "best case"; (3) a meeting or meetings for questioning and rebutting the best-case summaries; and (4) an opportunity to negotiate a settlement.

In most cases, if the parties fail at this last stage to reach such a settlement, the judge or panel will present an analysis of the strengths and weaknesses of the positions heard.

All procedural aspects of a minitrial are negotiable, as the parties must feel comfortable with the process if settlement is to be reached. In general, there are only two essential aspects of a minitrial process: first, an opportunity for each side to state its case with an assurance of confidentiality; and second, the participation of leaders with the authority to enter into an agreement. (A neutral advisor, expert either in the subject matter of the dispute or in the processes of dispute or in the processes of dispute resolution, is also typically involved.) Negotiation by top corporate officials—preferably without their lawyers—can be a chief ingredient for success.

Corporate minitrials held so far have proven relevant in cases involving product liability, patent infringement, and employee grievances. They also have been successful in antitrust cases, in instances when competitive practices were in question, and in circumstances requiring an expert analysis of highly technical issues. These private sector applications suggest a number of potential public sector applications especially in disputes over standards (that is, cases in which scientific authorities disagree on such subjects as acceptable health risks). Scientific and technical portions of distributional disputes could then offer their views in an effort to encourage the disputants to settle.

To summarize: In nonbinding arbitration, the disputing parties still control the design of the process and must still approve the ultimate outcome, but the intermediaries take more responsibility for devising possible solutions. The disputing parties are no longer saying, "Help us help ourselves." Instead, they are saying, "Give us an answer." Obviously, then, the intermediaries in nonbinding arbitration must be substantively knowledgeable—even more so than mediators. Ideally, they understand not only the complexities of the issues in dispute, but also the legal processes that may come to bear if all else fails.

FROM ZERO-SUM TO INTEGRATIVE BARGAINING

Neutrals in any kind of dispute should seek to assist the parties in reaching satisfactory, as opposed to ideal, agreements. This process usually begins with an effort to ascertain that the parties understand their own interests, as well as what the others want and need. Once all the parties understand each other's interests, and they still find themselves in conflict, the neutral's next step is to assist the parties in exploring ways of reframing the dispute so that hidden common interests can be uncovered.

If it becomes clear that basic interests are in conflict (and more than just communication or personality problems are involved) and that there is little common ground, the neutral switches gears. That is, when it becomes clear that disputants are in a zero-sum situation (in which it appears that the only way for one to gain is for the others to lose), the intermediary seeks to "change the game" by introducing the possibility of trading things, especially things that the parties value differently.

There are obviously limits on what can be traded, including constraints on what the parties in their real-life situations can offer. Finally, if a package of trades that would satisfy all sides cannot be found, the helper must work privately with the disputants to be sure that they have calculated their BATNAs realistically. If they have, and their away-from-the-table options are likely to produce better results for some or all of them, the neutral should probably exit.

The search for satisfactory agreements, then, involves clarification of interests; the search for common ground; the creation of a setting in which the parties can work together to discover differences, which can then be exploited to produce joint gains; and the constant reassessment of alternatives to negotiation. If the parties have overlapping interests, a clarification of those interests and the search for common ground should produce a satisfactory agreement. If the parties have conflicting interests, the task of the neutral is to transform the dispute from a zero-sum situation to an integrative problem solving activity. There is, of course, no magic wand that the helper can wave, and neutrals are not in the business of cajoling disputants into making concessions in the name of harmony or peaceful coexistence. The transformation involves exploiting the multidimensionality of most conflict situations.

When there are lots of issues on the agenda and the parties rank them differently, this creates the possibility of trades. If the parties place a different value on certainty (or respond differently to risk), a small-but-certain victory sometimes can be traded for a larger-but- uncertain victory. If the parties calculate the time-value of money differently, this can open up trading possibilities. For example, one side may, for tax reasons, suggest a settlement that involves small payments, from the other side to them, each year for a number of years rather than a larger lump-sum payment. The other side may agree, finding this solution less of a strain in terms of cash flow. Even individual issues can be fragmented into smaller parts, permitting trades across elements of an issue. Symbolic commitments are a good example: They cost one side very little, and can often be exchanged for money or other tangible returns.

The transformation from zero-sum to integrative bargaining requires the invention and packaging of items to trade. A clear danger is that such trading may encourage extortionate behavior. If one side says to itself, "I get the idea; I'll gain by making my list of demands longer and longer," the game is then akin to blackmail. In such a case, the problem for the neutral is how to pursue the search for joint gains without encouraging excessive claiming.

Negotiation researchers have documented the inevitable tension between "creating and claiming value" in any dispute resolution situation.[4] This follows earlier studies of "mixed-motive bargaining." Every negotiation, whether zero-sum or integrative, recreates this tension.

In a zero-sum situation, the tension is obvious. Every proposal that one offers in an effort to discover possible joint gains—that is, to create value—will not be accepted by the others without promises in return. This is to be expected if the disputants are thinking solely in zero-sum terms. But even in an integrative bargaining situation, in which the parties have indicated a desire to find an all-gain outcome, the possibility exists that an honest statement of what one side might give up in exchange for something will be exploited by one of the other participants.

Even assuming that disputing parties have been successful in creating joint gains by exploiting differences, this fact alone is no guarantee that the gains they have created can or will be divided equally. So, for example, the parties may find things to trade that they value differently. One side may come out a little bit ahead and the other may come out way ahead. Nobody is worse off, but they are not equally better off.

Intermediaries in public disputes must be honest about this problem. When they say to the parties that they can help find all-gain outcomes, they should clarify that they are not promising that everyone will "beat their BATNA" (or satisfy their interests) to the same extent. We might imagine that everyone would be happy as long as assisted negotiation allowed them to satisfy their underlying interests; nevertheless, we are all aware of situations in which one side would rather not accept a gain if it means that another side gains even more. Thus, neutrals have to keep an eye on the overall "score card" as the parties search for joint gains. They should remind the parties that real costs are associated with not finding mutually beneficial trades. In addition, they should indicate that excessive or extortionate claiming will undermine the very process of inventing joint gains which leads to satisfactory agreements.

The transformation from a zero-sum perception of a conflict to a willingness to search for joint gains does not depend on the parties adopting "soft" (as opposed to "hard") negotiating styles. Based on extensive studies, negotiation researchers have established that cooperative negotiators are not necessarily more successful than competitive negotiators in reaching satisfactory agreement. Negotiators of either style can be effective or ineffective, and this is true regardless of the style of the negotiators they are matched against.[5] Thus, the search for joint gains does not require everyone to be "nice" or to make concessions; nor does it require one side to mimic the attitudes of the other. Effective but tough negotiators know their own interests, and they know that by participating in a collaborative process of creating joint gains they may be more likely to serve their own interests. They also know that there will be very little to claim if differences cannot be exploited through packaging and trading.

Creating and claiming, as noted earlier, are distinct activities. "Competitive-style negotiators are likely to stress the claiming part of the process, and may require tangible "victories" at each step along the way. By contrast, "cooperative-style" negotiators are less inhibited about throwing themselves into the creating part of the creating and claiming process. They are also more willing to wait until the end to tote up the score.

But claiming can preempt creating, and it is important for the participants to realize this. Some negotiators attempt to solve this problem by constandy switching their negotiating posture from claiming to creating and back again. It may be impossible to move back and forth between the two attitudes, however, if claiming creates tension or hostility. It may in fact be necessary in some disputes to go through a period of claiming, or zero-sum bargaining, so that the parties see what they might be able to achieve this way. Once the process of creating begins, though, and an integrative problem-solving mode is established, it is best to stay on this track.

Facilitators and mediators rarely try to convince the disputants to change their styles of negotiation. They do, however, take advantage of the emergence of the "group mentality" that develops as negotiations proceed.

As the parties "go at it" over an extended period of time, relationships develop, just as they do when a jury is sequestered. The group may begin as total strangers, but constant interaction at close quarters can lead to accommodation, if not friendship. Though the negotiators are there to advance the interests of the groups they represent, they cannot help but get caught up in the new "group" of which they are a part.

This new group may pressure an individual who has not been very forthcoming into changing his or her attitude. As it approaches closure, the group may also bring pressure to bear on a party that is holding out. Momentum in such situations is almost tangible. While the intermediary may encourage all the parties to check back with their constituents before concluding a draft agreement, the group may prefer to push toward a conclusion. There is almost a "team spirit" that emerges as the disputants reach the end of their joint task.[6]

An effective intermediary may use the emergence of group pressure to move the transformation along, saying to one party, for example, "I don't know how much longer the rest of the group will stick with this, if you don't give some sign of your willingness to accept the trades that have been proposed." This is not to say that the neutral will encourage a party to ignore or sell short its own interests; rather, the neutral may use the pressure of the group to encourage a party to change its behavior, make a more realistic calculation of its BATNA, or offer a counterproposal that the others are likely to be able to accept.

We generally hold the view that any distributional dispute in the public sector that appears to be a zero-sum conflict can be transformed into an occasion for integrative bar gaining assuming the parties have adequate assistance. These sorts of conflicts are uniformly complex, but creative negotiators in any dispute usually will be able to find some possible trades—whether they be across issues, over time, relative to risk, or whatever.

This is not to say, though, that every distributional dispute will yield to resolution through assisted negotiation. The parties may have utterly unrealistic BATNAs, and they may refuse to reassess them regardless of what happens in the negotiations. Even though legitimate interests could be met through the creation of joint gains, the parties may hold out for more gains than can possibly be created.

Even with the assistance of a skilled intermediary, the parties may not be willing to move from inflated demands to ways of satisfying their true interests—either because they do not want to be seen as having backed down from their stated positions, because they are caught in psychological traps that work against their own best interests, or because internal pressures within their organizations lead them to attach a higher value to sustaining the conflict than to resolving it.

ASSISTED NEGOTIATION: CONCLUDING COMMENTS

At present, three techniques are available for assisted negotiation in the resolution of public disputes: facilitation, mediation, and nonbinding arbitration. By any rational accounting, these tools are underutilized. These techniques are not mutually exclusive. They can be used sequentially in the same dispute; in some situations, the line between facilitation and mediation may be blurred as the neutral moves into a more active behind-the-scenes role. They are highly mutable and can be applied in different ways by individual dispute resolution practitioners. In all cases, though, they involve the search for all-gain outcomes through a move from zero-sum to integrative bargaining.

We have already alluded to the biggest obstacle to their acceptance: fear on the part of public officials that facilitation, mediation, and nonbinding arbitration will infringe on their authority. We contend that this fear is misplaced, given that the outcomes of all three processes remain entirely under the control of the parties, including these same public officials. [...]

NOTES

1 The debate on the role of the mediator is presented in Joseph B. Stulberg, *Taking Charge/ Managing Conflic*t. (Lexington, Mass.: Lexington, 1987).

2 The details of how the EPAs resource pool worked are reviewed in Lawrence Susskind and Gerard McMahon, "The Theory and Practice of Negotiated Rulemaking," *Yale Journal of Regulatio*n 3,1 (1985):133–165.

3 For more on minitrials, see Eric Green, "The CPR Mini-Trial Handbook," in *Corporate Dispute Managemen*t (New York: Matthew Bender, 1982).

4 David Lax and Jim Sebenius, *The Manager as Negotiato*r (New York: Free Press, 1986).

5 Gerald Williams, *Legal Negotiation and Settlemen*t (St. Paul, Minn.: West, 1983).

6 This point is further explained by Jacob Bercovitch, *Social Conflicts and Third Parties: Strategies of Conflict Resolutio*n (Boulder, Colo.: Westview, 1984).

In Chapter 6, Philippe Korda presents various strategies that professional negotiators use to set traps in negotiations. Ideally, we should be more concerned with avoiding their use against us, but there could be an occasion where you feel that a trap is warranted.

Chapter 6

How to Avoid the Traps of Professional Negotiators

by Philippe Korda

Carl RITCHIE (*with a knowing smile*): However, there were a few occasions when you went too far.

Margaret PEAKE (*feigning incomprehension*): Were there?

Carl RITCHIE: I'm talking about a couple of negotiating sessions when I was a new boy and you used one or two tricky maneuvers on me. What should I call them?

Margaret PEAKE: Traps?

Carl RITCHIE: If you like.

MARGARET PEAKE'S OFFICE, 10 YEARS EARLIER

Carl Ritchie is feeling ill at ease. He has been forced to wait for almost an hour in a small, overheated room before being allowed into the buyer's office. Once there, he has been obliged to sit on a low, uncomfortable chair. There's nowhere for him to

Philippe Korda, "How to Avoid the Traps of Professional Negotiators," *The Five Golden Rules of Negotiation*, pp. 95-108. Copyright © 2011 by Business Expert Press. Reprinted with permission.

put his documents. While she files away a few papers, Margaret Peake explains in a distant manner, "I can only spare you a little time today. As you are surely aware, I'm under a lot of pressure, particularly from your competitors, whose prices are much more attractive than yours. What's your best offer?"

Carl Ritchie tries to slow things down, asking how business is going and about trends in the market, but the buyer cuts him short: "Let me be clear. There's a 5% disparity between your proposal and the price offered by your main competitor. Let's stop beating about the bush. Just tell me whether you can get close to that price."

Carl Ritchie hesitates. The price quoted is his absolute bottom line and one beyond which he definitely cannot go. He considers this, then says, "No, I'm afraid I can't."

Margaret Peake approaches him and says, "I'm sorry to have to tell you this, but if you don't win this contract you are very unlikely to win another from us. I doubt that your senior management would appreciate losing a customer like us overnight. Am I making myself clear, Mr. Ritchie?"

Finally, she adds, "I'm presenting this deal to our board this evening, so I shall need an immediate response from you."

Carl Ritchie tries to play for time and claims that he will need to discuss the issue with his line management. "You can use my phone, Mr. Ritchie. Please go ahead! Or, if you prefer, I'll give you time to call on your cell."

Carl Ritchie realizes that his only option is to back down. He attempts to offer a 3.5% price cut, but the buyer sighs, "Please be serious, Mr. Ritchie; you must offer at least 4%."

Somewhat discouraged, Carl Ritchie quietly agrees. Margaret Peake smiles at last, looking visibly satisfied to have won the day: "I shall sign the purchase order this afternoon. You see, Mr. Ritchie, you've won your contract!"

Carl relaxes. All the time spent hanging around has not been in vain. Anyway, he really needed to clinch this deal to "get one over" on the competition. Now it is done and he can start planning for the weekend. The buyer is getting ready to stand up to escort Carl to the door. Then she pauses for a moment and seems to be trying to think of something. With a smile, she asks, "Of course, you'll grant us a 2% discount at the year's end, won't you?"

Carl is startled: "Why? We've not even discussed that!"

The buyer sits down, looking disconsolate: "Well, in that case, I'm afraid that we'll have to go back to the beginning."

Carl Ritchie feels cornered and frustrated. He opts to call for a break in the discussions and suggests that they reconvene for special negotiations about the terms of the contract. As she accompanies him to the door, Margaret Peake tries to reassure him: "Most of the work is done, Mr. Ritchie. We are agreed about everything except this discount issue, which is a key point for me. I'd really like to help you out, but in all sincerity, I can't give ground on that."

Once he is back in his car, Carl's hopes rise again. If he makes a good case to his sales manager, he should be able to get his customer the discount that she requires.

IN THE RESTAURANT

Carl RITCHIE: You certainly brought out the heavy artillery that day.

Margaret PEAKE (*a little embarrassed*): Yes, maybe.

Carl RITCHIE: You tried to undermine and pressure me from the start.

Margaret PEAKE: That's true.

Carl RITCHIE: Then there was the threat involving my senior management.

Margaret PEAKE (*relaxing*): And the urgency: "You can use my phone, Mr. Ritchie!"

Carl RITCHIE: But there's no doubt that the cruelest trap was the last one, when you cast doubt over the whole deal for the sake of one last demand.

Margaret PEAKE: I have to tell you that my favorite TV detective has always been Columbo! He always speaks very pleasantly to suspects, lulling them into a false sense of security.

Carl RITCHIE: And then waits until they are almost out the door before catching them off balance with a seemingly innocuous but loaded question.

THE TRAPS OF THE PROFESSIONAL NEGOTIATORS

It is neither necessary nor useful to try to "trap" your counterpart into agreeing to a good deal. Listening, understanding, convincing, and thinking up solutions acceptable to both parties are much more desirable objectives. It is therefore not a question of recommending that you use the techniques presented in this chapter. Instead, it is essential that you know how to thwart them.

UNDERMINING

A negotiator may seek to make her counterpart feel inferior, often insidiously or indirectly. For example, the buyer may make the seller wait for an hour, suggesting that he is ultimately of little importance, or the buyer may offer him a chair that is lower than hers or allow the meeting to be interrupted repeatedly by taking a series of phone calls. Such undermining can also be direct, maybe involving insulting statements about the supplier's company or occupation. This makes the other person uncomfortable: Having been treated like a child, he is less capable of resisting pressures or demands.

WHAT ARE THE POSSIBLE RESPONSES?

- Refuse to be undermined: Leave after waiting for 20 minutes, ask for a different seat, suggest that all phone calls be diverted, and so on.
- Demonstrate your refusal to be undermined: when waiting in reception, keep working on another deal and pretend not to notice your counterpart's arrival.
- Put the issue on the table, while not offending the other person's sensibilities: "Some buyers resort to odd practices, such as making visitors sit on a lower chair. I know that you have no need to do that, Mrs. Peake."

THREATS

In negotiations, threats are a weapon of last resort. They may take various forms. At best, you are warned about what is at stake if you do not meet the terms demanded. At worst, you are told nothing: The threat is indirect, taking the form of hearsay, unexplained incidents, and the like, encouraging you to believe that a breakdown in negotiations could have serious consequences.

Under these circumstances, the party doing the threatening is hoping that, under pressure, the other party will give more ground than she had planned. When faced with a threat, you really must avoid giving ground out of fear— and without adopting a defiant attitude toward the other party, even if you do not believe that her threat is credible.

WHAT ARE THE POSSIBLE RESPONSES?

- It is sometimes preferable to pretend not to understand the threat: rephrase things, without paying much attention to your counterpart's intimidating remarks. Adopting a calm approach focused on seeking precise information and resolving problems may be enough to encourage your counterpart to adopt a more relaxed approach.
- If the threat is confirmed, the best thing is to calmly examine what is at stake: recognize the existence and reality of the risk, citing its potentially damaging effects for both parties, while allowing it to appear that you are prepared to take that risk (without saying so provocatively): "Of course, that would cause problems for me, but ultimately that's up to you."
- In all cases you will need to carefully analyze the probability of the threat being put into effect: What would be the consequences for both parties?

URGENCY

Your counterpart demands an instant reply: "I'm ready to issue the PO right now"; "I've only got one left in stock"; "the committee is meeting tomorrow morning"; "If you want, you can call your senior managers right now"; and so on. This is a trap offering many benefits to the party laying it. The urgency pressures the counterpart as she faces an imminent risk of permanently losing an opportunity if she does not give way. Furthermore, if your counterpart calls her boss, the boss will be unprepared for negotiations: Which arguments should she use (Golden Rule No. 2)? What should she ask in exchange (Golden Rule No. 3)? How can she give concessions gradually (Golden Rule No. 4)? Thus urgency very often leads to the giving of greater concessions than would have been the case if there had been sufficient time for reflection. Therefore it is important that you avoid the classic errors: immediately capitulating under pressure, phoning your line management in front of the other party (unless there is a prior agreement to adopt a particular set of tactics), and so on.

What are the possible responses?

- Take no account of the urgency expressed by your counterpart if you suspect she is bluffing.
- Negotiate firmly over the deadline: Ask for 5 or 8 days to adapt your stance.
- Impose an even shorter deadline to put pressure on the other party (e.g., "I can only keep this offer open until midday tomorrow").

The Columbo Effect

Your counterpart seems satisfied and is bringing negotiations to a positive conclusion when she suddenly makes an unexpected demand: "Naturally, you'll need to sign this little amendment to our general terms, but that shouldn't be a problem for you, should it?"

You are helpless. You have just started to relax, thinking it is a done deal, and you do not know how to respond. You are afraid of losing everything at the very last minute. If you still have some room to maneuver in the negotiations, it will be tempting to use it in order to grant the concession demanded.

What are the possible responses?

- Close down the discussions: "Nice try, Mrs. Peake, but you know very well that I've quoted you my best offer and you got a great deal."
- Launch a war of nerves: "I wasn't aware of that demand. If it really is a priority, then we'll have to start again from scratch. I'll have to take my offer and the benefits agreed to off the table."
- Get something in return. Start by refusing to concede, argue, and then maneuver your counterpart into a position where he offers a further benefit. Then partially grant the concession demanded by the other party and seal the deal.

THE "GOOD COP, BAD COP" ROUTINE

Two negotiators combine forces to deal with a seller. The first adopts a very hard-line stance and speaks forcefully. Any negotiation is practically impossible. Then the second negotiator intervenes, trying to "reason" with his partner, and makes the other party an apparently more acceptable proposal. This is yet another trap that is often highly effective: You are distressed by the confrontation with the "bad cop" and tend to place great trust in the "good cop," viewing his proposal as a lifeline to cling to.

You need to avoid common errors in situations of this type. Do not lose your cool with a "bad cop" when the real negotiation has not even started yet. It is also important to remain on your guard and not be too quick to see the more conciliatory negotiator as an ally.

WHAT ARE THE POSSIBLE RESPONSES?

- If you are also operating with two negotiators, divide the roles between you: One takes on the "bad cop" in a struggle where nothing is really at stake, while the other adopts a more affable stance and prepares to conduct the real negotiations.
- If you are operating on your own, allow the "bad cop" to speak, but do not respond, then negotiate with the "good cop" without taking any account of the "bad cop's" demands.
- You can also highlight the technique employed in order to defuse it: "That's strange, it looks like you're deploying the 'good cop/bad cop' routine and you're doing it very well, but I do think that we should now come together to find a solution acceptable to everyone, so I suggest that we look again at the issue of . . ."

THE "LIMITED BUDGET"

Almost regretfully, the buyer claims that he cannot commit more than a given sum to this purchase, although your product or service is indeed worth more. This "limited budget" argument is an extremely cunning one, as it puts the seller in a difficult position: He cannot defend his product, as it has not been criticized, nor can he seek to justify the price, as the buyer is not saying that the price is inappropriate as such. Furthermore, this technique allows negotiations to proceed in a constructive climate, with the seller trying "to help" the customer to buy the product while keeping within his budget.

Lastly, the buyer can obtain useful information from the seller: for example, "If you take it without the aluminum guardrail, we can supply you with the same machine, with a plastic component, for $7,000 less."

The "limited budget" argument may be genuine or purely tactical. It will be all the more effective if the buyer can use documentary evidence or the testimony of others to bolster his credibility. The seller may even be manipulated in advance: The buyer asks for a quotation "for information only" on a basic model; the seller then makes an approximate commitment-free price quotation; the buyer then comes back asking for a more sophisticated model, with a view to an imminent purchase, saying, "I'm sorry, but I only have a limited budget."

If you are acting as the seller, you may find an idea for an effective response from among those suggested below.

WHAT ARE THE POSSIBLE RESPONSES?

- Obtain as much information as possible about the buyer's budgets (i.e., how and when they are decided, etc.) to verify the credibility of the argument.
- Find out who has the power to revise the budget. If necessary, ask to meet that person, with your own line managers, if appropriate.
- Demonstrate that the benefits provided are worth the extra cost.
- Look for a way of splitting the cost: between two financial years (e.g., by offering a part-sale this year, with the balance being paid early next year) or between two different budget headings (e.g., certain machine parts from a linked budget, or you could reduce the price of the machine and increase contractual service charges).
- Stand firm on price, but offer concessions that are less costly to you and that might justify his exceeding his budget.
- Look for potential recompense for a price cut: for example, simplified product specifications, certain services covered directly by the customer, supply of a demonstration model used at trade fairs, an increase in order volumes,

a customer commitment to order consumables, payment of a large deposit, changes in the delivery schedule, and so on.

IN THE RESTAURANT

Carl RITCHIE: Then there was that time when you saw me with your assistant.
Margaret PEAKE: A very pleasant young man, who went on to make a good career for himself.
Carl RITCHIE: Yes, I thought he was very pleasant, too.

BOARDROOM, 9 YEARS EARLIER

Carl Ritchie is facing two people across the negotiating table. Margaret Peake is leading the discussions with great determination and combativeness. She raises some very tough demands:

> Let's be clear, Mr. Ritchie. It's out of the question for me to agree to pay more than $72,000 for this product. Furthermore, I will not accept payment terms of less than 60 days. That's how we operate and you'll need to adapt to that; otherwise we might as well call this off right now.

The assistant buyer remains silent, just taking notes. When his boss raises her voice, he seems embarrassed and ill at ease. Carl tries to play his hand to the best of his ability. He offers to reduce the initial $87,000 starting price to $82,000, but says he can go no further, although on an exceptional basis he is prepared to accept her payment terms to seal the deal. This proposal apparently falls well short of Margaret Peake's expectations. She becomes quite aggressive:

> We're wasting our time, Mr. Ritchie, and I have no time to spare. I'll give you the opportunity to think it over and to come

back with a more reasonable offer. However, I must stress that I shall pay no more than $72,000.

With these words, the buyer leaves the room, heading for an "important" meeting. She asks her assistant to make a note of Ritchie's new proposals and to make a decision, if appropriate. Carl Ritchie sees some light at the end of the tunnel.

The assistant finally speaks up: "I know she's not an easy person to deal with, but she's under constant pressure. Please understand her position, Mr. Ritchie."

The young man thinks for a moment and then announces, "I think your product suits our needs perfectly. Furthermore, you have presented it with great conviction and talent."

Carl Ritchie tries to stifle a smile of satisfaction, while awaiting objection to the price. But the assistant says, "I'd add that the price seems to be justified both by the quality of the components and by the standard of your after-sales service."

This time Carl Ritchie breaks into a grin: At last things are falling into place.

"However," the assistant continues, "my hands are tied by our exceptionally tight budget. Between you and me, I know that we are allowing for a maximum budget of $75,000, not $72,000, as Mrs. Peake claimed. Anyway, under no circumstances can I go higher than $75,000. What can we do?"

Carl Ritchie again tries to stress the benefits of his proposal, but the assistant interrupts him: "I know and I completely share your view, but I'd never get my boss to accept an expenditure of more than $75,000. Can you suggest a solution?"

Carl hesitates: $75,000 is too low a price, but still much more reasonable than the $72,000 demanded by the buyer. An idea comes to him.

"The problem," says Carl, "is that you're comparing my product, which has a 2-year warranty, with competing products that only have a 1-year warranty. That makes a big difference!"

The assistant buyer seems to find this point interesting: "I could use that argument to justify my decision to Mrs. Peake. In your view, what is the monetary value of the second year of your warranty?"

Carl opts to bluff a little to bolster his case: "At least $5,000."

The assistant looks him straight in the face and replies, "OK, Mr. Ritchie; if you cut your price by $5,000 that gives you $77,000. If you then give just a little bit more,

I'll buy that product from you for $75,000 with just a one-year warranty. I'll sign up right now."

Carl Ritchie thinks for a moment and then gets out a purchase order.

IN THE RESTAURANT

Carl RITCHIE: You won yourself a good deal that day!

Margaret PEAKE (*modestly*): Yes, let's just say that my young assistant played his part rather well.

Carl RITCHIE: You mean to say that you divided the roles between you?

Margaret PEAKE: If you watch detective films, when two policemen are interviewing a suspect there is the bad cop, who is aggressive and violent, and the good cop, who offers the suspect a cigarette.

Carl RITCHIE: It's often to him that the suspect opens up.

Margaret PEAKE: Particularly if he's afraid that the bad cop may come back!

Carl RITCHIE: It was difficult for me not to allow your assistant his concessions when he agreed with every aspect of my proposal. He just had to work within a limited budget.

Margaret PEAKE (*smiling*): Yes, that limited budget …

SOME OTHER TRAPS OF THE PROFESSIONAL NEGOTIATOR

THE DECOY

This involves starting off by "exhausting" your counterpart by spending hours demanding a concession that you know to be completely nonnegotiable. The negotiator then suddenly lifts the pressure by waiving that demand, but in exchange asks his counterpart to immediately grant another demand, which is depicted as being of little consequence. This second demand, in reality a major demand, was the negotiator's main objective from the outset.

BLOWING HOT AND COLD

Otherwise known as the "solo" version of the "good cop/bad cop" routine.

THE FALSE FRIEND

"If you significantly improve your offer, together we shall have better arguments with which to convince my boss."

THE SHOPPING LIST

Your counterpart artificially increases the number of items for negotiation to induce you to accept a number of significant concessions.

THE VULTURE

As soon as you offer a concession, your counterpart minimizes it to show that the real negotiations have not yet begun.

THE LEADER OF THE PACK

The seller faces a large group of buyers who simultaneously attack different aspects of the seller's proposal like a pack of wolves. The negotiations seem chaotic. In reality, a leader is continuously directing the pack so as to dismember its prey.

The Fait Accompli

If an item has not been addressed, it is deemed to have been granted automatically on the terms that your counterpart wants.

The Secret Agent

I don't really want to go into this, but we know that you're giving one of our competitors better terms than us. That's serious. Before we take things any further, let's try to resolve that problem.

This scene takes place one Sunday morning at an antiques stall.

A woman stops in front of a dealer's stall and says, "I've just bought a completely unfurnished vacation home and I'm looking to give it a bit of life. What is your price for all these knickknacks?" The secondhand dealer looks at the dozens of objects in his stall. For weeks he has been hauling them around, packing, unpacking, and dusting them (with a few breakages), while struggling to sell them as individual items. A bulk sale would be an unexpected opportunity not to be missed. "$100 cash," he replies.

The woman thinks about this and then suddenly notices a china plate, partially hidden behind a large vase. "May I?" Looking excited she picks up the plate and murmurs, "It can't be, can it?" She shakes her head, visibly dumbfounded by her discovery: "He'll never believe it!"

The dealer looks at her quizzically. The woman explains, "Every Sunday for years, my husband has been out looking for this plate. It's the only one missing from his collection and we've not been able to find it anywhere—and this one is in great condition. I just can't believe it." Then she gives the dealer an anxious glance: "How much?"

The dealer suppresses a smile. This is an unexpected opportunity.

"It is indeed a very rare piece, but I'll let you have it for $80, as you've been so nice to me"

The woman looks pensive and gazes at the plate, nodding her head gravely.

"Well, I'm going to have to think about the plate." Then she looks the dealer straight in the eye, smiling innocently, and says, "For today, I'll just take the rest, for $20, naturally."

AVOIDING THE TRAPS OF THE PROFESSIONAL NEGOTIATOR: FOUR RECOMMENDATIONS

1. *Keep your cool.* Do not allow yourself to be overcome by either enthusiasm or anger. Remain an observer as well as a participant in the negotiations.

2. *Show empathy.* Before and throughout the discussions, ask yourself *what you would do if you were in the other party's shoes.* What would be your objectives? How could you achieve them? Judging the other party serves no purpose. Trying to understand him is more useful.

3. *Talk little, listen a lot.* Everything that you say may be noted and used against you, particularly if it involves information about your internal constraints, your price or cost structure, your processes, your alternatives, and so on.

4. *Be patient— and show it.* Do not be in too much of a rush to complete the deal. Even when you are nearing the finishing line, be prepared to start again from scratch if the situation so requires. Do not make any major decision without taking the time to reflect and consult.

KEY POINTS TO MEMORIZE

- If you encounter attempts to undermine you, remain courteous but ask for better negotiating conditions.

- When your counterpart makes a threat, assess the risks and avoid an emotional response.

- If you face claims of great urgency, negotiate a deadline.

- If ambushed by the "Columbo effect," stand firm.

- When faced with two people using the "good cop/bad cop" routine, focus your attention and vigilance on the "good cop," who is generally the real negotiator.

- Never view a "budgetary limit" as fixed without verifying the true position.

SOME SENSIBLE QUESTIONS TO ASK YOURSELF

- Which of these traps have I already encountered in my work?

- In which situations am I most vulnerable?

- What instincts must I acquire in order to deal with these situations?

Chapter 7 concludes the unit with James Altucher's humorous look at behaviors to avoid during a negotiation. Altucher presents examples from his own life of things to avoid and more effective approaches. Enjoy the lighthearted approach, but there are nuggets of advice here, particularly avoiding using the word "no" in a negotiation.

Chapter 7

The Ten Worst Things You Can Do in a Negotiation

by James Altucher

The best negotiator I knew always acted like an idiot. He acted so well that I thought he was really stupid. I also thought at the time that he was my best friend.

That was probably an act also. Just two years later he stopped talking to me forever.

I ran into him in the street the other day. He smiled and shook my hand. I felt warm, like he liked me again. Then he was gone.

Negotiation is first about warmth. Two sides deciding if they want to be friends with each other. If they want to be in the same tribe, fighting side by side in this harsh world.

After that it's about vulnerability. Making yourself into the type of person someone else wants to take care of.

This is not a mystery. When a baby is born the negotiation begins. It lasts until at least the baby is an adult.

My oldest turns 16 tomorrow. She negotiates with me every day. I love her. But maybe that's what makes her such a tough negotiator.

I'm not so good at realizing where all the boundaries are.

James Altucher, "The Ten Worst Things You Can Do in a Negotiation," http://www.jamesaltucher.com/2015/03/the-ten-worst-things-you-can-do-in-a-negotiation/. Copyright © 2015 by Altucher Confidential. Reprinted with permission.

Between the outer me and the inner me. Between the me that always loves her and the me that wants her to love me back.

I guess that's how I am with everyone. If they don't love me back, I'm afraid, I'll be less happy.

If I'm honest where the boundaries are, then we can begin to set up the rules. Then love begins.

Tricky!

—

I've probably seen over 1000 negotiations in action. I've probably been directly involved in 100 or so.

Every day life is a negotiation. I'm not talking in this post about the every day negotiations although the same rules apply. I'm talking about negotiations where careers and money and reputations and maybe love is at stake.

For me, that latter is the hardest. So take my advice with a grain of salt. In fact, I'd rather tell you all the ways in which I've messed up in negotiations. Because this is really the classroom I learned in.

IF YOU HAVE A SMALL LIST OF TERMS, YOU LOSE

Let's say you are selling a company. One side is usually focused on the final price. That side will henceforth be called "the loser".

Make your list bigger: what are the terms of the non-compete, what is the length of the earn out, what are the salaries of the new top executives, what are the perks, what are the options packages.

Or if it's a job: what are the responsibilities, what are similar people being paid, what is the path to higher promotions, what are the details of health, vacation, moving expenses, reviews, etc.

The side with the bigger list can give up the nickels for the dimes to the loser.

IF YOU DON'T GET ENOUGH SLEEP, YOUR WILLPOWER WILL BE ZERO

Carl Icahn, one of the best investors in the world, uses this technique.

He schedules his negotiations for the early evening.

Our peak mental ability (according to Dan Ariely, author of Predictably Irrational, and many other books) is approximately 2 hours after we wake up until about 4 hours after we wake up.

And then throughout the day, our willpower slowly leaks away until we sleep again. That's why we watch TV and eat donuts at night rather than when we first wake up.

So Carl Icahn will sleep until 4pm and then go to the negotiation at 6pm.

On the other side of the table are exhausted lawyers who have been working all day.

BAM! Who do you think will win that negotiation.

MOST PEOPLE THINK SHORT-TERM. BE THE VISIONARY AND YOU WIN

Applied Semantics didn't want to sell to Google in 2001. They had raised some money and thought they could make it.

A few months earlier I had made the mistake of turning them down when they were raising money. "The search engine business is dead!" said the greatest prophet of modern times.

Me.

Larry Page told the CEO of Applied, "I'm not getting off the phone until you say yes".

So Applied Semantics sold themselves in exchange for 1% of Google. ONE PERCENT.

This was before Google went public. So it was a total unknown what those shares would be worth. Larry Page had the vision of where they would be.

Applied Semantics became the Adsense division of Google. Which now accounts for 99% of Google's revenues.

Are they upset? Shouldn't they have sold for more?

Of course not. They sold for over a billion in value and created the end goal of making one of the best companies in the world.

You can only get rich once. Don't worry so much about maximizing your percentage of something. One percent of $250 billion is better than 100% of nothing, as the saying goes.

—

I'm going to take a break for a second and say something that has saved me considerable stress.

NEVER WORRY ABOUT WHAT IS IN SOMEONE ELSE'S POCKET.

Let other people do well. Then you will do well.

Ok, back to what you shouldn't do in a negotiation.

—

DON'T SAY NO

I say this even though I wrote the book, "The Power of No". What I really mean here is, bury your NO inside of a YES.

I was negotiating with one company once. They wanted me to be an advisor. I said, "no". But not like that. What I really said was, "You have a great company and I am happy to give advice."

What a great way to say no! They kept calling. They really wanted me. I said, "Here's what you should do without me" and I totally laid out the plan they should do. I did it for free. That was another way of saying "no".

This made them want me as an advisor even more. Eventually they offered enough that I said, "yes". They followed my advice exactly. The advice that I had already given for free.

There's a well-known improv technique of "Yes, and…"

In improv, the first performer creates the premise. The second performer can't change it or reject it, he can only build on it.

In a negotiation if someone says, "well, you're only worth $1 because you have X" you can say, "yes, and we also have Y so let's take that into consideration."

Suddenly your value is higher because you didn't start a fight. You agreed and added

MANY PEOPLE NEGOTIATE WITH THE WRONG MATH.

This is the part many people don't get right and it's hard to explain. I'll take a simple example. I don't know if the negotiation took place this way but it describes what I mean.

Why did Facebook buy Instagram for $1 billion. Instagram had 11 employees and zero revenues.

On that basis, maybe Instagram was worth…nothing. Or close to it.

But maybe the negotiation went something like this:

Instagram: Let's agree to a formula first on how we should value our company.

Facebook: Err…Ok.

Instagram: Forget about our revenues for a second. But let's just assume we can earn $X for every user you have (call that number $Y). Pay us $X * Y.

Facebook: Err. Ok.

Instagram probably then showed how they could add $1 in value for every customer Facebook had. Facebook has a billion users. So a billion dollars.

Come to the negotiation with your formula. Know how to fill in the variables before the other side does. Every good negotiator does this.

The reason I know this? Because this is how I've lost many negotiations to good negotiators. I've had very good mentors on this one aspect of negotiation.

Because we all negotiated the formula, but not the price, in advance, then everyone has already said "Yes" to something and they basically have to stick with it.

(Well, they don't have to. But it's high stakes and you don't want to seem like you don't live up to your word.)

IF YOU HOPE FOR ONLY ONE OUTCOME, YOU NEVER GET IT

I really wanted my company, Stockpickr, to be bought by Google. I threw everything I could into the basket. I would send them love notes in the middle of the night.

Seriously, I was in love with the woman doing the negotiating.

I didn't have a technical team was the problem. We built the whole site for a few thousand dollars. I had one partner. We had 99% margins on our revenues but Google likes technical teams.

Oh well.

I then focused on getting alternatives. I called AOL, Yahoo, Reuters, Forbes. Then thestreet.com bought us.

Sometimes people write me and say, "I sent my ten ideas to my favorite company but they haven't called back. Should I call them again?"

That's the wrong question. The right question is: "What's the next 100 companies I should write to?"

It's no secret that being able to walk away from a negotiation is the best starting point in a negotiation.

SMARTER PEOPLE LOSE

This is what I like to say: you guys are the experts at this, we've just been focused on building our product, company, art, whatever.

Then I say, "if you were me, what would you ask for?"

I ask them advice. Because they are the experts. It's not a lie.

If you are applying for a job with someone more senior than you, why not ask the more senior guy for advice? He knows more than you.

Very often they give very good advice.

IF YOU NEGOTIATE WITH A LOSER, YOU LOSE

If two sides are negotiating, you need at least one champion for what you are doing on the other side.

One time I was working with a company and GE offered us a billion dollars for the company. Yes, a BILLION.

They laid out the time frame. "The deal will be closed by November 15" said the highest ranking person in the room from GE.

I went back to the CEO of the company I was advising and told him that.

He said, "Who were you talking to?" I told him.

He said, "100% chance this deal doesn't happen".

But they offered! I told him. They actually made an offer.

"Trust me. No way. There's no real champion for you on the other side who is close to being a decision maker. She is 5 rungs below the decision maker and she's your only champion."

And he was right. That deal did not happen. They found a better way to get what they wanted for 1/200 of the price.

You can only cross the bridge to the other side if someone strong is there holding out their hand to pull you in.

THE DEAL IS NOT THE FINAL DEAL. DON'T RELAX!

People think when they agree on a deal, that's the end of the negotiation.

I'm sorry to say, that is only the beginning of the negotiation.

There's agreeing, there's signing, and there's closing.

The final two steps are equally important and everyone assumes they are easy.

They aren't. They are excruciatingly painful. The honeymoon period lasts for two days after you agree. Then there can be another six months to go.

Agreeing is easy. "I'll buy your product or business for $X."

Signing a deal involves all the little things that are the nickels and dimes (see above).

Closing a deal means both sides delivering everything they represented in a deal.

At each stage of this is buyer's remorse and seller's remorse and often things have to be renegotiated.

So every day after agreement, make it a point to stay in touch, be friends, keep focusing on the vision (particularly with the champion for your deal on the other side), have just as much energy to close all the details, keep in touch with the lawyers to make sure paperwork is going through, keep working on the alternatives (since the negotiation is not done til it's DONE), and so on.

So many deals fall apart after agreement. You don't need this pain in your life.

—

LOVE IS A NEGOTIATION

Taking another break here in the post. Please forgive me for not laying it out all perfect.

When I used to go on a first date I was both scared and excited. I'd get excited first, "she wants to date me!" And then I'd get scared. "Ugh, what do I do now?"

I'd literally do homework for the date. I'd find out her interests and read books on them. I'd watch comedy beforehand. I'd think of things to say and questions to ask. I'm not saying preparation is bad.

One time I was an expert on Kaballah. Another time I had to be an expert on Al Gore (long story). Another time I had to bribe the counter girl to pretend she knew me before my date arrived.

I'd be too scared to show my real self so I'd have to get her to like my fake self long enough for me to feel comfortable showing the real me.

Sometimes that never happened. In many cases I never had a real me. I was always jumping through hoops to keep the fake me going. I had to keep bribing the counter girl everytime we went for yogurt.

This is the difference between agreeing on a deal (the first date) and closing (trust, love, real compassion). This is a problem I'm afraid I will always have. I hope I am getting better bit by bit.

—

MOST DEALS DON'T WORK OUT.

You agree, you sign, you close, and STILL it's not the end.

Don't be the guy (or woman) who falls apart now that all the energy of the deal has been expended.

It's a negotiation and a deal because NOW there is work to do. There is a common vision to be achieved. There is a fantasy that must be made into reality.

Be that person. Be the one who delivers. You have a new baby in your hands as the result of this negotiation.

Now the hard work begins. Raise that baby to be a good adult.

POST-READING QUESTIONS AND ACTIVITIES

Answer the following questions to help you fully understand the Unit 1 readings:

- Think of a recent negotiation that you have had. How would you have done things differently in the preparation, presentation of offers, and conclusion?

  - Would you have taken more time?

  - What obstacles did the other side prevent?

  - Were there multiple issues introduced, or was it a straight price negotiation?

- List common reasons or explanations for not accepting a deal and for presenting counter offers.

  - Why is a non-confrontational approach the best during the offer period?

- When negotiations have stalled, what are some suggestions to keep the process alive?

- What are the benefits of unassisted versus assisted negotiations?

- Which form of non-partisan intermediary would have been best for the land use negotiation in Chapter 4?

- Which traps are most effective to use in price-only negotiations?

- Review the traps in Chapter 5, and develop counters to each of them for a typical negotiation situation that you have had (at work, at school, with a roommate, etc.).

- Analyze a negotiation that you are familiar with or have studied in school (such as the resolution of the Troubles in Northern Ireland or the UPS Strike). In three to four pages, briefly discuss the background of the situation, the major positions of each side, what they bargained with and their respective goals. How was the negotiation resolved, and what could/should have been done differently?

UNIT 2 OVERVIEW

NEGOTIATIONS IN INTERCULTURAL SITUATIONS

The goal of Unit 2 is to analyze how negotiations can differ when intercultural paradigms are added to the equation, following up on the Native American land negotiation in Chapter 4 (Unit 1). In Chapter 8, the authors examine cross-cultural encounters in business settings, using the research technique of the critical incident analysis, which focuses on key behaviors or events that can impact business success or failure. Subsequent chapters focus on principles-first, compared with applications-first, reasoning (Chapter 9) and an empirical test of conflict within international partnerships (Chapter 12), followed by examples of negotiations in diplomatically challenging situations.

Some of the key concepts in this unit include:

- Key elements of cross-cultural communication
- Common errors in cross-cultural encounters
- Principles-first versus applications-first reasoning
- Strategies for persuading across cultures
- The importance of face-saving in many cultures
- The importance of heightened listening skills in cross-cultural situations
- An application of diplomatic work versus humanitarian work and their different perspectives

In Chapter 8, Andre Pekerti, et al., discuss communication problems in cross-cultural negotiations, including the danger of stereotyping. The chapter concludes with three different examples of negotiating cross-cultural misunderstandings, featuring three Anglo-Saxon acculturated individuals within three Asian markets and various explanations for interpretation.

Chapter 8

Valuing Cultures Through Critical Incidents: Analyses of Cross-Cultural Encounters and Their Implications for International Business Behaviors

by Andre A. Pekerti, Sarah Woodland, and Steven Diack Anugerah Pekerti

VALUING CULTURES THROUGH CRITICAL INCIDENTS

The present day view that cultures can influence one another has been developed through many centuries of trade between nations, immigration patterns, and exchange of information between nations. However, it is only in recent decades that

Andre A. Pekerti, et al., "Valuing Cultures through Critical Incidents: Analyses of Cross-Cultural Encounters and Their Implications for International Business Behaviors," *Journal of International Business Education*, pp. 43-74. Copyright © 2011 by NeilsonJournals Publishing. Reprinted with permission.

the degree and intensity of the above processes have become a significant factor in management and business. Technological developments, among other things, have been attributed as the main cause of the rapid increase in economic and financial interdependence worldwide (Arnett, 2002; Rycroft, 2003). One of the major implications in the present globalized environment is that exposure to multiple cultures is rapidly becoming a new reality for many individuals. This creates situations where people have to function with differing backgrounds and cognitive frameworks in the same context while at the same time having to complete tasks together.

A number of eminent scholar have, however, rejected the convergence of cultures phenomena as a function of globalization. For example, Dorfman, Hanges and Brodbeck (2004)—based on the Global Leadership and Organizational Behavior Effectiveness (GLOBE) study—rejected the culture convergence hypothesis. They argued that societal cultures are relatively enduring (Cushner & Brislin, 1996), thus the idea of technology, globalization and global communication creating a "one world managerial culture" is limited. They went as far as to argue that cultural differences might actually be exacerbated as a reaction of people trying to adapt to modernization and maintain their cultural identity. Thus modernization may in fact contribute to societies 'striving to preserve their cultural heritage' (Dorfman et al., 2004, p. 709; Blyton 2001). Taken together, these views echoed Mittleman's (1994, p. 428) insight that 'although often portrayed as a totalizing or homogenizing force, globalization articulates with local structures in diverse ways, accentuating, not eroding, national and regional differences'.

Keeping in mind Dorfman et al. (2004) and Mittleman's (1994) views, numerous scholars have highlighted potential issues in the multicultural work environment, and enlightened us with the cultural underpinnings of the issues. On the one hand, these issues can range from simple embarrassing misperceptions that lead to misunderstandings (Brislin & Yoshida, 1994; Boyacigiller, Goodman, Phillips, & Pearce, 2003; Cutler, 2005; Cushner & Brislin, 1996), and on the other, the behaviors can be contextually inappropriate or unacceptable. Both of which can be costly to all parties involved. It is our view that one of the most common situations where these *faux pas* and/or costly inappropriate behaviors are likely to occur are during initial cross-cultural communication situations and also upon subsequent interactions between interactants who are not yet familiar with each other's cultures (Cushner & Brislin, 1996; Pekerti & Thomas, 2003).

The purpose of this article is to explore cultures through a number of critical incidents, thus an analytical learning approach, that requires individuals to understand another's objective and subjective culture; namely in a particular culture or situation that one is not familiar with. We begin with a brief theoretical introduction to the major causes of cross-cultural misunderstanding, then suggest that cultural frameworks such as individualism-collectivism, the low- and high-context dimensions, plus other *communication rules* that can serve as start-up tools, can be applied to analyze unfamiliar cultures. These tools in turn can assist individuals to understand different behaviors in cross-cultural situations. This is followed by a discussion on some of the common errors likely to occur in cross-cultural encounters. Using similar techniques and a critical incident format introduced in Cushner and Brislin's (1996) "Practical Guide", we then present three different incidents involving six different cultures that can be used as discussion materials and initial learning resources about these six cultures and situations. All three incidents contain cross-cultural issues including communication; the first two surrounding the concept of *face*, and the third is more complex requiring culture specific knowledge to solve. Self-contained teaching notes are presented to offer insights and implications for teaching in international business and international organizational behavior courses.

THEORETICAL FOUNDATIONS

In cross-cultural situations it is understood that misunderstanding and/or cultural clashes can arise when the cognitive frameworks or schema of people involved do not match with those of others in the situation, especially when each person is functioning with a different set of goals and expectations (Kashima & Kashima, 1993; Newman, 1993; Sanchez-Burks, 2002). In other words, misunderstandings arise due to variations in perceptions caused by different schemas that are used in the interaction (Catrambone & Markus, 1987; Markus, Smith, & Moreland, 1985), which tend to be culturally based. Even within the same culture, two individuals may interpret a set of information in a different manner depending on his/her frame of reference (McArthur & Baron, 1983), previous experiences, goals, and expectations at the time. The differing frameworks consequently lead individuals to attune to different elements of the environment (Hall, 1976; Pekerti & Thomas, 2003), which produces different interpretations of the information set.

McArthur and Baron (1983) proposed that the differences in attunement is culturally bound since information acquisition processes are learnt during socialization, thus through the way cultures educate the attention processes of its members, including their subsequent goals, expectations and actions. Recent research corroborates McArthur and Baron's (1983) assertion and suggests that different cultural socialization patterns leads to differing developments of individual self-perceptions and in turn differing causal explanations (Pekerti, 2005; Pekerti & Kwantes, *in press*). In short, findings suggest that individuals socialized in an individualistic society are more likely to have an *independent self-concept* that causes the tendency to make internal causal explanations or attributions. Individuals socialized in a collectivistic society are more likely to have an *interdependent self-concept*, and thus have a tendency to make external attributions (Pekerti, 2005; Pekerti & Kwantes, *in press*).

CAUSES OF CROSS CULTURAL CLASHES IN COMMUNICATION SITUATIONS

HIDDEN DIMENSION OF CULTURE

Triandis (1989) and Hofstede's (1980) view of culture suggests that there is a hidden dimension of culture, and it is understood that this hidden dimension generally revolves around the assumptions and values associated with particular cultures. We believe that one of the best ways to understand this hidden dimension is to think of cultures as a living tree. Similar to the analogies that have been used in extant literature (iceberg, onion), a tree has a hidden part—its roots and a visible part—its trunks, branches, stems and leaves. However, unlike an iceberg or unplanted onion, a tree is a living thing. We believe this living attribute is an important characteristic of cultures that people have to interact with in international business settings, since it is active in the psyche of people that we interact with. Furthermore, research indicates that there is a direct and proportional link between the hidden dimension and the visible dimension of societal culture, i.e., a direct and proportional link between the roots and surface area respectively (Enquist & Niklas, 2002). In short, we view the roots as the hidden dimension of culture consisting of assumptions which are the most difficult to change or adjust. The trunks and branches are the links between the hidden dimension of culture (subjective culture) such as assumptions, and the visible part of culture (objective culture) are the branches and leaves. Thus, they resemble people's expressions of their assumptions, which manifest themselves as values and beliefs (subjective culture). In turn, these values and beliefs are then exhibited through the artifacts of cultures such as in norms and behaviors (objective culture). So, just like a tree, artifacts, norms and behaviors of societal culture, are the visible part and the most malleable part of culture.

We believe that it is this hidden dimension of societal culture—the assumptions, the subjective values, and beliefs—that is the source of many misunderstandings and cultural clashes during cross-cultural encounters. The next section provides some examples of value dimensions that have been found to influence cross-cultural interactions.

VALUE DIMENSIONS THAT INFLUENCE CROSS-CULTURAL INTERACTIONS

A number of theoretical perspectives suggest dimensions along which communication styles might vary across cultures and cause *faux pas* and/or costly inappropriate behaviors. The rationale is that communication behaviors are logical extensions of internalized cultural values, and therefore govern the style, conventions, and practices of communication. One way in which cultures vary is the extent to which language itself is used to communicate the message as a function of the culture's norms and social beliefs (*axioms*; Bond et al., 2004).

The low- and high-context communication typology is one of the theoretical dimensions that illustrate how language is influence by cultural norms and values (Hall, 1976). In low-context cultures, the message is largely conveyed by the words spoken. In high-context cultures, a good deal of the meaning is implicit and the words convey only a small part of the message. The receiver must fill in the gaps based on past knowledge of the speaker, the setting, or other contextual cues.

Scholars of culture and communication have documented the link between communication style and cultural values, namely, that there is a close agreement between the position of countries on the low- and high-context communication continuum and their location on individualism-collectivism index respectively (Gudykunst, Ting-Toomey, & Chua, 1988; Hofstede, 1980). The logic of this relationship is suggested by the two primary functions that communication serves (Honeycutt, 1993). One function is *reducing uncertainty*, which serves a functional purpose; and the other is *affiliation*, which serves a relational purpose. The emphasis of communication on uncertainty reduction or affiliation may vary according to the situation, but also according to culturally based motives for communication (Thomas et al., 2008; Pekerti & Thomas, 2003).

For example, in the United States, which has been described as a relatively *idiocentric* society (Hofstede, 1980; Triandis et al., 1993), effective verbal communication is expected to be explicit and unambiguous (Gallois & Callan, 1997). People are expected to say exactly what they mean, thus more aligned to the functional purpose of communication. In contrast, communication styles in some other cultures, such as Indonesia—a relatively allocentric society (Hofstede, 1980; Triandis et al., 1993; Pekerti & Thomas, 2003)—are considerably more inexact, ambiguous, and implicit which is more aligned to the affiliative purpose of communication.

As Pekerti and Thomas (2003) explained, the communication social exchange between individuals is tied to how people view themselves and their relationship to others, which is then used as an information processor that selects, interprets and evaluates the meaning of actions and intentions (subjective culture). Research suggests that people with a collectivistic cultural orientation place more value on social order or harmony, which motivates behaviors that are relational, people-oriented, and focus on interdependence (Triandis, et al., 1993). Triandis et al. (1993) labeled the behaviors stemming from a relationship maintenance motive, indicated by associative, high-context, and indirect actions as *allocentric* behaviors.

In contrast, explicit, and unambiguous communication (Burgoon & Hale, 1987) implies a functional approach to communication with a primary motive of task accomplishment through direct means. These motives are often associated with members of individualist cultures (Kluckhohn & Strodbeck, 1961). While all communication has both relational and functional purposes, a task-oriented style relegates the affiliative function to a secondary role (Burgoon & Hale, 1987).

Triandis et al. (1993) labeled behaviors associated with this task accomplishment motive as *idiocentric*—indicated by abstractive, low-context, and direct actions.

UNCERTAINTY REDUCTION THEORY

Shannon and Weaver's (1949) numerical approach to communication has fuelled the development of a number of theories in the field of communication. One of the theories that have been significant in the field of interpersonal communication is Uncertainty Reduction Theory. As a precursor to Honeycutt (1993) plus Burgoon and Hale's (1987) work, Uncertainty Reduction Theory posits that when strangers meet and interact, their primary concern is to reduce uncertainty about each other (Berger, 1979). Based on the literature presented above, we argue that this can be achieved via the task-oriented, direct, uncertainty reduction approach and/or via the relational, indirect, affiliative approach since it is not an all-or-nothing phenomenon. Furthermore, this process can be facilitated through assessing and selecting his/her own behavioral repertoire that are considered most appropriate in the situation (Miller, 1963). Regardless of which communication function is prioritized in a given communication situation, there are expectancies that are associated with the communication situation, as well as implicit theories and/or rules governing the interactions (Berger 1993; Honeycutt, 1993).

COMMUNICATION RULES IN DIFFERENT CULTURES

Ferguson's (1981) work on structure and use of politeness formulas in communication suggests that deviations and/or absence of certain elements from formulas in specific social interactions may cause discomfort to others who are expecting individuals to follow the particular formula. We assert that in any communication encounters, not knowing these so called *communication rules* can cause discomfort and misunderstanding; hence, would be exacerbated during initial cross-cultural communication situations.

Firth (1972) views conversational exchanges including greeting and parting routines as formal rituals that have the effect of regularizing social situations. The function of conversational routines has been analyzed by using the concept of *politeness* in relation to the concept of *face* in social interactions (Brown & Levinson, 1987; Cocroft & Ting-Toomey, 1994). For example, Sunnafrank (1986) claimed that communication behavior in initial interactions between two individuals (in Western cultures) is ritualized in order to reduce behavioral uncertainty in the immediate situation. According to Lebra (1976), in Eastern or collectivistic cultures, similar behaviors of adhering to rules in ritualized and initial encounters also exist. However, the communication interaction in these ritualized situations stems from the attempt to maintain *face*. Scholars (Bonavia, 1982; Earley & Randel, 1997; Hu, 1944) have described the concept of *face* as something that is both tangible and abstract and essential in understanding some cultures, especially East and Southeast Asian cultures (Bonavia, 1982; Cocroft & Ting-Toomey, 1994; Lebra, 1974).

In a seminal piece, Hu (1944) conceptualized two categories of face—*lien* and *mien-tzu*—identifying an internal personal and external social character respectively. Lien was described as "… the respect of the group for a man with good moral character, the loss of which makes it impossible for him to function properly within the community. Lien is both a social sanction for enforcing moral standards and an internalized sanction" (Hu, 1944, p. 45). It is accepted that lien is an internal experience of the person, thus a *private concept* (Brown & Levinson, 1987; Triandis, 1989), implying that a person can experience a loss of lien without an external experience.

Mien-tzu is "the kind of prestige that is emphasized in this country (China); a reputation achieved through getting on in life, through success and ostentation. This prestige is accumulated by means of personal effort or clever maneuvering" (Hu, 1944, p. 45; brackets added). It is understood that mien-tzu is acquired as a function of the social interaction and tends to vary depending on the social situation of the interaction; therefore, it is an external or *public-face* (Brown & Levinson, 1987; Triandis, 1989).[1]

As a tangible concept, face is the respectability an individual can claim for oneself as a function of his/her place within a society. Face can be acquired through

---

[1] Lebra's (1976) use of face refers to the Eastern-Collectivistic usage, thus both *lien* and *mien-tzu*.

behaviors and accumulations of a person's experiences and life (Hu, 1944), which also implies that in can be *lost*. Research in the field of organizational behavior has documented that the concept of face is applicable in an organizational framework (Earley & Randel, 1997). As an intangible concept face is an "un-written set of rules by which people in society cooperate to avoid unduly damaging each other's prestige and self-respect" (Bonavia, 1982; p. 73).

Brown and Levinson (1987) proposed all competent members of society have face or the public self-image that one wants to project, and that all competent members of society have certain rational capacities to achieve a public-face. Thus it is both a characteristic of a person, as well as an emergent property.[2] Brown and Levinson's (1987) conceptualization of face is a combination of Hu's (1944) face construct with conflict negotiation. As such, face maintenance behavior in Brown and Levinson's terms are conflict avoidance behaviors, or applied *politeness rules* (Oetzel, Garcia, & Ting-Toomey, 2008). Ting-Toomey's (2005) recent work updating the face-negotiation theory suggested that face can be used in a strategic manner. We argue that Ting-Toomey's (2005) application of the politeness formula in negotiation describes situations when people behave using a *mutual-face* strategy, thus being concerned with maintaining one's *own face* (self-face) and maintaining an *other's face* (other-face). It is of interest that Ting-Toomey's work also documented the link between a person's independent self-concept with a self-face strategy, while a person with an interdependent self-concept is more akin to use an other-face strategy.

Ting-Toomey (2005), similar to Bonavia (1982), acknowledges that in conflict situations, people can also use a *face-obliteration* strategy, thus rather than attempting to maintain each other's prestige and self-respect. "People implacably hostile to one another may refuse to cooperate in this way (avoid damaging) and will do what everything they can to make each other lose 'face'" (Bonavia, 1982; p. 73; brackets added). As one can imagine, there are many aspects of interactions where face is at risk for both parties in an encounter. Depending on the goal of the interaction, a number of strategies can be used, however if the goal is to maintain or build an ongoing relationship, then the risk of face loss must be minimized by using appropriate (prescribed) polite behavior or conflict avoidance behavior (Oetzel

---

[2] In this context, we are ascribing Brown & Levinson's (1978) usage of face as the public-face, i.e., Hu's (1944) concept of *mien-tzu*.

et al., 2008).[3] In other words, adherence to the politeness formula is governed by the degree of risk individuals perceive in the interaction. The norm suggests that the greater the degree of risk to face, the more constrained deviations from polite routines should be. In other words, accepted polite routines are maintained to minimize the degree of risk to face (Firth, 1972; Goffman, 1967; Lebra, 1976).

The above discussion illustrates the importance of routines and formulas and two significant functions in human interactions. First, they function as guides for communication to reduce uncertainty in ambiguous and/or novel situations. Second, they serve to maintain and regulate social relationships, such as maintain the *faces* of people involved in the interactions. The implication is that in any situation both functions are fundamental for clear and effective communication to occur. However, we stress that misunderstanding may occur and be exacerbated during initial cross-cultural encounters, especially if both parties are not familiar with each other's cultures. With that in mind, we now discuss some of the common errors that are likely to occur during cross-cultural encounters. We present this discussion of common errors both as a preventative and self-awareness tool, since Thomas' work (Thomas, 2010; Thomas, et al., 2008) suggest that self-awareness is a crucial element for *cultural intelligence*. Furthermore, the discussion also provides explanations as why these errors are common so that one can be conscious of them during cross-cultural encounters.

COMMON ERRORS IN CROSS-CULTURAL ENCOUNTERS

Before we present the critical incidents, it is useful to discuss a number of common errors that one may make in initial cross-cultural encounters. In line with Cushner and Brislin's (1996) approach, as well as the *keep it simple and stupid* (KISS; we prefer the term *systematic* for the last S) principle of design, we have categorized the

---

[3.] Goffman (1967) identified two types of face-related actions, *avoidance* and *corrective*. Avoidance refers to a person not engaging in actions that would threaten the face of others or self. Corrective refers to a proactive reestablishment of someone else's face their face has been threatened. We argue that avoidance behaviors are still proactive as opposed to passive or reactive since it is aimed at protecting self or other's face.

common errors under two major categories. They are cognitive-processing errors and errors linked to cultural knowledge—both of course are interlinked. These categories are presented as starting points when dealing with unfamiliar cultures, thus are not exhaustive.

CROSS-CULTURAL ERRORS RELATED TO PROCESSING INFORMATION

Conclusions based on expectations and personal beliefs. One of the most common errors that people make in cross-cultural encounters is making a judgment when there is too little information, and not making an effort to find more information. Cognitive psychologists (Miller & Carol, 1988; Taylor, 1981) suggest this is common since people are effectively *cognitive misers* due to their cognitive limitations, and will make many judgments on preconceptions and expectations. Although, this error is common, scholars (Brislin & Yoshida, 1994; Cushner & Brislin, 1996; Pekerti, 2005) have documented that it is likely to occur in cross-cultural encounters since a majority of people do not have expert knowledge on the myriad of cultures that exist in the world. As Pekerti (2005) proposed, depending on the context, the outcomes of making judgments on lack of information can lead to errors (e.g., *attribution* error) that will disadvantage individuals in the short- and long-term. Cushner and Brislin (1996) reported that misattributions can the lead to negative emotional reactions from both parties involved in the interactions, and thus ideally should be avoided.

Minimizing the impact of expectations and personal beliefs. One simple and systematic suggestion to minimize the impact of one's personal expectation and belief is as follows. In the absence of other information, try to assess whether the cultures involved fall under the categories of individualistic or collectivistic and/ or low- or high-context cultures. As a starting point, knowing whether a person comes from one of these cultures can help predict and understand some behaviors, but not others—thus it is a first best guess (Adler, 1997).

Ecological fallacy and sophisticated stereotyping. A caveat that must be stressed at this point is related to our suggested technique of using either the individualistic or collectivistic and/or low- or high-context dimensions to analyze unfamiliar cultures. Numerous scholars, including Cushner and Brislin (1996), have warned of the dangers of using stereotypes, especially negative stereotypes when dealing with groups of people one is not familiar with (e.g., this group of people are lazy). There are a number of pitfalls in using stereotypes. To name one: since the information generally comes from second-hand experience, the information can be incorrect, thus again leading to incorrect conclusions, regardless of whether the stereotype is positive or negative. Another danger in the use of stereotypes revolves around the *ecological fallacy,* which can be considered an error and cause of stereotypes. Again numerous scholars including Hofstede (1980; 1993), present a caveat in relation to this work. Hofstede warned the public of making judgments about individuals based on aggregated statistical data collected from a group to which a person belongs, that is an ecological fallacy. In short, he was cautioning people against using findings from his work to predict behavior of individuals since it can lead to fallacies if one does not go beyond these finding and learn more about particular individuals. Scholars have used the term *sophisticated stereotyping* (Osland & Bird, 2000) when one simplifies a culture to a shorthand description based on theories and empirical findings, and not going beyond this information.

Minimizing the impact of stereotyping. Our solution to stereotyping including sophisticated stereotyping is similar to the one we made previously—go beyond the stereotype. Our rationale is, even if stereotypes are useful, and/or based on empirical research, they are limited since they ignore context and individual personality (Osland & Bird, 2000). Although sophisticated stereotypes are generally not negative descriptions, they are still at best a first best guess. Therefore, one still needs to go beyond the general understanding of concepts such as individualism-collectivism and/or low- or high-context cultures and know individuals personally. It is a good idea to use more than one source of information, such as using multiple dimensions from multiple studies in an attempt to analyze another's behavior (Pekerti, 2005), plus get to know individuals personally. For example, analyzing *Incidents A* and *B* presented in this article (in the Cross-Cultural Incidents Section) using the individualism-collectivism or the low- and high-context dimension may help us to understand some of the behaviors manifest in the incident. However, using the individualism-collectivism or the low- and high-context dimensions on their own to analyze *Incident C* will not lead to the insights required to understand the behaviors manifest in this incident since it requires in-depth culture specific knowledge. The point is that one needs to be very conscious of using these simplification heuristics and then go beyond them.

Recommended Resources. In line with the above prescription, we also suggest readers to go beyond our present article and read the following resources as aids to analyze unfamiliar cultures. A) DiStefano and Maznevski's (2000) work on "Creating value with diverse teams in global management" in *Organizational Dynamics,* Volume 29, pp. 45-63. B) Osland and Bird's (2000) article on "Beyond sophisticated stereotyping: Cultural sensemaking in context", in the *Academy of Management Executive,* Volume 14, pp. 65-78.

CROSS-CULTURAL ERRORS RELATED TO CULTURAL KNOWLEDGE

Limited Cultural Knowledge. Committing a faux pas due to lack of cultural knowledge is an obvious error people make in cross-cultural encounters (Brislin & Yoshida, 1994; Boyacigiller, Goodman, Phillips, & Pearce, 2003; Cutler, 2005; Cushner & Brislin, 1996). A logical solution to this error is to do one's *homework* and inform one's self about the particular culture of one's counterpart. However, when dealing with an unfamiliar culture, the answer is not as simple as picking up a book or going on the internet to Google information about the culture. Often times the particular context and participants involved make it complex. For example, the use of idioms, slang and/or colloquialisms and thus an expression that has figurative meaning, is a common error that people make when interacting with people from a different culture. Usage of these *figures of speech* are in essence also information processing errors since people have a tendency to behave in ways that they are accustomed to (i.e., using availability heuristics; Kahneman, Slovic & Tversky, 1982), such as, using everyday language that people use with members of the same group. The issue is that cultural misunderstanding occurs when the receiver of a message who is not familiar with the usage misinterprets the meaning during the decoding process. The fundamental problem with errors related to idioms, slang and/or colloquialisms is that the meanings are generally very parochial and can change very rapidly, thus the appropriate and accurate meaning of latest terminology may not be available in print or online.

Minimizing the impact of and everyday language usage. A simple suggestion to minimize the impact of everyday language usage is to avoid using idioms, slang and/or colloquialisms. Alternatively, be very conscious of it usage and attune to people's feedback during interactions to ensure that the correct meaning has been perceived, or go as far as explaining the meaning after it usage. We also would assert that, depending on the goal of the cross-cultural interaction, using idioms, slang and/or colloquialisms may actually be appropriate; for example, when one is helping people adapt to a new culture. Therefore, our caveat when using everyday language during cross-cultural interactions is similar to the use of stereotypes—be aware of its usage then ensure accuracy, that is, ensure that the counterpart perceives meanings correctly.

Ethnocentrism and cultural insensitivity. We contend that *ethnocentrism* and *cultural insensitivity* can be both an error and a mistake respectively, linked to both cultural knowledge and processing errors. Ethnocentrism is the belief in the superiority or correctness of one's ethnic or cultural group, thus involves a tendency for individuals to evaluate a foreigner or outsider's behaviors by the standards of one's own culture. We believe that this is more likely to occur when a person lacks cultural knowledge of another culture. For example, in Linowes' (1993) article, he gives examples of ethnocentric views from both the Japanese and American perspectives. The Japanese behavior of being equivocal and ambiguous is sometimes exhibited to avoid conflict and to maintain face. American observers, however, view these behaviors as being insincere and condescending. In contrast, Americans who blurt out the facts and truth directly are viewed as being rude by Japanese observers. It is possible that both the American and Japanese individuals lack knowledge of each other's cultures. At the same time, it is also possible that they have sufficient knowledge about each other's cultures and understand the behaviors, but still choose not to accommodate their judgments appropriately.

Norman (1988) in his analysis of everyday things classified a number of actions and argued that errors and mistakes are different. The former involves actions that are unintended with negative and/or unwanted outcomes, while the latter are intended actions but also with negative and/or unwanted outcomes. Based on Norman's classifications, we categorize ethnocentrism as an error. We assert that for the most part everyone has the tendency to be ethnocentric because it is natural for people to evaluate using self-referent information unless one makes a conscious effort not to do so (Pekerti, 2005; Pekerti & Kwantes, *in press*). Furthermore, since one's own culture is one that an individual is most familiar with or in some cases the only that one knows, it is normal to be ethnocentric. In short, ethnocentrism may be caused by people's unconscious use of the availability heuristic in their working memory (Kahneman et al., 1982), which in turn can cause evaluations of behaviors to be made solely on one's own culture. Cutler (2005) suggests that when one interacts with other cultures and comes away making judgments such as *rude, dirty, lazy, dishonest, disrespectful,* etc. (i.e., negative judgments) then one is probably being ethnocentric.

On the other hand, it is also possible that individuals are very much aware of a counterpart's culture, but choose not to acknowledge the norms, traditions and/ or values. We believe that unless the norms, traditions and/or values are directly in conflict with one's own cultural norms, traditions and/or values, the person may be behaving in an insensitive manner. In turn, the behaviors may lead to negative or unintended outcomes, thus in effect a mistake (Norman, 1988). The point is that both ethnocentrism and cultural insensitivity involve cultural knowledge. The former may involve the lack of knowledge while the latter may involve having knowledge about another's culture, but choosing not to value it.

Minimizing the impact of ethnocentrism. We acknowledge the fact that sometimes when the norms, traditions and/or values are directly in conflict with one's own cultural norms, traditions and/or values; it is the prerogative of the individual to not accommodate. Thomas et al. (2008) and Thomas (2010) suggests that this is part of what makes up cultural intelligence. We also acknowledge that not cooperating with norms of behavior can be a strategy in particular contexts (Bonavia, 1982; Ting-Toomey, 2005). Our suggestion is to be conscious that clashes of norms, traditions and/or values during cross-cultural encounters are not necessarily a personal attack on an individual's value system, as such. One's response should be aimed at protecting both one's face and the other's face at the same time.

MINIMIZING POTENTIAL CROSS-CULTURAL ERRORS

To conclude this section and as a preamble to the critical incidents we present a number of questions in an attempt to minimize the potential errors that one can make during cross-cultural encounters. These questions are posed from the realistic perspective that one person can never have expert knowledge about every culture that exists in the world. More importantly, they also serve as caveats that everyone is subject to the errors we discussed above.

In line with the KISS principle, we pose five simple and systematic questions and suggestions concerning the following areas in cross-cultural situations: *Cultures, Individuals, Different Behaviors, Understanding of,* and *Disagreement with values* (CIDUD). Please note that some of the suggested solutions have been discussed in more detail in previous sections of this article.

1 - C) Do I have sufficient *cultural* knowledge to function effectively with the person from the other culture? *If not, inform yourself about the culture, and withhold judgments until sufficient knowledge is gained.*

2 - I) Do I have sufficient knowledge about the *individual(s)* from the other culture? *If not, withhold judgments, then inform yourself about the counterpart(s).*

3 - D) Is the person(s) behaving *differently* to the available information I have about the culture? *If so, withhold judgment then inform yourself about the individual, especially if you come away with judgments such as, rude, dirty, lazy, dishonest, disrespectful, etc.*

4 - U) Do I *understand* the reasons/causes for the behavior(s)? *If not, go through the first three steps again in more depth, or consult a cultural informant and/or trusted person to provide explanations about the particular behavior(s).*

5 - D) Do I *disagree* with the reasons/causes of the behavior(s)? *If so, then try to behave in ways that protect the face of all parties.*

We now present three cross-cultural mini cases as learning and discussion tools with the aim of valuing the cultures depicted through the critical incidents. Each incident is self-contained including references and a number of explanations, which allows the reader to choose the best one that elucidates the events described in the incident. Analyses of the explanations provides readers with insights into each of the cultures involved in the cases. We hope that the cross-cultural incidents will serve as starting points for further discussion and learning regarding international business and organizational behavior of the cultures portrayed and/or similar situations depicted.

CROSS-CULTURAL INCIDENT A

AN AUSTRALIAN IN CHINA

BY SARAH WOODLAND AND ANDRE A. PEKERTI

While Sarah was in China as an international student, she had a *huxiang* (language partner) and friend named Tommy. Sarah and Tommy would spend time together a couple of times a week discussing all sorts of topics, in English and Chinese. He would mostly speak Chinese and she would speak English so they could practice their listening skills. On one particular occasion, Sarah invited Tommy over to her dormitory; they chatted as usual when Sarah suddenly felt hungry and wanted to go out for lunch. Sarah had assumed that going out for food with a friend had a similar meaning in China as it did in Australia. In Australia, eating together was an expression of friendship, but was primarily a functional activity, that is of sustenance. The following conversation ensued.

INCIDENT

Sarah: (In English) I am hungry, let's go eat. (In Chinese) Where is good food?

Tommy: (In Chinese) Canteen.

Sarah: (In English) No, I mean *good* food! (emphasizing *good*)

Tommy: (In English) Oh, I don't know.

Sarah: (In English) Let's go to that fish restaurant someone recommended to me.

Tommy: (In English) Oh, yeah that is a good place.

Sarah: (In English) What kind of fish do you want to eat?

Tommy: (In English) *Long pause* Oh, no, maybe not that place. *At this point, he looked rather worried, and he furrowed his brow.*

Sarah: (In English) I'll pay, don't worry, fish is expensive but it is delicious.

Tommy: (In English) *Another pause* Maybe some other time... *He didn't seem to want to look at Sarah, and was very non-committal.*

Sarah: (In English) Oh, well, hrmmm.... *At this point, she read out the following Daoist phrase* – "Keep your belly full and your head empty". So how about we go, and get some fish and we eat, and then we don't worry about that will happen next?

Tommy: (In English) OK.

After managing to go out for lunch, Sarah was confused and disconcerted as to why Tommy seemed unwilling to commit to the activity. His initial verbal and non-verbal behavior seemed to indicate he wanted to go, yet it took an inordinate amount of time to convince him. She still felt that maybe she had made an error in how she approached the interaction, and that she was missing important information, which would help her better understand Tommy's behavior.

DISCUSSION QUESTIONS

Sarah is wondering what had actually happened.
What would you do if you were Sarah now, and why?
What would you have done if you were Sarah to avoid the current situation?

All of these alternatives below may have something to do with the problem, but which one best explains the situation?

Explanation A. First, different communication styles may have hindered clear communication between Sarah and Tommy during their interaction. Interpretation of messages across cultures is more difficult and less accurate than communication between members of one culture. Therefore, while Sarah may have been conveying the desire to satisfy her hunger and spend time with a friend, Tommy may have interpreted her behavior or conversation differently, perhaps as having some kind of social expectation or obligation associated with the act of going out for lunch together.

Explanation B. Alternatively or as in addition to this, Sarah's request to go to lunch together may have been interpreted as a proposition. A woman asking a man over to her dormitory, then suggesting going out for lunch at a relatively expensive restaurant may have been interpreted as a romantic or forward gesture, akin to asking someone out on a date. This situation may have made Tommy uncomfortable or uncertain as to Sarah's intentions, and therefore less willing to agree immediately.

Explanation C. Another possible explanation is that Tommy and Sarah were unfamiliar with how to act politely in each other's cultures and thus were unable to use appropriate *facework* or *politeness* strategies when making requests or refusing an invitation. When Sarah requested that Tommy come with her to lunch, this required Tommy to give an appropriate response, which would not offend Sarah. The reason for his refusal is not as significant as the way in which he refused the offer. However, his refusal may have been related to financial capacity. Given he was a domestic Chinese student at the time; Tommy's disposable income would likely have been far lower than Sarah's. Therefore, in order to avoid *losing face*, he may have tried to delay or avoid going with her to an expensive restaurant.

Explanation D. Last, the language barrier between Tommy and Sarah may have caused the misunderstanding between them. The lack of language ability of both parties may have caused Sarah's invitation to sound too rough, demanding or overly casual. It may have also made an elegant rejection (for whatever reason) more difficult for Tommy.

ANALYSIS OF THE CROSS-CULTURAL INCIDENT

Socialization into a particular culture has implications for behaviors of members of that culture. In Sarah and Tommy's case, differences in socialized cultural orientations relating to communication styles, gender roles/expectations, languages, and the importance of *face* are all evident within their interaction. These cultural differences likely contributed to the miscommunication, which occurred between the two parties.

Culturally, Sarah and Tommy sit in different positions along the continuum of individualism and collectivism dimensions (Triandis & Singelis, 1998; Triandis, 2000). Compared to Sarah, Tommy is from a relatively collectivist culture, which also implies that his communication pattern reflects that of a high-context communicator. That is, Tommy relies heavily on situational and nonverbal cues in order to understand the messages being conveyed by others. Due to the large amount of information implied in the environment, he conveys relatively little information directly and/or verbally (Luthans & Doh, 2009). These characteristics are somewhat evident in Sarah and Tommy's conversation. Whilst Sarah uses direct verbal and self-referent communication, Tommy speaks less directly, relying more on non verbal communication such as kinesics (e.g., eye contact and facial expressions) and para-language (e.g., pauses) (Luthans & Doh, 2009; Pekerti & Thomas, 2003) to convey his emotions. This means that when communication occurs between Tommy and Sarah, culture adds to the *noise* between them, and creates difficulties in message interpretation.

Also embedded within the socialization patterns of most cultures, and evident in the cross-cultural incident described, are ideas relating to gender roles. Gibbons, Hamby and Dennis (1997, p. 153) state that "cross-cultural investigations of gender role development have shown that despite similarities in many facets of gender roles, some cultures do hold different perspectives of what characteristics males or females should exhibit". Essentially, "Gender roles are culturally defined concepts" (Brannon, 2005 cited by Yu & Xie, 2008, p. 1519). These roles are reinforced through regional and national levels, and social, economic, and political systems (Tu & Liao, 2005). Gender roles can relate to issues such as labour division and power distribution within relationships. Practices such as foot-binding and banning women from working, along with forms of discrimination embedded within the language are examples of the traditional patriarchal attitudes towards women, which have been observed in China (Zhang, 2006). Whilst contemporary attitudes are perhaps not so extreme, by inviting Tommy to lunch with her, Sarah still may have inadvertently violated Chinese cultural norms surrounding appropriate behavior for men and women. Her actions may have been interpreted as being too forward, and therefore caused Tommy to become uncomfortable.

Another concept that is highly influential within Chinese culture is the notion of *face*. There are many complex cultural nuances, which are associated with the preservation of one's own and other's *face* in order to maintain social harmony (Zhang, 2006). The analysis of this cross-cultural incident therefore warrants consideration of the theory of facework, or politeness theory. Politeness/facework theory essentially states that individuals are motivated to preserve and enhance their own public self-image as well as the public self-image of others during an interaction. This public self-image is referred to as face, and has two subsets—positive and negative face. Positive face relates to the desire to be "appreciated and approved of by others", whilst negative face involves a person's desire to be able to freely pursue their goals (Mao, 1994, p. 451).

It is suggested by Brown and Levinson, and cited by researchers such as Mao (1994), Gagne (2010), Johnson (2007), and Morand (2003), that certain actions, statements or behaviors, such as requesting, ordering, inviting, or criticizing may be considered to be *face-threatening*. That is, these aspects of an interaction threaten the face of one or both members involved. In order to communicate effectively and maintain positive relations between individuals and groups, strategies are developed in order to either avoid threatening face altogether or to redress any acts which may cause damage to another's face (Mao, 1994; Johnson, 2007; Gagne, 2010). These strategies are culturally specific, and may be chosen by individuals based on the perceived "appropriateness and availability of strategies in a given context" (Gagne, 2010, p. 156). If incorrectly chosen, a facework strategy can backfire; for example, the refusal of a request may see the requester persist rather than accept the refusal (Johnson, 2007; Johnson, Roloff & Riffee, 2004). At this point, compliance may eventually be attained by the requester, but at the cost of damaging the relationship between the parties (Johnson, 2007). This risk of relationship deterioration is reduced, however, if the parties share some familiarity or common ground with each other that can be used to overcome difficulties in communication (Chen, 2002).

Further work by researchers such as Mao (1994) argue that there are flaws in Brown and Levinson's approach to the concept of politeness. It is important to take note of the impact culture has on the development and applicability of cross-cultural theories in general. For example, Mao argues that there are important distinctions between the concept of self-image in individualistic societies, as put forward by Brown and Levinson, and self-image in sociocentric societies such as China. Self-image as per the original model is closely related to individually-centered needs. However, in China, the concept of self-image is inextricably linked to fulfillment of social expectations and the maintenance of group harmony (Mao, 1994).

Analysis of the dialogue in the cross-cultural incident, shows that it is evident that facework has played a significant role in how Sarah and Tommy have interacted. By inviting Tommy to lunch with her, Sarah put herself in a position where she could be rejected, which required Tommy to respond using a facework strategy in order to try to preserve his own face as well as Sarah's. Whilst he rejected her offer, he quickly redressed the situation by softening his rejection, using a common strategy which employs pauses and "maybe not", instead of a direct "no"(Morand,

2003). However, because this redress was ineffective, it resulted in Sarah persisting, even to the point of offering to pay. By offering to do this, Sarah may have exacerbated the face threat towards Tommy by elevating herself above him in terms of financial capacity (Johnson, 2007). Again, she was rejected and this time Tommy made amends by offering to go with her some other time. Recognizing that there was a difficulty in communication at this point, Sarah drew upon common ground, in this case, a Daoist phrase, in order to communicate across the cultural gap (Morand, 2003; Chen, 2002). By referring to established common ground, in this case a philosophy, which they both shared, Sarah and Tommy were able to communicate more effectively and come to a mutually beneficial outcome.

EVALUATION OF THE FOUR POSSIBLE EXPLANATIONS

Explanation A. While different communication styles seem to have, in part, contributed to the miscommunication that occurred between Sarah and Tommy, they are not the primary reason for the incident. This conclusion is supported by research, which shows that as individuals develop a closer relationship, they in fact become familiar with each other's communication styles, and become less likely to misinterpret each other (Morand, 2003). Furthermore, research by Elfenbein and Ambady (2003) states that if either Tommy or Sarah had been exposed to another culture before, communication cues such as facial expressions may have been easier for them to identify than if they had no cross-cultural experience (Elfenbein, 2006). So whilst initial encounters are particularly vulnerable to miscommunication due to differing communication styles (Chen, 2002), this may have been less of a factor for Sarah and Tommy, as they were already somewhat familiar with each other and each other's culture.

Explanation B. In terms of the violation of gender norms or roles, whilst it is true that China was traditionally associated with strongly masculine views and had very strict roles for women and men, the ideological shift to Communism from the 1950s onward may have introduced some more egalitarian ideological perspectives (Zhang, 2006). However, research by Zhang indicates that traditional gender perspectives are still dominant within Chinese society, and these views are positively related to age (Zhang, 2006). According to this research, since Sarah and Tommy are young university students, their views would have been more egalitarian than older students or members of society. Gender roles therefore may have been a peripheral issue in the cross-cultural incident, but were unlikely to be the root cause of the miscommunication.

Explanation C. The difficulty in communication between Tommy and Sarah most likely arose from each party's attempts to communicate whilst engaging in face-work strategies. There is a large body of evidence that outlines the difficulties, which can arise from the meeting of complex systems of politeness that are used in cross-cultural interactions. In the earlier cross-cultural incident, both parties seem unsure of each other's true meaning, and thus repeatedly put each other in the position where they could *lose face*. As discussed earlier, the Chinese form of face-work is different to the Western form, and particular behaviors associated with politeness vary across cultures (Mao, 1994). Sarah and Tommy's conversation is a classic example of two parties who are struggling to understand what is considered polite in each other's culture and to act accordingly. Only by drawing on common ground did they manage to get past the difficulty and come to an agreement. The miscommunication may have been avoided altogether if Sarah and Tommy had a better understanding of the notion of face, and a basic grasp of strategies for avoiding causing confusion or offence in each other's culture.

Explanation D. The language barrier between the two parties was a contributing factor to the situation as well, since communicating effectively in a particular culture depends partially on one's ability to use correct language in the correct context (Luthans & Doh, 2009). This idea is perhaps epitomized by the complex system of *keigo* used within the Japanese culture (Gagne, 2010). The Chinese language also has many politeness maxims, which are a critical part of communication within that culture, and which may be difficult for a person of a different language base to identify and use correctly (Si, 2008). More generally, even basic conversation between two parties who do not speak the same native language can at times be difficult and cause miscommunication to occur. However, language is not the sole determinant of effective communication (Luthans & Doh, 2009). As mentioned earlier, non-verbal communication is highly valued within high-context cultures, and is used in place of verbal language. Furthermore, the parties would have anticipated language deficiencies to some degree, since they were engaging in a language exchange partnership specifically for improving their skills. Thus, language deficiencies alone are unlikely to be the cause of the misunderstanding.

CONCLUSION

Cultural issues were the primary reason for the miscommunication that occurred between the two parties involved in the cross-cultural incident. Specifically, different notions of politeness were the primary issue. Other contributing factors included different views of gender roles, communication styles and language orientations. However, the positive outcome of the incident shows that there are ways of overcoming these difficulties, and that people can learn from their experience in order to establish and maintain good relationships with members of other cultures.

ADDITIONAL TEACHING IDEAS

1) Remove the four possible answers at the end of the scenario and just use the questions to initiate discussions surrounding the incident.
2) Or leave the four possible answers, but ask the questions prior to asking students to make a choice of the best explanation.

REFERENCES

Chen, L. (2002), "Perceptions of Inter-cultural interaction and communication satisfaction: A study on initial encounter", *Communication Reports, 15*(2), pp. 133–147.

Elfenbein, H. & Ambady, N. (2003), "When familiarity breeds accuracy: Cultural exposure and facial emotion recognition", *Journal of Personality and Social Psychology, 85*(2), pp. 276–290.

Elfenbein, H. (2006), "Learning in emotion judgments: Training and the cross-cultural understanding of facial expressions", *Journal of Non-verbal Behaviour,* 30(1), pp. 21–36.

Gagne, N. (2010), "Re-examining the notion of negative face in the Japanese socio-linguistic politeness of request", *Language & Communication,* 30, pp. 123–138.

Gibbons, J., Hamby, B. & Dennis, W. (1997), "Researching gender-role ideologies internationally and cross-culturally", *Psychology of Women Quarterly,* 21(1), pp. 151–170.

Johnson, D. (2007), "Politeness theory and conversational refusals: Associations between various types of face threat and perceived competence", *Western Journal of Communication,* 71(3), pp. 196–215.

Johnson, D., Roloff, M., & Riffee, M. (2004), "Politeness theory and refusals of requests: Face threat as a function of expressed obstacles", *Communication Studies,* 55(2), pp. 227–238.

Luthans, F. & Doh, J. (2009), *International Management: Culture, Strategy and Behaviour,* 7th Edition, pp. 94–202. McGraw- Hill Irwin, New York,

Mao, L. (1994), "Beyond politeness theory: Face revisited and renewed", *Journal of Pragmatics,* 21, pp. 451–486.

Morand, D. (2003), "Politeness and the clash of interaction orders in cross-cultural communication", *Thunderbird International Business Review,* 45(5), pp. 521–540.

Pekerti, A. A. & Thomas, D. C. (2003), "Communication in intercultural interaction: An empirical investigation of idiocentric and sociocentric communication styles", *Journal of Cross-Cultural Psychology,* 34(2), pp. 139–154.

Si, Y. (2008), "A pragmatic study of politeness maxims in contemporary Chinese", *International Forum of Teaching and Studies,* 4(2), pp. 1–12.

Triandis, H. C. & Singelis, T. M. (1998), "Training to recognize individual differences in collectivism and individualism within culture", *International Journal of Inter-cultural Relations,* 22, pp. 35–48.

Triandis, H. C. (2000), "Culture and conflict", *International Journal of Psychology,* 35(2), pp. 145–152.

Tu, S. & Liao, P. (2005), "Gender differences in gender-role attitudes: A comparative analysis of Taiwan and Coastal China", *Journal of Comparative Family Studies,*

36(4), pp. 545–566. Yu, L. & Xie, D. (2008), "The relationship between desirable and undesirable gender role traits, and their implications for psychological well-being in Chinese culture", *Personality and Individual Differences, 44,* pp.1517–1527.

Zhang, N. (2006), "Gender egalitarian attitudes among Chinese college students". *Sex roles, 55,* pp. 545–553.

CROSS-CULTURAL INCIDENT B

AN AMERICAN IN JAPAN

BY STEVEN DIACK AND ANDRE A. PEKERTI

INCIDENT

This cross-cultural incident takes place in a small business in Tokyo, Japan between John Smith, from New York, USA and his senior supervisor Aki Saito. John has been working in Japan for three months; he is still learning Japanese culture with very basic Japanese language skills. Aki Saito has lived in Japan all his life.

Two months into his tenure at the company, John, catches his supervisor off-guard and asks to speak with him in private. Aki Saito is a bit hesitant to speak with him at such short notice, however he agrees to do so. John wanted to request some time off for a holiday in two weeks time.

Throughout the meeting, which took part in English, John kept fixed eye contact with his supervisor and continued talking in his usual manner as he was prompted and encouraged by the supervisor with frequent murmurs of "mmm" accompanied by head nodding. His supervisor seemed reluctant to indicate a clear decision. John continued to ask for clarification only to be met by more nodding and "mmm" sounds. Due to the content and feedback of the conversation during the meeting, John assumed that his request would be approved. John thanked his supervisor for allowing him to a take holiday at such short notice at the conclusion of the meeting. After the meeting, he left work early so he could go home and make plans for his upcoming holiday. However, two days later he was informed by the second in charge (2IC) of the department that his supervisor did not approve his request for the holiday as per John's schedule, stating that others are not taking time off.

This outcome left John feeling frustrated, offended and confused since he did not understand why the supervisor had changed his mind, as well as why he heard the news from the 2IC.

DISCUSSION QUESTIONS

John Smith is wondering what had happened.

A) *What would you do if you were John Smith now, and why?*

B) *What would you have done if you were John Smith to avoid the current situation?*

All of these alternatives below may have something to do with the problem, but which one best explains the situation?

Explanation A. John Smith's lack of cultural awareness caused him to misinterpret his supervisor's message both verbal and non-verbal communication. As prescribed by Japanese norms, Aki Saito did not immediately reject John's request in order to save face, despite thinking that John Smith was out of line as a subordinate to be so forward and informal in requesting time off only after two months into his tenure at work.

Explanation B. John Smith communicated effectively and made a reasonable and perfectly valid request for leave. However, Aki Saito has underdeveloped English skills and was too embarrassed to ask John to slow down during their meeting. Not understanding what John entirely said during the meeting, Aki Saito decided to reject his request to avoid approving something he would not usually endorse.

Explanation C. John Smith communicated effectively and made a reasonable and perfectly valid request for leave just as he would usually do back in the USA. However, Aki Saito has a personal dislike for John and has decided to reject his request in an attempt to get him to leave the organization.

Explanation D. John Smith did not convey his request clearly given his current knowledge of Japanese culture, hence, making a few fundamental communication errors and assumptions. However, this did not affect Aki Saito's interpretation of the request, as Aki knew what John was requesting, but thought that it was a particularly busy part of the business year.

ANALYSIS OF THE CROSS-CULTURAL INCIDENT

In the cross-cultural incident described above, there are several misunderstandings, miscommunications and misperceptions between the two parties, which can be attributed to a lack of cultural knowledge. Stier (2004, p.7) states that, "we are unable to observe the very eyes with which we are viewing the world putting us in a dilemma that to a large extent we are trapped in our own culture and frame of mind".

Hall's (1976) low- and high-context theory of communication is useful to explain John Smith and Aki Saito's behaviors in the incident above. According to Ahlstrom & Bloom (2010, p.41), "Japan is a high-context culture and the USA is a low-context culture".

"In a high-context culture, communication is less direct, speech is unhurried and drawn out, a great emphasis is placed upon non-verbal communication (rather than the content), interpretation is loose and face is very important" (Alstrom & Burton, 2010, p. 41). In the incident, Aki Saito demonstrates several high-context culture characteristics. One of the most important aspects of high context culture in the incident is the concept of *face*. According to Ting-Toomey (1994, p.1), "face entails the presentation of a civilized front to another individual within the webs of interconnected relationships in a particular culture". "The Japanese tend to have low *self-face* and high *other-face* relative to that of other cultures" (Oetzel et al., 2001, p.240). This means that Japanese tend to prioritize concern for another's image more than their own face. The concept of other-face can be used to explain Aki's behavior in the scenario as he withheld his decision from John Smith and had the 2IC communicate this to him. "In low-context cultures the concept of self-face is more important than other-face" (Ting-Toomey & Kurogi, 1998, p.192), hence the reason why John Smith was frustrated by being informed through the 2IC of the final decision.

Other aspects of high-context cultural communication used by Aki Saito are *backchannels* such as "mmm" coupled with nodding of the head, as a type of non-verbal communication. Backchannels are "short utterances e.g. 'uh-huh' produced (by the listener) while the interlocutor speaks" (Ward, Escalante, Al Bayyari, & Solorio, 2007, p. 385). According to Maynard (1990, p. 406) and Maynard (1993; cited in Kita & Ide, 2007; p. 1247), "nodding accompanies 63% percent of *aizuchis* (backchannels) in Japanese conversation and Japanese speakers nod three times more frequently than American English speakers". "By giving feedback signals, the listener backs up the speaker not only by signaling understanding, but also by indirectly granting the speaker the right to go on talking by defining himself as a listener" (Miyata & Nisisawa, 2007, p. 1256). Given the large amount of head nodding and backchannels in Japanese conversation, it is no surprise that John Smith misinterpreted Aki's actions. Non-Japanese speakers become disturbed by the frequent responses of Japanese listeners and fail to understand their meaning: attentiveness, comprehension and interest (Mizutani, 1982, p.33).

"In a low-context culture the primary interest is information (not context), the listener requires a lot of information, ambiguity is seen as a negative, interpretation is unequivocal, and face saving is not very important" (Alstrom & Burton, 2010, p. 41). In the incident, the behaviors displayed by John Smith are typical of a person from a low-context culture. This is depicted by John's behavior of asking for clarification about the issue in question (holiday leave) and prolonged direct eye contact. According to Schneider and Barsoux (2003, p.44), "in a low-context situation everyone should be able to understand the message and have equal access to information". In this instance, Aki, being from a high-context culture may have felt pressured and threatened by John's directness. Moreover, "in Japan, eye contact shows that you are being aggressive, rude, insistent to be equal or belligerent" (Nishiyama, 2000, p.23). According to Nishiyama (2000, p.23), contrary to the Japanese meaning, "In America, establishing eye contact during a conversation shows interest, honesty and sincerity". As such, Aki Saito would have viewed these particular behaviors displayed by John Smith as severely unfavorable, whereas in American culture they are the accepted and expected norm.

Regarding behaviors displayed throughout the incident, it is likely that either or both parties made attributions to explain behavior that they did not understand.

According to Hall (1959, p.15), "others may blame their lack of understanding on the other party's stupidity, deceit or craziness". On the other hand, "they may attribute superior wisdom to them" (Deresky & Christopher, 2008, p.130). These are internal attributions, however, certain cultures will also make external attributions for example when they believe that "events are beyond their control or for example religious people make external attributions to acts of God" (Deresky & Christopher, 2008, p.130). In general, "members of high-context cultures tend to look for explanations externally whilst members of low-context cultures tend to attribute internally" (Deresky & Christopher, 2008, p.130).

Furthermore, only after two months into his tenure at work, it would be seen as inappropriate for John to go on leave due to the following cultural and social attitudes that he is seemingly unaware of. According to Turner (2005, p.18), "the average Japanese worker takes less than half (47.5% in 2001) of his or her allocated holidays and the rate is falling every year". Suggested reasons for not taking leave include sense of achievement from work, fear of being replaced and blurred job description i.e. it is hard to distinguish where the job starts and stops, therefore making it harder to take holidays (Turner, 2005, p.18). According to Gilbert and Terrata (2001, p. 70), "When Japanese individuals do not work hard, they tend to feel the shame that this brings upon their families, companies, and societies, which consequently leads them to suffer from feelings of guilt". Aki Saito may have felt ashamed upon John Smith's behalf and therefore felt it in his duty to decline his leave application.

EVALUATIONS OF THE FOUR POSSIBLE EXPLANATIONS

Explanation A. After evaluating the behaviors displayed in the incident, rationale A can be offered as the best explanation of the incident since it accurately describes both parties involved in the incident by forming accurate representations of the subjects and their behaviors, whilst highlighting the misperceptions attributed by each party to the other. As John Smith has only been in Japan a short period and is still at the *unconscious incompetence stage* (Bhawuk, 2001) of his cross-cultural expertise development, it is unlikely that he understood the intended meaning of

Aki Saito's actions through backchannels, non-verbal communication methods and the concept of other-face. At the same time, due to the difference in the contexts of their cultures, it is evident that Aki Saito may have misinterpreted the apparent directness John Smith's behaviors, hence adding to the cultural misunderstandings of the incident (Hall, 1976).

As stated in the previous section the following statements support this rationale as the best explanation. Non-Japanese speakers become disturbed by the frequent responses of Japanese listeners and fail to understand their meaning: attentiveness, comprehension and interest (Mizutani, 1982; p.33). Furthermore, "in a low-context situation everyone should be able to understand the message and have equal access to information" Schneider & Barsoux (2003, p.44). These views suggest that by using a low-context mode, John Smith had interpreted the information expressed in the interaction causing the misunderstanding.

Explanation B. Explanation B is an incorrect interpretation of the incident since several misunderstandings have occurred. Analysis of the behaviors presented Hall's (1976) high- and low–context theory suggests that this rationale is invalid. Furthermore, it would be wrong to draw assumptions about Aki Saito's English skills, and attribute the outcome to Aki's English skills without more information or evidence. Doing so would be in accordance with Hall's (1959, p.15) statement that, "others may blame their lack of understanding on the other party's stupidity, deceit or craziness".

Explanation C. Explanation C is an incorrect interpretation of the incident since several misunderstandings have occurred. Attributing the outcome to Aki Saito's personal dislike for John Smith is simplistic and an assumption that cannot be reached without personally asking Aki. There are better explanations, so using this one would be an example of misattribution.

Explanation D. Attributing the outcome to John Smith's communication errors given his current knowledge of Japanese culture seems to be valid in this situation. However, the second part of this rationale that suggests that Aki Saito may have had legitimate reasons to reject John Smith's request (e.g., particularly busy part of the business year), cannot be made without having proper information to support it.

A combination of Explanation A and D is a good option, but Explanation A can stand-alone.

ADDITIONAL TEACHING IDEAS

1) Remove the four possible answers at the end of the scenario and just use the questions to initiate discussions surrounding the incident.

2) Or leave the four possible answers, but ask the questions prior to asking students to make a choice of the best explanation.

REFERENCES

Alstrom, D. & Burton, G. D. (2010). *International management: Strategy and culture in the emerging world.* South-Western Cengage Learning, Mason.

Bhawuk, D. P. S. (2001), "Evolution of cultural assimilators: Toward theory based assimilators", *International Journal of Intercultural Relations, 25,* pp. 141–163.

Deresky, H. & Christopher, E. (2008), *International Management: Managing across borders and cultures,* Pearson Education Australia, Frenchs Forest.

Gilbert, D. & Terratta, M. (2001), "An exploratory study of factors of Japanese tourism demand for the UK", *International Journal of Contemporary Hospitality Management, 13*(2), p. 70.

Hall, E.T. (1959), *The silent language.* Doubleday, New York.

Hall, E.T. (1976), *Beyond culture.* Doubleday, New York.

Kita. S. & Ide, S. (2007), "Nodding, aizuchi, and final particles in Japanese conversation: How conversation reflects the ideology of communication and social relationships", *Journal of Pragmatics, 39*(7), pp. 1242–1254.

Maynard, S. K. (1990), "Conversation management in contrast: listener response in Japanese and American English", *Journal of Pragmatics, 14,* pp. 397–412.

Miyata, S, & Nisisawa, H. (2007), "The acquisition of Japanese back channeling behavior: observing the emergence of aizuchi in a Japanese boy", *Journal of Pragmatics, 39,* pp. 1255–1274.

Mizutani, N. (1982), "The listener's responses in Japanese conversation", *Sociolinguistics Newsletter, 13*(1), pp. 33–38.

Nishiyama, K. (2000), *Doing business with Japan: successful strategies for intercultural communication.* University of Hawaii Press, Honolulu.

Oetzel, J. G., Ting-Toomey, S., Masumoto, T., Yokochi, Y., Pan, X., Takai, J., & Wilcox, R. (2001), "Face and facework in conflict: A cross-cultural comparison of China, Germany, Japan and the United States", *Communication Monographs, 68*, pp. 235–258.

Schneider S. C. & Barsoux, J. (2003), *Managing across cultures*, 2nd ed. Pearson Education Limited, Essex.

Stier, J. (2004), "Intercultural competencies as a means to manage intercultural interactions in social work", *Journal of Intercultural Communication, 7*, pp. 1–17.

Ting-Toomey, S. (1994), *The challenge of facework*. State University of New York Press, Albany.

Ting-Toomey, S. & Kurogi, A. (1998), "Facework competence in intercultural conflict: An updated face-negotiation theory", *International Journal of Intercultural Relations, 22*, pp. 187–225.

Turner, D. (2005), "All work and no play should worry Japan's bosses Economic problems", *Financial Times,* December, 22, p. 18.

Ward, N. G., Escalante, R., Al Bayyari, Y., & Solorio T. (2007, "Learning to show you're listening", *Computer Assisted Language Learning,* 20(4), pp. 385–407.

CROSS-CULTURAL INCIDENT C
A NEW ZEALANDER IN INDONESIA – DEATH OF A WORKER

BY ANDRE A. PEKERTI AND ANUGERAH PEKERTI

INCIDENT

James Dexter was a subsidiary manager of a New Zealand paper and pulp plant in Central Java, Indonesia. He had been managing the subsidiary for 2 years and had built up a good rapport with his Javanese workers.

One unfortunate morning, one of the workers dropped a chlorine drum spilling its contents on the warehouse floor. The chlorine mixed with other residue of chemicals found in the warehouse causing a toxic mixture. As a consequence of being exposed to the toxic gas, one of the workers died a few days later. The operation was closed for a few days for decontamination and a review of the safety procedures undertaken.

During the shutdown, James Dexter ordered a review of the safety procedures in the plant as well as safety checks on all equipment in the firm. As a result of the review a revised policy concerning the storage of chemicals was devised. The new policy ensured that no chemicals stored in the same warehouse would produce toxic reactions. James also revised all other safety procedures in the plant and all workers were to be re-trained in emergency and safety procedures concerning chemicals and all equipment in the plant.

One day before the plant was to re-open, James called a meeting with all the workers. It was held at a nearby auditorium at the workers' request. The workers also requested a traditional ceremony to be carried out and all night *Wayang kulit* (shadow puppet) performance was made to honor their fallen colleague. James had agreed to the alternate venue since the plant did not have a venue to accommodate all the workers. However, James did not agree to the all night Wayang performance since he thought it would affect the productivity of the workers and cause a potential safety hazard. He decided to have an *Ulamah* (Islamic cleric) pray for the fallen worker and safety of all. James also assured the workers that all equipment had safety checks that had been passed. Those that did not had to be upgraded and now all passed international safety standards. Since the worker was not insured, the firm further guaranteed that the worker's family would be compensated.

The next day James came to work early and enthusiastic to greet the workers at the gate. At 7:00 am, after waiting for 2 hours for his first shift of workers to arrive, none had come in. He proceeded to enter the plant to call one of his Javanese managers at home to ask where all his workers were. Before he made the call James found out that the night shift had not shown up for work.

DISCUSSION QUESTIONS

James Dexter is wondering what had happened.

A) What would you do if you were James Dexter now (7:00 am with an empty work-place), and why?

B) What would you have done if you were James Dexter to avoid the current situation?

All of these alternatives below may have something to do with the problem, but which one best explains the situation?

Explanation A. The workers did not think that the compensation for their colleague's family was enough. As such, they refused to go to work until the compensation was increased.

Explanation B. The workers viewed the new safety standards as too stringent and thought that they could not work under the new regulations.

Explanation C. The workers thought that the Gods were angry and that was the reason their colleague had died. They feared that the Gods were still angry hence did not dare to go to work.

Explanation D. With all the drama surrounding the death of the worker and the new regulations, it had slipped James's mind that the day the plant was scheduled to re-open was a traditional Javanese Hindu holiday.

EVALUATIONS OF THE FOUR POSSIBLE EXPLANATIONS

Explanation A. Although Indonesia's labor market regulations are changing for the better, many of Indonesia's worker are not insured ("Most workers still lack insurance", 2004). As such, accident compensation payments from firms may still be perceived as diminutive even if they have worked for the company for more than 10 years (Manning, 1997; Manning 2003). This is a probable explanation, however, it is more likely that only a few close friends would have known the compensation amount, thus only a few workers would have boycotted the job rather than the whole workforce. Another explanation should be sought.

Explanation B. Similar to explanation A, consistent with changes in labor market regulations, health and safety regulations are improving in Indonesia. For the most part, improvements in safety regulations benefit workers, thus this is not the best explanation for workers not showing up on the day.

Explanation C. The most appropriate answer is choice C. The workers thought that the Gods were angry and the reason for the accident which resulted in their colleague's death. Their request to have a traditional ceremony and Wayang performance to honor their fallen colleague was a polite way to ask for a ceremony to ward away evil spirits and appease the Gods.

After discussions with the community leaders and workers representatives James learnt the workers real request was to have a *Wayang kulit* performance where the scenes depicted evil spirits being exorcised. James learnt that the ceremony and Wayang performance serves to ward away evil spirits and appease the Gods. James immediately organized the Wayang performance and all the workers went back to work happily the next day.

Wayang is a Javanese word meaning "shadow" or "ghost" and is a theatrical performance of shadow images projected before a backlit screen (*Wayang kulit*).

Wayang kulit in Central Java is probably one of the oldest continuous traditions of storytelling in the world, and certainly among the most highly developed. Wayang is well integrated in Javanese society, and it is considered a highlight of Javanese culture. Far more than mere entertainment, the wayang kulit is an extremely important vehicle of culture, serving as a carrier of myth, a morality play, and a form of religious experience all rolled into one (Lysloff, 1993; Sunarya, Gamelan & Foley, 2001). See Irvine's (1996) work for a rich (high-context) description of the characters and symbolism embodied by the puppets.

Explanation D. Indonesia celebrates a number of official national holidays. Since it recognizes five major religions; Islam, Protestantism, Catholicism, Hinduism and Buddhism, Indonesia's national holidays revolve around the five major recognized religions (www.expat.or.id; Howell, 2003). Although Indonesia functions on the Roman (Julian, 365 days) calendar, the religious holidays of the five recognized religions follows the lunar calendar, and as such, the dates of the holidays change each year. The exceptions are Independence Day, Christmas Day, and New Year's Day. The Chinese New Year has also recently been recognized as a National Holiday, which also changes each year. Although religious Hindu traditions are recognized in Hindu communities around Indonesia, only *Nyepi*, which is a Hindu Day of Silence or the Hindu New Year, is considered an official holiday in the Balinese

Saka calendar (www.expat.or.id). It is therefore not an official hiliday in Java and another explanation should be sought

ADDITIONAL TEACHING IDEAS

1) Remove the four possible answers at the end of the scenario and just use the questions to initiate discussions surrounding the incident.
2) Or leave the four possible answers, but ask the questions prior to asking students to make a choice of the best explanation.
3) Link the scenario with external locus of control.

REFERENCES

Irvine, D. (1996), *Leather Gods and wooden heroes*, Singapore; Times Editions. Howell, J.D. (2003).

"Islam, the New Age and Marginal Religions in Indonesia: Changing Meanings of Religious Pluralism". The CESNUR International Conference. Vilnius, Lithuania, April 9–12 2003. [Online], retrieved 15/11/2005, Available at: http://www.cesnur.org/2003/vil2003_howell.htm

"Most workers still lack insurance", (2004, May 18) *Jakarta Post*. [Online], retrieved 14/11/05, available at: http://www.asianlabour.org/archives/001620.php

Lysloff, R. T. A. (1993), "A wrinkle in time: The shadow puppet theatre of Banyumas (West Central Java)", *Asian Theatre Journal, 10*(1), pp. 49–80.

Manning, C. (2004), "Legislating for labour protection: Betting on the weak or the strong?" Working paper No. 20004/08. [Online], retrieved 14/11/2005, available at: http:// rspas.anu.edu.au/economics/publish/papers/wp2004/wp-econ-2004–08.pdf

Manning, C. (1997), "A new era of labour market regulation in developing East Asia? The case of Indonesia", *Asian Economic Journal, 11*(1), pp. 111–129.

Sunarya, A. Gamelan G. H. & Foley, K. (2001), "The Origin of Kala: A Sundanese Wayang Golek", *Asian Theatre Journal, 18*(1), pp. 1–58.

www.expat.or.id (n.d.), retrieved, 22/02/2011, from http://www.expat.or.id/info/holidays.html

ARTICLE REFERENCES

Adler, N. J. (1997), *International dimensions of organizational behavior*, 3rd. Ed. Cincinnati: South-Western.

Arnett, J. J. (2002), "The psychology of globalization", *American Psychologist, 57*(10), 774–738.

Berger, C. R. (1993), "Uncertainty and social interaction". In S. A. Deetz (Ed.), *Communication Yearbook, 16*, pp. 491–502. Newbury Park; Sage.

Blyton, P. (2001), "The general and the particular in cross-national and comparative research", *Applied Psychology: An International Review, 50*, pp. 590–595.

Bonavia, D. (1982), *The Chinese*. Ringwood, Victoria: Penguin Books.

Bond, M., Leung, K., Au, A., Tong, K-K., Reimel de Carrasquel, S. (2004), "Culture-level dimensions of social axioms and their correlates across 41 cultures", *Journal of Cross-Cultural Psychology, 35*(5), pp. 548–570.

Boyacigiller, N. A., Goodman, R. A., Phillips, M. A., & Pearce, J. L. (2003), *Crossing Cultures: Insights from Master Teachers*. New York, NY: Routledge.

Brislin, R. W. & Yoshida, T. (1994), *Improving intercultural interactions*. Thousand Oaks, CA: Sage.

Brown, P. & Levinson, S. (1978), "Universals in language usage: Politeness phenomenon". In E. Goody (Ed.), *Questions and politeness: Strategies in social interactions*. Cambridge: Cambridge University Press.

Burgoon, J. K. & Hale, J. L. (1987), "Validation and measurement of the fundamental themes of relational communication", *Communication Monographs, 54*, pp. 19–41.

Catrambone, R. & Markus, H. (1987), "The role of self-schemas in going beyond the information given", *Social Cognition, 5*(4), pp. 349–368.

Cocroft, B-A. K. & Ting-Toomey, S. (1994), "Facework in Japan and the United States", *International Journal of Intercultural Relations, 18*(4), pp. 469–506.

Cushner, K. & Brislin, R. W. (1996), *Intercultural interactions*. Thousand Oaks, CA: Sage.

Cutler, J. (2005), *The cross-cultural communication trainer's manual, Vol 1 &Vol 2*. Burlington, VT: Gower.

Dorfman, P.W., Hanges, P.J., & Brodbeck, F.C. (2004), "Leadership and Cultural Variation". In R.J. House, P.J. Hanges, M. Javidan, P.W. Dorfman and V. Gupta (Eds.),*Culture Leadership and Organizations: The GLOBE Study of 62 Societies*, pp. 669–722, London: Sage.

Earley, C. P. & Randel, A. E. (1997), "Self and other: 'Face' and work group dynamics". In C. Granrose & S. Oskamp (Eds.), *Claremont Symposium on Applied Social Psychology*. Sage Publications.

Enquist, B. J. & Niklas, K. J. (2002), "Global allocation rules for patterns of biomass partitioning in seed plants", *Science, 295*, pp. 1517–1520.

Ferguson, C. A. (1981), "The structure and use of politeness formulas". In F. Coulmas (Ed.), *Conversational routine*, pp. 21–36. New York: Mouton.

Firth, J. R. (1972), "Verbal and bodily rituals of greetings and parting". In J. S. La Fontaine (Ed.), *Interpretation of ritual*, pp. 1–38. London: Tavistock.

Hu, H. C. (1944), "The Chinese concept of 'face'", *American Anthropologist, 46*, pp. 45–64.

Gallois, C. & Callan, V. (1997), *Communication and culture: A guide for practice*. Chichester, UK: Wiley.

Goffman, E. (1967), *Interaction ritual: Essays in face-to-face behavior*. Chicago: Aldine.

Gudykunst, W. B., Ting-Toomey, S., & Chua, E. (1988), *Culture and interpersonal communication*. Beverly Hills, CA: Sage.

Hall, E. T. (1976), *Beyond culture*. New York, NY: Doubleday.

Hofstede, G. (1980), *Culture's consequences*. Beverly Hills, CA: Sage.

Hofstede, G. (1993), "Cultural constraints in management theories", *Academy of Management Executive, 7*(1), pp. 81–94.

Honeycutt, J. M. (1993), "Components and functions of communication during initial interaction, with extrapolations to beyond". In S. A. Deetz (Ed.), *Communication Yearbook, 16*, pp. 461–490. Newbury Park: CA: Sage.

Kahneman, D., Slovic, P., & Tversky, A. (Eds.) (1982), *Judgment under uncertainty: heuristics and biases*. New York: Cambridge University Press.

Kashima, E. S. & Kashima, Y. (1993), "Perceptions of general variability of social groups", *Social Cognition, 11*(1), pp. 1–21.

Kluckhohn, F. R. & Strodbeck, F. L. (1961), *Variations in value orientations.* Evanston, IL: Harper & Row.

Lebra, T. S. (1976), *Japanese pattern of behavior.* Honolulu: University of Hawaii Press.

Linowes, R. G. (1993), "The Japanese manager's traumatic entry into the United States: Understanding the American-Japanese cultural divide", *Academy of Management Executive, 7*(4), pp. 21–38.

McArthur, L. Z. & Baron, R. M. (1983), "Toward an ecological theory of social perception", *Psychological Review, 90*(3), pp. 215–238.

Markus, H., Smith, J., & Moreland, R. L. (1985), "Role of the self-concept in the perception of others", *Journal of Personality and Social Psychology, Vol. 49*(6), pp. 1492–1512.

Miller, D. R. (1963), "The study of social relationships: Situation, identity, and social interaction". In S. Koch (Ed.), *Psychology: A study of a science Vol. 5*, pp. 639–737. New York: McGraw-Hill.

Miller, D. T. P. & Carol, A. (1988), "Errors and biases in the attribution process". In L. Y. Abramson (Ed.) *Social cognition and clinical psychology: A synthesis*, pp. 1–30. New York: The Guilford Press.

Mittleman, J. H. (1994), "The globalization challenge: Surviving at the margins", *Third World Quarterly, 15*(3), pp. 427–443.

Newman, L. S. (1993), "How individualist interpret behavior: Idiocentrism and spontaneous trait inference", *Social Cognition, 11*(2), pp. 243–269.

Norman. D. A. (1988), *The psychology of everyday things.* New York, NY: Basic Books.

Oetzel, J., Garcia, A. J., & Ting-Toomey, S. (2008), "An analysis of the relationships among face concerns and facework behaviors in perceived conflict situations: A four-culture investigation", *International Journal of Conflict Management, 19*(4), pp. 382–403.

Osland, J. & Bird, A. (2000), "Beyond sophisticated stereotyping: Cultural sensemaking in context", *Academy of Management Executive, 14*(1), pp. 65–78.

Pekerti A. A. & Kwantes, C. (*In press*), "The effect of self-construals on perceptions of organizational events", *International Journal of Cross-Cultural Management.*

Pekerti, A. A. (2005), "Cross-Cultural Perceptions in the Leadership Process: Theoretical Perspective on the Influence of Culture on Self-Concepts and Leadership Attributions", *Thunderbird International Business Review, 47*(6), pp. 711–735.

Pekerti, A. A. & Thomas, D. C. (2003), "Communication in intercultural interaction: An empirical investigation of idiocentric and sociocentric communication styles", *Journal of Cross-Cultural Psychology, 34*(2), pp. 139–154.

Rycroft, R. W. (2003), "Technology-based globalization indicators: the centrality of innovation network data", *Technology in Society, 25*(3), pp. 299–317.

Sanchez-Burks, J. (2002), "Protestant relational ideology and (in)attention to relational cues in work settings", *Journal of Personality and Social Psychology, 83*(4), pp. 919–929.

Shannon, C. & Weaver, W. (1949), *The mathematical theory of communication.* Urbana: University of Illinois Press.

Sunnafrank, M. (1986), "Predicted outcome value during initial interactions: A reformulation of uncertainty reduction theory", *Human Communication Research 13*, pp. 3–33.

Taylor, S. E. (1981), "The interface of cognitive and social psychology". In J. H. Harvey (Ed.), *Cognition social behavior and the environment,* pp. 189–211. Hillsdale, NJ: Lawrence Erlbaum.

Thomas, D.C., Stahl, G., Ravlin, E. C., Poelmans, S., Pekerti, A. A. (2008), "Cultural Intelligence: Domain and Assessment", *International Journal of Cross-Cultural Management, 8*(2), pp. 123–143.

Ting-Toomey, S. (2005), "The matrix of face: An updated face-negotiation theory". In W. B. Gudykunst (Ed.), *Theorizing about intercultural communication,* pp. 71–92. Thousand Oaks, CA: Sage.

Triandis, H. C., McCusker, C., Betancourt, H., Iwao, S., Leung, K. (1993), "An eticemic analysis of individualism and collectivism", *Journal of Cross-Cultural Psychology, 24,* pp. 366–383.

Triandis, H. C. (1989), "The self and social behavior in differing cultural context", *Psychological Review, 96*(3), pp. 506–520.

In Chapter 9, Erin Meyer discusses principles-first vs. applications-first styles of reasoning, along with strategies for cross-cultural persuasion.

Chapter 9

Why Versus How

The Art of Persuasion in a Multicultural World

by Erin Meyer

The art of persuasion is one of the most crucial business skills. Without the ability to persuade others to support your ideas, you won't be able to attract the support you need to turn those ideas into realities. And though most people are unaware of it, the ways you seek to persuade others and the kinds of arguments you find persuasive are deeply rooted in your culture's philosophical, religious, and educational assumptions and attitudes. Far from being universal, then, the art of persuasion is one that is profoundly culture-based.

That was the hard lesson learned by Kara Williams, an American engineer newly working as a research manager for a German firm in the automotive industry. As one of the leading experts in her field Williams had extensive experience presenting recommendations and influencing her American colleagues to follow her ideas. But when Williams began working in a German environment she didn't realize that being persuasive would require a different approach. "When I think back to my first presentation to my new German bosses, I wish I had understood the difference and hadn't let their feedback get under my skin. If I had held my cool I might have been able to salvage the situation."

Williams has faced many challenges in her career. Before taking the job with the German firm, she worked for an Australian company from her home office in Boston, traveling frequently to the Sydney headquarters to give presentations and

Erin Meyer, "Why Versus How: The Art of Persuasion in a Multicultural World," *The Culture Map: Breaking Through the Invisible Boundaries of Global Business*, pp. 89-114, 260. Copyright © 2014 by Perseus Books Group. Reprinted with permission.

offer advice. "A lot of my job relies on my ability to sell my ideas and influence my internal clients to take the best path," she explains. "I'm good at what I do, but I hate constant long-distance travel. When offered a similar position working for a German auto supplier, I jumped at the opportunity for shorter travel distances."

Williams's first project was providing technical advice on how to reduce carbon emissions from one of the group's "green" car models. After visiting several automotive plants, observing the systems and processes there, and meeting with dozens of experts and end users, Williams developed a set of recommendations that she felt would meet the company's strategic and budgetary goals. She traveled to Munich to give a one-hour presentation to the decision makers—a group of German directors.

"It was my first internal presentation, and its success would be important for my reputation," Williams recalls. In preparation for the meeting Williams thought carefully about how to give the most persuasive presentation, practicing her arguments, anticipating questions that might arise, and preparing responses to those questions.

Williams delivered her presentation in a small auditorium with the directors seated in rows of upholstered chairs. She began by getting right to the point, explaining the strategies she would recommend based on her findings. But before she had finished with the first slide, one of the directors raised his hand and protested, "How did you get to these conclusions? You are giving us your recommendations, but I don't understand how you got here. How many people did you interview? What questions did you ask?"

Then another director jumped in: "Please explain what methodology you used for analyzing your data and how that led you to come to these findings."

"I was taken aback," Williams remembers. "I assured them that the methodology behind my recommendations was sound, but the questions and challenges continued. The more they questioned me, the more I got the feeling that they were attacking my credibility, which puzzled and annoyed me. I have a Ph.D. in engineering and expertise that is widely acknowledged. Their effort to test my conclusions, I felt, showed a real lack of respect. What arrogance to think that they would be better able to judge than I am!"

Williams reacted defensively, and the presentation went downhill from there. "I kick myself now for having allowed their approach to derail my point," she says. "Needless to say, they did not approve my recommendations, and three months of research time went down the drain."

The stone wall Williams ran into illustrates the hard truth that our ability to persuade others depends not simply on the strength of our message but on how we build our arguments and the persuasive techniques we employ.

Jens Hupert is a German director at the company Williams worked for. Having lived in the United States for many years, he had experienced similar failures at persuading others, though the cultural disconnect ran in the opposite direction. Hupert recalled the problems he'd had the first few times he tried to make a persuasive argument before a group of his American colleagues. He'd carefully launched his presentation by laying the foundation for his conclusions, setting the parameters, outlining his data and his methodology, and explaining the premise of his argument. He was taken aback when his American boss told him, "In your next presentation, get right to the point. You lost their attention before you even got to the important part."

Hupert was unsure. "These are intelligent people," he thought. "Why would they swallow my argument if I haven't built it carefully for them from the ground up?"

The opposing reactions that Williams and Hupert received reflect the cultural differences between German and American styles of persuasion. The approach taken by the Germans is based on a specific style of reasoning that is deeply ingrained in the cultural psyche. Hupert explains:

> In Germany, we try to understand the theoretical concept before adapting it to the practical situation. To understand something, we first want to analyze all of the conceptual data before coming to a conclusion. When colleagues from cultures like the U.S. or the U.K. make presentations to us, we don't realize that they were taught to think differently from us. So when they begin by presenting conclusions and recommendations without setting up the parameters and how they got to those conclusions, it can actually shock us. We may feel insulted. Do they think we are stupid—that we will just swallow anything? Or we may question whether their decision was well thought out. This reaction is based on our deep-seated belief that you cannot come to a conclusion without first defining the parameters.

Hupert's time in the United States taught him that Americans have a very different approach. They focus on practicalities rather than theory, so they are much more likely to begin with their recommendations. Unfortunately, this reasoning method can backfire when making presentations to an audience whose method of thinking is the opposite—as Kara Williams discovered.

TWO STYLES OF REASONING: PRINCIPLES-FIRST VERSUS APPLICATIONS-FIRST

Principles-first reasoning (sometimes referred to as *deductive reasoning*) derives conclusions or facts from general principles or concepts. For example, we may start with a general principle like "All men are mortal." Then we move to a more specific example: "Justin Bieber is a man." This leads us to the conclusion, "Justin Bieber will, eventually, die." Similarly, we may start with the general principle "Everything made of copper conducts electricity." Then we show that the old statue of a leprechaun your grandmother left you is 100 percent copper. Based on these points, we can arrive at the conclusion, "Your grandmother's statue will conduct electricity." In both examples, we started with the general principle and moved from it to a practical conclusion.

On the other hand, with *applications-first reasoning* (sometimes called *inductive reasoning*), general conclusions are reached based on a pattern of factual observations from the real world. For example, if you travel to my hometown in Minnesota one hundred times during January and February, and you observe every visit that the temperature is considerably below zero, you will conclude that Minnesota winters are cold (and that a winter visit to Minnesota calls for a warm coat as well as a scarf, wool hat, gloves, and ear warmers). In this case, you observe data from the real world, and, based on these empirical observations, you draw broader conclusions.

Most people are capable of practicing both principles-first and applications-first reasoning. But your habitual pattern of reasoning is heavily influenced by the kind of thinking emphasized in your culture's educational structure. As a result, you can quickly run into problems when working with people who are most accustomed to other modes of reasoning.

Take math class as an example. In a course using the applications-first method, you first learn the formula and practice applying it. After seeing how this formula leads to the right answer again and again, you then move on to understand the concept or principle underpinning it. This means you may spend 80 percent of your time focusing on the concrete tool and how to apply it and only 20 percent of your time considering its conceptual or theoretical explanation. School systems in Anglo-Saxon countries tend to emphasize this method of teaching.

By contrast, in a principles-first math class, you first prove the general principle, and only then use it to develop a concrete formula that can be applied to various problems. As a French manager once told me, "We had to calculate the value of pi as a class before we used pi in a formula." In this kind of math class, you may spend 80 percent of your time focusing on the concepts or theories underpinning the general mathematical principles and only 20 percent of your time applying those principles to concrete problems. School systems in Latin Europe (France, Italy, Spain, Portugal), the Germanic countries (Germany, Austria), and Latin America (Mexico, Brazil, Argentina) tend to emphasize this method of teaching.

I felt the full force of the applications-first method when I studied Russian in my American high school. We walked into Mr. Tarasov's class on the first day of school, and he immediately fired questions at us in Russian. We didn't understand a thing. But gradually we started to understand, and, after a few lessons, we began to speak, putting words together any which way we could. Then, with Mr. Tarasov's guidance, we began using sentences whose structure we did not understand to create a conceptual grammatical framework.

By contrast, in a principles-first language class, learning starts with understanding the grammatical principles underpinning the language structure. Once you have a solid initial grasp of the grammar and vocabulary, you begin to practice using the language. This is the way my husband learned English in his French school, and ironically, his knowledge of English grammar is far superior to that of many Americans. The disadvantage is that students spend less time practicing the language, which may mean they write it better than they speak it.

In business, as in school, people from principles-first cultures generally want to understand the *why* behind their boss's request before they move to action. Meanwhile, applications-first learners tend to focus less on the *why* and more on the *how*. One of the most common frustrations among French employees with American bosses is that the American tells them what to do without explaining why they need to do it. From the French perspective, this can feel demotivating, even disrespectful. By contrast, American bosses may feel that French workers are uncooperative because, instead of acting quickly, they always ask "Why?" and are not ready to act until they have received a suitable response.

COUNTRY POSITIONS ON THE PERSUADING SCALE

In general, Anglo-Saxon cultures like the United States, the United Kingdom, Australia, Canada, and New Zealand tend to fall to the far right on the Persuading scale (see Figure 9.1), where applications-first cultures are clustered. As we move across the scale there's a Nordic cluster, where we find Scandinavia and the Netherlands. Latin American and Germanic cultures are considerably more principles-first than the United States but much less so than their Latin European cousins, so we put them around the middle of the scale. France, Russia, and Belgium appear on the principles-first side of the scale.

As always, remember the importance of cultural relativity. Where a given country falls on the scale matters less than where two cultures fall relative to one another. The British tilt rather far toward the applications-first end of the scale. But Yasser Tawfik, an Egyptian manager for Merck Pharmaceuticals, has this to say about his experience of studying in both the United Kingdom and the United States:

> In the U.K., the learning was all about concept. Only after we struggled through the theoretical did we get to the practical application. The U.S. was exactly the opposite. Even before I attended a course I was already given a case study as pre-work—an example of practical application. In the classroom it was all about the three Ls of leadership or the

six Cs of customer satisfaction. From moment one, we were immersed in practical solutions and examples of how to apply the solutions.

Compared with other European cultures, the United Kingdom is quite applications-first. But when the United Kingdom is measured against the United States, it appears strongly principles-first—a vivid illustration of the power of cultural relativity to shape our perceptions.

(You may be wondering where the Asian cultures fall on the Persuading scale, since they don't appear in the diagram. Actually, the view of the world most common in Asian cultures is so different from that of European-influenced cultures that an entirely different frame of reference, unrelated to the Persuading scale, comes into play. We'll discuss that uniquely Asian perspective later in this chapter.)

FIGURE 9.1   PERSUADING

Italy	Russia	Germany	Argentina	Sweden	Netherlands	Australia	
France	Spain		Brazil	Mexico	Denmark	UK	Canada	US

Principles-first   Applications-first

Applications-first Individuals are trained to begin with a fact, statement, or opinion and later add concepts to back up or explain the conclusion as necessary. The preference is to begin a message or report with an executive summary or bullet points. Discussions are approached in a practical, concrete manner. Theoretical or philosophical discussions are avoided in a business environment.

Principles-first Individuals have been trained to first develop the theory or complex concept before presenting a fact, statement, or opinion. The preference is to begin a message or report by building up a theoretical argument before moving on to a conclusion. The conceptual principles underlying each situation are valued.

WHEN PHILOSOPHY MEETS BUSINESS

Different cultures have different systems for learning in part because of the philosophers who influenced the approach to intellectual life in general and science in particular. Although Aristotle, a Greek, is credited with articulating applications-first thinking (induction), it was British thinkers, including Roger Bacon in the thirteenth century and Francis Bacon in the sixteenth century, who popularized these methodologies among modern scholars and scientists. Later, Americans, with their pioneer mentality and disinclination toward theoretical learning, came to be even more applications-first than the British.

By contrast, philosophy on the European continent has been largely driven by principles-first approaches. In the seventeenth century, Frenchman René Descartes spelled out a method of principles-first reasoning in which the scientist first formulates a hypothesis, then seeks evidence to prove or disprove it. Descartes was deeply skeptical of data based on mere observation and sought a deeper understanding of underlying principles. In the nineteenth century, the German Friedrich Hegel introduced the *dialectic* model of deduction, which reigns supreme in schools in Latin and Germanic countries. The Hegelian dialectic begins with a thesis, or foundational argument; this is opposed by an antithesis, or conflicting argument; and the two are then reconciled in a synthesis.

Clear examples of applications-first and principles-first reasoning styles can also be found in the legal systems of different societies. The British and American systems are based on common law, in which a judgment in one case sets a precedent for future cases—a clear example of applications-first thinking.

By contrast, most European Union states use the civil law system that originated in Roman law and the Napoleonic Code, in which a general statute or principle is applied on a case-by-case basis, mirroring the principles-first approach. Interestingly, Scandinavia uses a hybrid legal system that does not fall neatly into either camp. Note the middle position of the Nordic countries on the Persuading scale.

As we've seen, the way different societies analyze the world depends on their philosophical roots. These, in turn, define how we learn in school and how we behave as adults at work. It's what Frenchman Stéphane Baron realized when he found his highly persuasive writing was not having much effect on his British colleagues. A graduate of the prestigious Polytechnique engineering school, now on the fast track at a large French industrial company, Baron was working for Michelin in Clermont Ferrand, France, as part of a global team whose other members were located mainly in the United Kingdom. Baron recalls:

> My British colleagues were not reading many of my e-mails, especially the most important ones. It was starting to annoy me. I liked my British colleagues a lot, and when we were face-to-face we had a great connection. But I had multiple indications that, when I sent e-mails to my team, they simply didn't read them. And I knew the British were big e-mail writers themselves, so I didn't think it could be cultural.

For example, Baron recalls carefully crafting a persuasive e-mail written to propose a number of key changes to company processes. The structure of his message looked something like this:

> Paragraph 1: introduced the topic.
> Paragraph 2: built up his argument, appealing to his teammates'
>
> sense of logic and developing the general principle.
> Paragraph 3: addressed the most obvious potential concerns with Baron's argument.
> Paragraph 4: explained Baron's conclusion and asked for his teammates' support.

Well educated in one of the most principles-first cultures in the world, Baron instinctively followed the dialectic method so carefully taught in the French school system. Notice how his second, third, and fourth paragraphs neatly present the thesis, antithesis, and synthesis Baron developed after much pondering of his topic.

On reflection, however, it's pretty obvious why Baron's British colleagues did not read this e-mail. Raised on the applications-first principle of *Get to the point quickly and stick to it*, they got through paragraph one and, seeing no clear point up front, moved the e-mail message to their "read at some undefined date in the future" file.

If Kara Williams and Stéphane Baron had a better understanding of the applications-first and principles-first cultural tendencies, they would each have had the chance to be a good deal more persuasive.

If Williams had realized she was presenting to an audience of principles-first Germans, perhaps she would have begun by presenting the parameters of her study and explaining why she chose this specific study method. She might then have introduced specific data to show her reasoning before presenting conclusions and recommendations. She wouldn't have needed to spend thirty minutes building her argument; five solid minutes describing her method before jumping to her results would probably have created a lot of buy-in. In addition, if Williams had recognized the crucial role of the antithesis—the counterargument—in the deductive process, she might have welcomed the challenges from her audience as a sign of interest instead of a lack of respect.

Similarly, if Baron had realized he was writing for a group raised on applications-first approaches, perhaps he would have started his e-mail with a few bullet points summarizing his proposal and explaining what he needed from the group. He might then have continued with a bit of background data, presented briskly with the recognition that "shorter is sweeter" for people with an applications-first orientation.

Baron subsequently learned this lesson. "One British colleague told me that, if my e-mail doesn't fit on the screen of an iPhone, it risks not getting read," Baron laughs. "That's the test I use now before I send out my e-mail."

The moral is clear. Presenting to Londoners or New Yorkers? Get to the point and stick to it. Presenting to French, Spaniards, or Germans? Spend more time setting the parameters and explaining the background before jumping to your conclusion.

STRATEGIES FOR PERSUADING ACROSS CULTURES

Effective leadership often relies on the ability to persuade others to change their systems, adopt new methods of working, or adjust to new trends in markets, technologies, or business models. So if you are a manager of a team whose members come from a culture different from your own, learning to adapt your persuasive technique to your audience can be crucial.

Jorge Da Silva, a Brazilian engineer with a steel company headquartered in southern Brazil, explains how he learned to use a different approach when seeking to influence a new team of colleagues located in Houston, Texas:

> We had developed a new method for monitoring safety risks in our plants that was working beautifully and required less oversight than the status quo. Our Latin American offices were in the process of adopting the new method, but our U.S. office was resisting. They felt the method they used worked fine.
>
> We kept trying to explain to them *why* the new process was so important. However, we didn't seem to be persuading them. So we developed a very detailed presentation that explained, slide by slide, the key concepts addressed in the new method. But the more detailed we became, the less responsive our American teammates were.
>
> Finally, I called one of my colleagues in the U.S., Jake Kuderlee. I went to undergraduate school with Jake in São Paulo and have
>
> had a great relationship with him for years. Jake asked, "Have you tried showing the decision-makers in the American office an example of what could happen if the new process is well implemented?"
>
> Based on this discussion, we invited two of the American decision-makers to our Brazilian plant to witness how the new safety process worked. We took two days to show them around the plant, to have them interview the workers on the assembly lines, and to review the production reports. They got a really good look at the process in action, and they asked a lot of questions. And when they got back to the U.S., they got the ball rolling. Now we have the same safety process in the U.S. that we have in Brazil.
>
> I learned my lesson. What is persuasive in Brazil may not be persuasive in an American environment.

As Da Silva learned, applications-first thinkers like to receive practical examples up front; they will extract learning from these examples. In the same vein, applications-first learners are used to the "case method," whereby they first read a case study describing a real-life story about a business problem and its solution, and then induce general lessons from it.

Principles-first thinkers also like practical examples, but they prefer to understand the basis of the framework before they move to the application. And for anyone raised in a principles-first culture, the American case method may seem downright odd. One Spanish executive told me, "In Spain, we have had it drilled into us since we were young that every situation is different and you can't assume that what happens in one situation will happen in another. So, when we are supposed to review the situation of one specific protagonist and extract general learning points, it may feel not just weird but even a bit dumb."

Shifting your persuasive style to match the preferences of your audience can be a bit challenging. However, it is still more complicated to choose the best approach if you have Brazilians, Americans, Germans, and French all attending the same presentation. As Jens Hupert, the German manager working with Kara Williams in the automotive industry, says, "My reality today is no longer a neat group of American or Germans but a large mix of participants from around the world."

The best strategy for managers in Jens's situation is to cycle back and forth between theoretical principles and practical examples. Provide practical examples to capture the interest of your applications-first listeners. The principles-first participants will enjoy them also. But you may find the latter asking theoretical questions, and, while you are answering them, the applications-first learners get bored. Try ignoring their boredom for a moment. Avoid the temptation to push away conceptual questions, as you risk sacrificing the interest and respect of your principles-first audience. Instead, take the time to answer the questions well and then quickly provide a couple of practical examples to recapture the waning attention of the applications-first students.

You may find that, no matter how well you shuttle back and forth, it will be difficult to satisfy all of your listeners all of the time. But if you are aware of the Persuading scale and the challenges it presents, you can read the cues from your audience more clearly and react accordingly.

The same differences that make it hard to persuade a multicultural audience can also make it difficult to improve collaboration among members of a multicultural team. Such teams are often much slower to make decisions than monocultural ones, and, if you consider the Persuading scale for a moment, it is easy to see why. If some team members are using principles-first logic and others are using applications-first logic to reach a decision, this can lead to conflict and inefficiency from the beginning. To make matters worse, most people have little understanding about the logic pattern they use, which leads them to judge the logic patterns of others negatively.

If the performance of your global team is suffering because its members are operating at different ends of the Persuading scale, consider the following strategies:

- Build team awareness by explaining the scale. Have everybody read this chapter and discuss it during a team meeting.
- A cultural bridge can help a lot. If you have team members who are bicultural or have significant experience living in different cultures, ask them to take responsibility for helping other team members.
- Understand and adapt to one another's behaviors.
- Patience and flexibility are key. Cross-cultural effectiveness takes time. Developing your own ability to recognize others' reactions and adapt accordingly will help you to be increasingly persuasive (and therefore effective) when working internationally.

HOLISTIC THINKING: THE ASIAN APPROACH TO PERSUASION

Across Western countries, we see strong differences between applications-first and principles-first patterns of thinking. But when considering the differences between Asian and Western thought patterns, we need to use a different lens. Asians have what we refer to as *holistic* thought patterns, while Westerners tend to have what we will call a *specific* approach.

I ran into the Chinese holistic pattern while teaching a course for a group of seventeen top-level Chinese executives, preparing them to work in Europe. They came from different Chinese companies and different regions of China. Four were women. Six lived in Poland, Hungary, and the Netherlands, and the rest in China. Although some spoke English, I taught the session through simultaneous translation into Mandarin.

I started by covering the Communicating, Leading, and Trusting scales (the latter two of which we'll discuss later in this book). The audience was so enthusiastic that they took photos of the classroom and my slides and even recorded video clips on their iPhones. I then asked them to break out into groups to discuss how they might handle different attitudes about confrontation on a global team consisting of French and Germans (who see confrontation as a key aspect of the decision-making process) and Chinese (who see confrontation as an affront to team relationships). They discussed the issue animatedly in their separate rooms and came back to the classroom for the debriefing.

We started by asking, "What steps should the team leader in this case take to manage different attitudes toward confrontation on the team?"

Lilly Li, a bird-like woman with thick glasses and a pleasant smile who had been running operations in Hungary for two years, raised her hand:

> Let me give my thoughts. In Hungary, we have people from many different countries—from all over Europe, in fact. The Trusting scale has been a big challenge for us, as the Hungarians do not take the same time to build personal relationships as we do in China. Let me explain some of the negative impact of not having a trusting relationship in our organization.

Now I was a little confused, because the question I'd asked was about confrontation, not about trusting—and there were no Hungarians in the case study we just read. I pushed the earpiece closer to my ear to make sure I was hearing the translator correctly. Lilly Li continued to talk for several minutes about trust, hierarchy, and her experiences in Hungary, and the Chinese participants listened carefully. After several long minutes of interesting comments that had—from my perspective—absolutely zero to do with the question I'd asked, Lilly Li came to the point: "In this case, if the team leader had spent more time helping the team build relationships outside of the office, that would have been very helpful during the meeting. The team would have been much more comfortable dealing with open debate and direct confrontation if the relationships on the team had been stronger."

Then another participant, Mr. Deng, raised his hand, I restated the specific question: "What steps should the team leader in this case take to manage different attitudes toward confrontation on the team?" Mr. Deng began:

> Let me give my perspective. I have been working in the technology industry for many years. In my company, we have lots of young people who are very eager and hardworking. Yet hierarchy is still strong in our company. During a meeting, if a young person is asked a question, he will look to his boss first to see if the boss's face indicates approval. If the boss approves, the younger employee will also express approval.

By now I was thinking to myself, "Mr. Deng, please don't forget the question!" After several long minutes' worth of comments about the role of hierarchy in his own organization, Mr. Deng observed, "On a global team, such as in this case, Chinese employees may confront their colleagues, but they will certainly never confront the boss. The team leader could remove himself from the meetings in order to allow for more comfortable discussions amongst his team members."

All morning long, the students' comments followed a similar pattern: After taking several minutes to discuss peripheral information, during which they would loop back to topics we had already discussed, they would then get to their point and come to a conclusion about the topic at hand. Gradually it became clear to me that this behavior did not reflect the idiosyncratic style of one person or even of one group, but rather a wider cultural norm—one that has been revealed by some of the most intriguing research in the cross-cultural field.

Professors Richard Nisbett and Takahiko Masuda presented twenty-second animated video vignettes of underwater scenes to Japanese and American participants (see an illustration of one of the vignettes in Figure 9.2 [...]).[1] Afterward, participants were asked what they had seen, and the first sentence of each response was categorized.

The results of the study were remarkable. While the Americans mentioned larger, faster-moving, brightly colored objects in the foreground (such as the big fish visible in the illustration), the Japanese spoke more about what was going on in the background (for example, the plants or the small frog to the bottom left). In addition, the Japanese spoke twice as often as the Americans about the

FIGURE 9.2

interdependencies between the objects up front and the objects in the background. As one Japanese woman explained, "I naturally look at all the items behind and around the large fish to determine what kind of fish they are."

In a second study, Americans and Japanese were asked to "take a photo of a person." The Americans most frequently took a close-up, showing all the features of the person's face, while the Japanese showed the person in his or her environment instead, with the human figure quite small in relationship to the background (see Figure 9.3).

In a third study, Nisbett and Masuda asked American and Taiwanese students to read narratives and watch videos of silent comedies—for example, a film about a day in the life of a woman, during which circumstances conspire to prevent her from getting to work—and then to summarize them. In their summaries, the Americans made about 30 percent more statements referring to the central figures of the stories than their Taiwanese counterparts did.[2]

FIGURE 9.3. Left: American portrait. Right: Japanese portrait

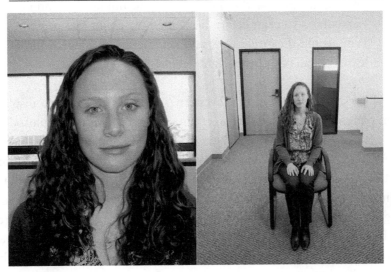

Photos by Melissa Veronesi

Notice the common pattern in all three studies. The Americans focus on individual figures separate from their environment, while the Asians give more attention to backgrounds and to the links between these backgrounds and the central figures. I have found these tendencies to be borne out in my own interviews with groups of multicultural managers. While Western European and Anglo-Saxon managers generally follow the American tendencies of specific thinking patterns, East Asians respond as the Japanese and Taiwanese did in Nisbett's research.

In addition, I've often watched Westerners and Asians discuss these studies. Here's a bit of dialogue taken directly from a classroom debate about the photo study:

> Western participant: But the instructions said to take a photo of a person, and the picture on the left is a photo of a person. The picture on the right is a photo of a room. Why would the Japanese take a photo of a room when they have been asked to take a photo of a person?
>
> Asian participant: The photo on the left is not a photo of the person. It is a close-up of a face. How can I determine anything about the person by looking at it? The photo on the right is a

photo of the person, the entire person, including surrounding elements so you can determine something about that person. Why would the Americans take a close-up of a face, which leaves out all of the important details?

Perhaps it's not surprising that Westerners and Asians tend to display these different patterns of interpretation. A common tenet of Western philosophies and religions is that you can remove an item from its environment and analyze it separately. Aristotle, for example, emphasized focusing attention on a salient object. Its properties could then be assessed and the object assigned a category with the goal of finding rules that governed its behavior. For example, looking at a piece of wood floating in water, Aristotle said that it had the property of "levity," while a stone falling through air had the property of "gravity." He referred to the wood and the rock as if each was a separate and isolated object in its own right. Cultural theorists call this *specific thinking*.

Chinese religions and philosophies, by contrast, have traditionally emphasized interdependencies and interconnectedness. Ancient Chinese thought was *holistic*, meaning that the Chinese attended to the field in which an object was located, believing that action always occurs in a field of forces that influence the action. Taoism, which influenced Buddhism and Confucianism, proposes that the universe works harmoniously, its various elements dependent upon one another. The terms *yin* and *yang* (literally "dark" and "light") describe how seemingly contrary forces are interconnected and interdependent.

With this background in mind, let's reconsider my class of seventeen Chinese executives. Here's a comment from one of the Chinese participants after we'd discussed the fish and photo research studies:

> Chinese people think from macro to micro, whereas Western people think from micro to macro. For example, when writing an address, the Chinese write in sequence of province, city, district, block, gate number. The Westerners do just the opposite—they start with the number of a single house and gradually work their way up to the city and state. In the same way, Chinese put the surname first, whereas the Westerners

do it the other way around. And Chinese put the year before month and date. Again, it's the opposite in the West.

It's easy to see how these differences in the characteristic sequence of thinking may cause difficulty or misunderstanding when people from Asian and Western cultures are involved in conversation. A typical example is that Westerners may think that the Chinese are going all around the key points without addressing them deliberately, while East Asians may experience Westerners as trying to make a decision by isolating a single factor and ignoring significant interdependencies.

This difference affects how business thinking is perceived in Western and Asian cultures. In the eyes of Asian business leaders, European and American executives tend to make decisions without taking much time to consider the broader implications of their actions. As Bae Pak from the Korean motor company Kia explains, "When we work with our Western colleagues, we are often taken aback by their tendency to make decisions without considering how their decisions are impacting various business units, clients, and suppliers. We feel their decisions are hasty and often ignore the surrounding impact."

INCREASING YOUR EFFECTIVENESS

In a *specific* culture when managing a supplier or team member, people usually respond well to receiving very detailed and segmented information about what you expect of each of them. If you need to give instructions to a team member from a specific culture, focus on what that person needs to accomplish when. If you explain clearly what you need each person to work on, that allows them to home in effectively on their specific task.

In *holistic* cultures if you need to motivate, manage, or persuade someone, you will be more influential if you take the time to explain the big picture and show how all the pieces fit together. When I interviewed Jacek Malecki, an unusually big man with a friendly round face and quiet voice, he was working for Toshiba Westinghouse. He provided this example of how he had learned to manage his staff in a more holistic manner.

> I had recently been promoted and for the first time I was managing not just Europeans and Americans but also Japanese. I have managed teams for sixteen years, and I've learned over the years to do it well. When I took my first trip to meet with my Japanese staff, I managed the objective-setting process like I always had. I called each person on the team into my office for a meeting. During the meeting we discussed what each individual on the team should accomplish. I outlined each person's short-term and long-term goals and the individual bonus plan for meeting and exceeding expectations.

But as Malecki later realized, his approach had not worked well for his Japanese team. "If they don't understand what others are working on and how the pieces fit together, they don't feel comfortable or persuaded to move to action. Although I noticed they asked a lot of peripheral questions during the meetings, none of them actually explained to me that my approach was not ideal for them so I went back to Poland with a false sense of comfort."

When Malecki returned to Tokyo several weeks later he saw that the way he had divided up the tasks and set individual incentives didn't match the way his team was working.

> The team had spent a lot of time consulting with one another about what each person had been asked to do and how their individual objectives fit together to create a big picture. The team was now making good progress but not in the way I had segmented the project. I learned that the type of specific division of tasks as well as individual incentive plans don't work well in a Japanese environment.

The lesson Malecki learned is a good one for anyone who needs to manage or influence holistic thinkers. If you need to explain a project or set objectives or sell an idea to a holistic audience, begin by explaining the big picture in detail. Outline not just the overall project but also how the parts are connected before drilling down what specifically needs to be accomplished and when.

AVOIDING THE PITFALLS, REAPING THE BENEFITS

With words like "diversity" and "global" all the rage, many companies are seeking to create multinational, multicultural teams in an effort to reap benefits in the form of added creativity and greater understanding of global markets. However, as we've seen, cultural differences can be fraught with challenges. Effective cross-cultural collaboration can take more time than monocultural collaboration and often needs to be managed more closely. Here are two simple tips that can help you realize the benefits of such collaboration while avoiding the dangers.

First, on a multicultural team, you can save time by having as few people in the group work across cultures as possible. For example, if you are building a global team that includes small groups of participants from four countries, choose one or two people from each country—the most internationally experienced of the bunch—to do most of the cross-cultural collaborating. Meanwhile, you can leave the others to work in the local way that is most natural to them. That way, you can have the innovation from the combination of cultures, while avoiding the inefficiency that comes with the clash of cultures.

Second, think carefully about your larger objectives before you mix cultures up. If your goal is innovation or creativity, the more cultural diversity the better, as long as the process is managed carefully. But if your goal is simple speed and efficiency, then monocultural is probably better than multicultural. Sometimes, it is simply better to leave Rome to the Romans.

NOTES

1 Richard Nisbett, The Geography of Thought (New York: The Free Press, 2003), 48–78.

2 Richard Nisbett and Takahiko Masuda, "Culture and Point of View" (Special series of Inaugural Articles by members of the National Academy of Sciences), PNAS 100, no. 19 (September 2003): 11163–11170

In Chapter 10, Mading Deng presents 10 Principals of Negotiations, set against the background of the recent violence in Sudan over South Sudan's quest for independence.

Chapter 10

Ten Principles on Negotiations

by Francis Mading Deng

Negotiations with third-party mediation are the counterpart to violent confrontation. Since independence, Sudan has twice alternated between devastating violent conflicts and negotiations leading to the peaceful resolution of the conflicts. The seventeen-year war (1955–1972) was ended by the Addis Ababa Agreement and the twenty-two-year war (1983–2005) ended with the Comprehensive Peace Agreement. The search for durable peace and the prospects for achieving genuine consensual unity will continue to require an ongoing process of negotiations into the foreseeable future.

I see negotiation and the closely related field of diplomacy as essentially management of human relations involving individuals, groups, or nations. Some people would argue that conflict is the normal state of human interaction and that it is futile to try to prevent or resolve conflicts; the most that can be done is managing conflicts. This can only be valid if it is understood to mean that grounds for conflict exist in normal human relations and that the *occurrence* of conflict is therefore normal. If it means that conflict is the normal *pattern* of life, then I would consider that position both empirically questionable and normatively ambiguous. Far from seeing conflict as the normal state of human interaction, I believe that people are more apt to cooperate and harmonize their incompatible or potentially conflictual

Francis Mading Deng, "Ten Principles on Negotiations," *Sudan at the Brink: Self-Determination and National Unity*, pp. 44-50. Copyright © 2010 by Fordham University Press. Reprinted with permission.

positions, and that conflict is in fact a crisis that signifies a breakdown in the normal pattern of behavior. In this sense, conflict involves a collision of incompatible positions resulting from a failure to regulate, reconcile or harmonize the differences. In the normal course of events, society is structured around fundamental values and norms that guide behavior and regulate relations so as to avoid a destructive collision of interests or positions. If people observe the principles of the normative code, which they generally do, the normal pattern would be one of relative cooperation and mutual accommodation, even in a competitive framework. To call that state one of conflict would be to put a negative value judgment on positive motivations and endeavors, and on a relatively high degree of success in peaceful interaction.

Even more important than strict empirical interpretation would be the normative implications of holding conflict the normal state of human existence, which would tend to foster a disposition that is fundamentally adversarial, suspicious, and conflictual. The extent to which members in a community or group reflect this disposition may depend in large measure on the culture and its normative code, defined as a set of shared and enduring meanings, values, and beliefs that characterizes national, ethnic, or other groups and orient their behavior.

Culture itself is a product of education, both formal and informal, through which the norms of behavior that a society has developed over a long period of time are inculcated from early childhood and passed on from generation to generation. The family is the institutional foundation of education, and, in particular, of the inculcation of basic cultural values. And yet, despite the pivotal role of the family and the culture in shaping values, attitudes, and operational techniques in human relations, individuals differ even within a family in their understanding, appreciation, and application of the values involved. It is this combination of the collective cultural conditioning and the individual inclination to absorb, accept, and apply what is acquired that gives significance to personal experiences as particular applications of values, customs, and techniques of conflict resolution and diplomacy within a specific cultural framework. As a challenge to grossly inequitable order, conflict may be a positive quest for reform.

It is important to emphasize that the objective is not merely to resolve a conflict, but to resolve it in a mutually satisfactory manner. This means addressing the root causes and observing such fundamental norms as justice and human dignity. In other words, where change is urgently needed, the status quo cannot simply be supported for the sake of harmony and peaceful interaction.

Conflict in this context can be defined as a situation of interaction involving two or more parties in which actions in pursuit of conflicting objectives or interests result in varying degrees of discord. The principal dichotomy is between normally harmonious and cooperative relations and a disruptive adversarial confrontation, culminating at its worst in high-intensity violence. On the basis of this definition, conflict resolution is a normative concept aimed at reconciling, harmonizing, or managing incompatible interests by fostering a process of institutionalized peaceful interaction. Conflict resolution envisages strategies aimed at restoring or establishing the normal state of affairs and raising the level of peaceful, harmonious, cooperative, constructive, and productive interaction.

The achievement of peace and reconciliation becomes a common objective, but one that is only possible if both sides feel that the solution proposed is indeed in the mutual interest. Since both were prepared to enter into conflict in the first place, it means that each must have a subjective view of right and wrong that gives them some degree of right and places some degree of wrong on the opposing party. These subjective perspectives cannot be ignored when negotiation takes place or when proposals are made for resolving a conflict, even though they need not and should not be allowed to have too much influence on such processes. Ultimately, while there is indeed a hierarchy of rights and wrongs in resolving disputes through negotiations, there should be no absolute winner or loser.

If one comes from a culture, a society, or a family in which unity, harmony, and cooperation are highly valued, then the discord of conflict becomes a disruption that is destabilizing not only to the community, but also intrinsically to the individual. And if one assumes further that in any conflict there are contributing factors for which both sides share responsibility, albeit in varying degrees, then the degree of uncertainty involved must create a sense of shared responsibility for properly tutored or nurtured members of the community. The desire to normalize the situation and restore amicable relations therefore becomes as much a societal as it is an individual objective.

EXPOUNDING THE PRINCIPLES

The proposed principles on negotiation should be seen in the context of the normative framework outlined above. These principles derive from personal experiences and are rooted in values, norms and mores that emanate from a specific African family and cultural background among the Dinka of Sudan. They cover experiences in interpersonal relations, third-party mediation, and diplomatic negotiations, with overlaps. Although personal and rooted in the Dinka, Sudanese, and African cultural contexts, they represent values that can claim universal validity, despite cross-cultural variations on the details and their applicability.

Principle One: Rights and wrongs, though seldom equal, are rarely one-sided. Even when you feel sure that you are in the right, you must not only strive to fit yourself into the shoes of the other side, but must also make the other side recognize that you are genuinely interested in his or her point of view.

Principle Two: It is unhealthy to keep grievances "in the stomach" or "in the heart." *Talking It Out*, the title of a book I wrote on the theme, is not only the best way to resolve differences or grievances, but is also essential for one's mental and even physical health. Often "what is not said is what divides," to use the words of an article I wrote on that theme.

Principle Three: Face-saving is crucial to resolving conflicts. One must avoid saying anything that is humiliating to the other side, and, where possible, it is advisable to show deference, even to an adversary, provided it is not cheap flattery.

Principle Four: It is important to listen very carefully and allow the other party to say all that she or he considers significant or relevant. Resolving differences is not a game of wits or cleverness, but of addressing the genuine concerns of the parties in conflict. In Dinka folktales, the cleverness of the fox eventually turns against the fox. Ideally, resolutions must have an element of give and take, although the distribution should be proportional to the equations of the rights and wrongs involved. In assessing the outcome of a negotiated settlement of a dispute, it is unwise to boast of victory, for that implies defeat for the other side and therefore an unsatisfactory outcome.

Principle Five: Historical memory of the relations gives depth to the perspectives of the parties and the issues involved, but one must avoid aggravating the situation with negative recollections and emphases and should instead reinforce constructive dialogue with positive recollections or interpretations of past events, without, of course, distorting the facts.

Principle Six: The mediator must be seen to be impartial, but where there is reason to believe that he or she is closer to one side in whatever capacity, the mediator must reach out to the more distant party. However, this should not be at the cost of fairness to the party closer to the mediator. Impartiality does not mean having no position on the issues in dispute, even though voicing opinions should be carefully coached to maximize the bridging role and promote mutual understanding.

Principle Seven: The mediator must listen very patiently to both parties, and even when there are obvious flaws in what is said, the mediator must appear to give due weight to each party's point of view. The popular view that in the indigenous African system of dispute settlement, people sat under the tree and talked until they reached a consensus reflects a broadly shared African normative behavior. Where explaining the opponent's view on a specific issue might facilitate the bridging process, the mediator should intercede to offer an explanation as part of consensus building.

Principle Eight: While the wisdom of words and the ability to persuade are important, leverage is pivotal. This means that the mediator must have, or be believed to have, the ability to support the process with incentives or threats of negative consequences, according to the equations of the responsibility for the success or failure of the negotiations. In the past, among the Dinka, spiritual powers of divine leadership provided the required leverage. In the modern context, influencing the balance of power to create a "mutually hurting stalemate" and help advance the process of "ripening for resolution," to borrow the famous words of the renowned scholar of conflict analysis, William Zartman, is part of the leverage that can effectively facilitate the mediator's task.

Principle Nine: Diplomatic negotiations combine elements of both interpersonal relations and third-party mediation in that the negotiator represents his or her government and in a sense combines negotiating with mediating between the respective governments involved. Discretion and creativity in adapting the official position to the dynamics of the situation with a degree of flexibility is critical to the prospects of successful bridging.

Principle Ten: While the tendency of the negotiators is to see the outcome of their efforts in terms of winning or losing, especially for domestic consumption, the desired outcome should be one in which neither side sees itself as a total winner or loser, except where the rights and wrongs involved are incontrovertibly clear. The win-win formula should be the objective and whatever the equations of winning or losing in the mediated or negotiated outcome, as noted in Principle Four, neither side should boast about winning and by implication humiliate the other side as a loser. There must be a degree of parity in both sides winning or losing.

BALANCING THE UNIVERSAL WITH THE PARTICULAR

The principles presented above do not claim to be a panacea. Quite the contrary, they reflect a particular emotional value system that may be more relative than universal. On the other hand, it would also be presumptuous and even hazardous to assume that these are universal, scientifically proven negotiation techniques that are applicable to all situations and cross-cultural contexts. A case can, of course, be made for expert knowledge in negotiation and there is a particular role to be played by individuals with such expertise. But to be effective a synergy between universal techniques and culturally specific methods need to be developed.

In Sudan, chiefs and elders known as *ajaweed* in the North but with varying titles throughout the country are usually made effective use of to mediate in intertribal conflicts. Indeed, most tribal conflicts, which are pervasive throughout the country, are resolved by these traditional mediators, for the most part illiterate but endowed with indigenous knowledge and wisdom. When one recalls that the number of colonial administrators who controlled that vast country of nearly a million square miles was relatively small, it is easy to see how they made effective use of traditional leaders to maintain law and order, peace and security throughout the rural areas. Failure to use this indigenous capacity accounts for much of the intertribal warfare and criminal violence that has been the lot of the postcolonial administration in Sudan. This must be reversed if Sudan is to enhance its full capacity for promoting peace, security, and stability throughout the country.

> *This chapter is adapted from Francis M. Deng, "The Sudan: Education, Culture, and Negotiations," in* Even in Chaos: Education in Times of Emergency, *ed. Kevin M. Cahill, M.D. (New York: Fordham University Press, 2010).*

In Chapter 11, Jacob Sending discusses diplomatic negotiations abroad, as opposed to humanitarian efforts, particularly in conflict zones.

Chapter 11

United by Difference

Diplomacy as a Thin Culture

by Ole Jacob Sending

T he last two decades of research on globalization is replete with claims about the power of nonstate actors and the implied demise or transformation of diplomacy.[1] Posing the question in these terms, however, begets a more fundamental question: what characterizes diplomacy as a social practice? Answering this question is important if we want to know how diplomacy may be changing as other actors become more active in representing and governing between and beyond states. This is a task that is less straightforward than one might expect. We may, for example, draw up a list of tasks performed by diplomats and see whether others, too, are performing such tasks: if we can tick a given number of boxes—representation, communication, or negotiation, for example—that then constitutes diplomatic work. Or we can differentiate diplomats from other actors by adding prefixes, such as celebrity diplomacy or NGO diplomacy. But none of this tells us much about the meaning attributed to diplomacy by diplomats and

---

[1] David Held and Anthony McGrew, eds., *Governing Globalization: Power, Authority, and Global Governance* (Cambridge: Polity Press, 2002); Margareth Keck and Kathryn Sikkink, *Activists Beyond Borders* (Ithaca: Cornell University Press, 1998); Paul Sharp, "Who needs diplomats? The problems of diplomatic representation," *International Journal* 52, no. 4 (1997): 609-32; Andrew F. Cooper, "Beyond representation," *International Journal* 53, no. 1 (1997–8): 173–78.

Ole Jacob Sending, "United by Difference: Diplomacy as a Thin Culture," *International Journal*, vol. 66, no. 3, pp. 643-659. Copyright © 2011 by Canadian International Council. Reprinted with permission. Provided by ProQuest LLC. All rights reserved.

nondiplomats alike. What are the rules of diplomacy and what types of skills are valued? Stripped to its basics, what is it that constitutes diplomacy?

In seeking to answer these questions I draw on the analytical framework presented in the introduction—territorial versus nonterritorial representation and representation versus governance—and analyze diplomatic work by contrasting it with humanitarian work. I argue that what unites diplomats is simultaneously what separates them, namely the representation of different territorial units. For this reason, diplomacy is characterized by a "thin" culture in that it places a premium on communication and the management of friction in the absence of shared values. Humanitarian actors, by contrast, share a "thick" culture in that what constitutes humanitarian action is defined by a set of substantive values that underwrites their claim to the representation of groups in whose name they act.[2]

Underlying this difference in the constitution of diplomatic and humanitarian work is a more general mechanism: the culture that characterizes diplomatic work and humanitarian work, respectively, flows from the character of the relation that is established and continually reproduced between the actor and the object that the actor either seeks to represent and/or govern. Diplomats represent territorial units whose existence is given: there would not be diplomats as we know them if the system was suzerain, for example. Humanitarian and other nonstate actors, however, have to construct and continually reproduce the governance object (i.e., suffering individuals, the economy, the environment) that is the rationale for their existence. Humanitarianism is constituted by a set of substantive values whose existence is constitutive of humanitarianism as a social practice. Diplomacy, by contrast, is constituted by a set of procedural values that reflect the defining feature of the object that diplomats represent, namely sovereign, territorial units whose interests may differ.

The more general point is that we gain more in terms of understanding diplomacy and its evolution over time by seeking to unearth some of its core features than by drawing up a list of "typical" diplomatic tasks such as representation, communication, and negotiation. Other actors perform these same tasks, but that does not mean that they engage in diplomacy, nor are such actors fruitfully labelled diplomats. Unearthing the "logic" of diplomacy in terms of the character of the relation between diplomats and what they represent, then, offers added value for the study of diplomacy and global governance more generally. I argue, for example, that the thinness of

---

[2] See also Cecelia Lynch's contribution in this issue on religious actors and humanitarianism.

diplomatic culture is expressed in how diplomats are attentive to form in a way that other actors are not, and that this feature also helps account for its resilience.

I focus on humanitarian actors as a contrast to diplomats for three main reasons. First, humanitarian action has expanded considerably over the last two decades, and diplomats and humanitarian actors engage one another on a range of issues that are high on the international agenda.[3] Examples include debates about "humanitarian space" in Afghanistan and the invocation of the humanitarian principle of protection of civilians for the intervention in Libya. Second, humanitarianism is typically defined in opposition to the doings of diplomats, with the former defined as apolitical and the latter as inherently political. This makes the exploration of their interaction important as a tool to unearth the distinctive features of both—and how they are mutually constituted. Third, because of the growth in humanitarian action and the importance of humanitarian actors to global efforts to respond to emergencies, humanitarian actors take on diplomatic functions as they (claim to) represent victims of humanitarian crises and speak on their behalf.

I proceed as follows: I first discuss briefly what I mean by culture and then move on to present a stylized definition of diplomacy as being organized around a "thin" culture, and contrast it with humanitarianism, which I argue is organized around a "thick" culture. I then offer a set of illustrations that aims to highlight central aspects of diplomatic culture, offering contrasting views with humanitarianism along the way. Here, I highlight the attention to form and process among diplomats, and to authenticity and proximity to those in need among humanitarian actors. In the concluding section, I briefly discuss the resilience of diplomacy and hypothesize that—given the foundational role of the character of the relation between the actor and that which is to be represented and/or governed—humanitarian actors are *an* authority, whereas diplomats are *in* authority.

CULTURE AND RECOGNITION

Before we can proceed to identify how diplomats and humanitarian actors see each other and interact, it is necessary to specify how I conceptualize culture. Culture

---

[3] Michael N. Barnett, *The International Humanitarian Order* (London: Routledge, 2010).

here is a generic term for the symbolic tools that enable communication and evaluation. It is a view of culture as a set of criteria that others use in granting or withholding recognition.[4] In short, I locate the driver of both stability and change not in omnipotent discourses, nor in internalized norms, but in the shared registers for communication and evaluation that actors use in a given social space.[5] Thus, culture is a descriptive term for the raw material upon which actors draw when acting, and the criteria of evaluation that others use to assess such actions.

Actors are granted recognition by others with reference to shared evaluative criteria. Without a minimum of shared criteria of what is appropriate, effective, and so on, there is no basis from which to seek or be accorded recognition. In diplomatic circles, recognition may be accorded to those who can "hold a bracket" in negotiations vis-à-vis other states, or to those who can subtly signal different things to different actors when delivering a speech. Diplomats recognize and value certain skills in other diplomats even when these represent and advance different interests from their own.

Seen in this way, diplomacy is reproduced and may change over time in and through how different actors search for and are granted recognition. It changes when the criteria of evaluation change and these criteria are themselves very much at stake in the interaction between diplomats and other actors. Diplomacy constitutes a thin intersubjective social space inasmuch as it includes a minimum standard, or expectation, to keep on talking: diplomatic culture places a premium on consulting others, of taking note of others' concerns, as Vincent Pouliot's contribution to this issue also demonstrates. Pierre Bourdieu notes, for example, that in searching for recognition, actors are "continuously led to take the point of view of others on himself, to adopt their point of view so as to discover and evaluate in advance how he will be seen and defined by them."[6] This description fits diplomatic culture well, and I argue below that this helps explain how and why diplomats are so attentive to form and being diplomatic is associated with having tact and being sympathetic to others' views in ordinary language. In that sense, diplomacy is about (re)producing—through the

---

[4] For a discussion and application of the concept of recognition and related sets of "criteria of evaluation," see George Steinmetz, "The colonial state as a social field: Ethnographic capital and native policy in the German overseas empire before 1914," *American Review of Sociology* 73 (2008): 589–612.

[5] Ole Jacob Sending and Iver B. Neumann, "Banking on power: How some practices in an international organization anchor others," in Emanuel Adler and Vincent Pouliot, eds., *International Practices* (Cambridge: Cambridge University Press, 2011): 231–54. See also Ian Hurd's article in this issue.

[6] Pierre Bourdieu, *Pascalian Mediations* (Cambridge: Polity Press, 2000), 166.

attention to protocol, form, and recognition of difference—culture in the form of a minimum set of intersubjective tools for communication between distinct units.

For humanitarians, by contrast, a thick culture organized around substantive values puts a premium on speaking out and letting the world know about abuse, atrocities, and suffering. Humanitarianism can be said to be anchored in and through a claim to moral authority that is outside and above history, politics, and territorial borders.[7] The difference with diplomacy is striking, as it is organized around the representation of and communication among distinct units. Humanitarian actors deliver relief and defend and advocate humanitarian principles, as expressed in discussions about humanitarian space. There are also pragmatic decisions that humanitarian actors have to make to be able to operate in conflict zones, which are in turn central to their credibility as humanitarians, since proximity to and experience in dealing with victims of humanitarian crises is central. But such pragmatism takes place within a social space whose boundaries are defined by substantive values, making policing at the margins important. Sergio de Mello, for example, was highly respected as a humanitarian actor, but he was frequently chastised by many of his humanitarian colleagues for being too pragmatic and not upholding humanitarian principles.[8] Many labelled "humanitarian" the advocacy of the "save Darfur" campaign to get western governments involved in stopping the war there. Humanitarian organizations reacted strongly to this label, noting that their concern was always for the access and safety of their staff to attend to suffering individuals and not to argue for "humanitarian intervention."[9]

Below, I substantiate empirically the thinness of diplomatic culture and the thickness of humanitarian culture and identify some implications for our understanding of both.[10]

---

[7] Stephen Hoopgood, "Moral authority, modernity and the politics of the sacred," *European Journal of International Relations* 15, no. 2 (2009): 229–55.

[8] Samantha Powers, *Sergio: One Man's Fight to Save the World* (New York: Penguin, 2010).

[9] Author's interview, official with the Norwegian Refugee Council, Oslo, Norway, 16 February 2011.

[10] Here I draw mainly on interviews with diplomats and humanitarian actors in Oslo, South Sudan, and New York, on my experience working in the ministry of foreign affairs in Norway, and on documents from international policy debates concerning the relationship between diplomats and humanitarian actors.

DIPLOMACY AND HUMANITARIANISM

Hedley Bull defined diplomatic culture as "the common stock of ideas and values possessed by the official representatives of states."[11] Others have noted that this overly ideational reading of culture misses out on central aspects of diplomacy.[12] My approach here differs in that it seeks to describe this culture in terms of the relationship between the diplomat and that which the diplomat represents—and the converse for humanitarians. The tasks that these actors perform and the skills that are judged as important by relevant others flow from the character of the relationship between the actors and that which they represent. In terms of the analytical tools used in the framing article, diplomacy represents territorial units while humanitarians represent nonterritorial ones. Moreover, humanitarianism represents those in need of relief and/or protection as part of an effort to govern, whereas diplomats represent first and govern second: the job description of humanitarian actors is to act on the world, that of diplomats is to act on the world to the extent that it is seen to serve the interests of the units that they represent. As I discuss towards the end of the article, globalization and the attendant move to establish global governance efforts on a range of transnational phenomena have arguably resulted in governing becoming an increasingly important frame of reference for the representation of territorially defined interests. One may thus ask how the transnationalization of governance efforts affects diplomatic practice and diplomats' relations with other actors.

What is shared by diplomats is also what separates them, namely the representation of territorial units. Humanitarians, by contrast, share a substantive commitment that cuts across territorial units, namely (the claim to) humanity, universalism, and relief to suffering individuals. Diplomatic culture is geared towards the recognition of difference, management of friction, and the perpetuation of lines of communication. The professional identity of the diplomat is expressed or instantiated in and through a diplomatic culture that is focused on recognizing diplomatic peers' concerns and interests. Humanitarianism is defined not only by international legal treatises, such as the Geneva convention and relevant protocols, but also, and more fundamentally, by the idea that there is a common humanity

---

[11] Hedley Bull, *The Anarchical Society: A Study of Order in World Politics* (London: Macmillan, 1977), 316.

[12] Iver B. Neumann, "Returning practice to the linguistic turn: The case of diplomacy," *Millennium: Journal of International Studies* 32, no. 3 (2002): 627-52; Vincent Pouliot, *International Security in Practice: The Politics of NATO-Russia Diplomacy* (Cambridge: Cambridge University Press, 2010).

and that suffering individuals should be helped on the principle of needs only.[13] These ideals underwrite humanitarian principles of independence, impartiality, and neutrality, since these are meant to secure humanitarian actors access and freedom of movement in conflict areas. As Hugo Slim has observed, the humanitarian tradition has a "strong conviction that an ethic of restraint, kindness and repair in war is universal, a trans-cultural phenomenon that is found in all peoples."[14] The relationship between humanitarian professionals and those they represent is thus not only nonterritorial but is also infused with a moral ideal of care for distant others.

This amounts to a thick culture in that there is a set of substantive objectives around which humanitarian activity is organized. A crucial part of this culture is the proximity that humanitarians seek to achieve between themselves and those they help and claim to represent. The humanitarian ideal of *témoignage*—witnessing—is here central, as is the direct interaction, through medical treatment and food delivery, between humanitarians and those to which relief is offered. As several authors have argued, humanitarian organizations' extensive use of images of suffering can be seen as a technique for producing proximity, of bridging the distance between the suffering individuals and the constituencies that fund humanitarian work.[15] This feature of humanitarianism is linked, I argue, to the fact that the relationship between humanitarian actors and those in whose name they act is more precarious and in need of policing and reinvestment than is the case with the relationship between diplomats and those that they represent. This leads to ongoing debates within humanitarian circles about where to draw the line between humanitarian action and other practices. This is not to say that there is not policing of diplomats as well, as Pouliot's article in this issue demonstrates. But it is to say that this policing—qua diplomacy—concerns protocol and form and not substantive values as is the case with humanitarian action.

---

[13] Michael Barnett and Thomas Weiss, "Humanitarianism: A brief history of the present," in Michael Barnett and Thomas Weiss, eds., *Humanitarianism in Question: Politics, Power, Ethics* (Ithaca: Cornell University Press, 2008): 1-48.

[14] Hugo Slim, "Humanitarianism with borders? NGOs, belligerent military forces and humanitarian action," paper for International Council of Voluntary Agencies Conference on NGOs in a changing world order, Geneva, 2003, 1.

[15] Lisa Malkki, "Speechless emissaries: Refugees, humanitarianism, and dehistoricization," *Cultural Anthropology* 11, no. 3 (1996): 377-404.

DIPLOMACY

The attention to form is pervasive in diplomatic circles. The speeches of different states during the opening of the UN general assembly each fall is a testament to the ritualized character of diplomacy. Certainly, the UN—and the debate that kicks off each year's general assembly—is somewhat unique. Nonetheless, the diplomatic practice of praising others for their efforts, of thanking the chair, of duly noting past achievements, and for generally couching substantive arguments in language that appears trivial to outsiders but that carries a very specific meaning for diplomats seems to be a distinct, and in many ways unique, aspect of diplomacy. This feature of diplomacy is inherently linked to how diplomacy as a social practice is characterized by a thin culture.

When asked about what diplomacy is, diplomats offer a range of different formulations: "representation," "advance national interests," "implement foreign policy," "negotiate and communicate." Most would recognize that diplomats in the past had more autonomy from the political leadership and acted with considerably more room for maneuver due to lack of rapid communication. All diplomats interviewed for this project emphasized that what set them apart from colleagues in line ministries or issue-specific regulatory agencies is that they are in charge of the totality of national interests and are thus charged with balancing sectoral interests against each other. One described the difference with line ministries as follows:

> Line ministries will often operate within a national frame of reference.... We offer a global reality check—a filter if you like. I do think that we have—and I know that many refer to us as being arrogant and whatnot—seen different countries and the realities there and thus offer a different frame of reference.[16]

Another diplomat noted that issue-specific experts would typically not understand the whole international context.[17] In terms of the concepts set out in the introduction, these are diplomatic practice categories, used by diplomats to differentiate themselves from others and to evaluate other diplomats' behaviour. The

---

[16] Interview, ministry of foreign affairs official, Oslo, Norway, 8 March 2011.

[17] Interview, foreign affairs official, Oslo, Norway, 10 May 2011.

accent here is placed on being knowledgeable about other actors' (states') concerns, and taking these into account when advancing and formulating national interests. It concerns making the national frame of reference less dominant and inserting the reality and concerns of other countries. The same diplomat also pointed out, however, that those representing line ministries were often quite quick to learn how to operate as they were among peers within the same issue-area. This was underscored also by other diplomats, one noting that during the efforts to establish a ban on cluster munitions, a few humanitarian actors became adept at couching their interventions in a form that followed a diplomatic script. Humanitarian actors themselves also pointed to this fact.

A representative of a humanitarian organization that was involved in the campaign to ban cluster munitions said that they "learned over time how to deal with states" and to operate as diplomats. Interestingly, tensions emerged within the humanitarian caucus between those within the secretariat of the Cluster Munitions Coalition, where the secretariat representatives had to try to discipline some of their humanitarian colleagues not to rub diplomats the wrong way. She noted that, "I think some diplomats were a bit scared of some of the NGOs that operated in the hallways of the negotiation room. They were important for the CMC as a whole for their advocacy vis-à-vis the general public, but they could also jeopardize our relations with some key states."[18] Perhaps the most clear-cut expression of the distinctiveness of diplomatic culture is found in the following description of the added value of diplomats relative to other actors, where emphasis is very much on the unique skill-set of a trained diplomat to gauge others' reactions and to know what others' pet issues and red flags are:

> What you say and how you say it is extremely important in these settings. If you say the wrong things, even often just using the wrong words, you've destroyed the whole thing. And you can win over important allies by including key words in the speech or text that you know they care strongly about. You also signal support to others through body language and eye contact so as to make sure that they get that this paragraph here is for you, etc. An 'expert' will be totally lost in such a setting if he/she does not know how to operate. What are the different states' pet issues? What are the red flags? How far can

[18] Interview, official with Norwegian Peoples Aid, Norway, 16 February 2011.

you push that state? How do you win over other states? Who are the most important actors in this setting? All of this is the purview of the diplomat, and it takes time to perfect this skill and the network required to operate effectively.[19]

The premium placed on the *fingerspitzengefühl* for other actors' interests and concerns is, I submit, an instantiation of a diplomatic culture organized around making communication possible across political units. The recognition among diplomats that they do the same work and share a way of doing things yet do so to advance different territorial interests is brought home in how one diplomat described the tacit understanding that allows sharing of information:

> I can visit a diplomat in the UK, say, and get a read out on what is going on in a particular country or on a specific theme that I would never get from others. This information is the bread and butter for diplomats. It is assumed that 'I give you this information now in exchange for information from you at a later stage.' This is central to the diplomatic *corps d'esprit*.[20]

HUMANITARIANS

Humanitarian actors perform a range of tasks that are similar to those of diplomats: they negotiate, report, communicate, and do so to represent others. But, as Larry Minear notes, while humanitarian actors negotiate with others on a daily basis, they do not identify themselves as diplomats. Diplomacy, he notes, is seen as "well beyond— and quite separate from—what they do."[21] This is intimately linked to humanitarians' well-known self-identification as operating outside of the political realm. Being asked whether they are engaged in politics, one representative argued, for example, that "we defend humanitarian principles and seek to influence decision makers to adhere to

---

[19] Interview, foreign affairs official, Oslo, Norway, 8 March 2011.

[20] Interview, foreign affairs official Oslo, Norway, 8 March 2011.

[21] Larry Minear, "The craft of humanitarian diplomacy," in Larry Minear and Hazel Smith, eds., *Humanitarian Diplomacy: Practitioners and their Craft.* (Tokyo: United Nations University Press, 2007), 8.

them. But this is not politics, it is advocating on behalf of humanitarian principles."[22] This was reinforced also by foreign affairs officials working on humanitarian issues, with one noting that "what is distinct about humanitarian work inside the MFA is that it is in principle apolitical." This is a testament to the substantive values that humanitarian actors use to differentiate themselves from others and to seek recognition for and authority to self-regulate what they do.

The set of humanitarian principles that I argue make up a thick culture is thus important not only in producing conformity among humanitarian actors, but also in drawing boundaries around other actors outside of the humanitarian realm. Indeed, the maintenance of distance to things political—as in the case of debates about humanitarian space—is integral to the constitution of humanitarian objects of governance and thus also to the representation and governance that humanitarian actors engage in. Humanitarian actors as we know them would not exist in the absence of their jurisdictional control over humanitarian victims and crises. The construction and reproduction of humanitarian relief as a distinct set of tasks and of suffering individuals as a distinct group is central to the representation and governing in which humanitarian actors are engaged. The insistence on an apolitical stance—as manifest in the principles of independence, impartiality, and, not least, neutrality—persists despite humanitarians' gradual expansion to act on and be concerned also with the causes of conflicts.

The continual reproduction and policing of boundaries is inherently linked to the thickness of humanitarian culture. It is no coincidence that one close observer notes that humanitarians see debates about the boundaries of humanitarianism as an issue of identity rather than activities: "The main issue seems to be a feeling that humanitarian NGOs want to put *moral boundaries around what can rightfully be considered humanitarian action*. In doing so, they seem to be suggesting that such boundaries to humanitarian action are not about activities (*what* is being done: food, water, shelter, etc.) but agents and motives (*who* is doing these activities and for what reason)."[23] This feature of humanitarian action is intimately linked to the aforementioned criteria of evaluation employed by humanitarians in judging others: if actors who claim to be humanitarian are seen to violate core humanitarian principles, they are not to be trusted. One humanitarian actor noted, for example,

---

[22] Interview, Norwegian Refugee Council official, Oslo, Norway, 10 February 2011.
[23] Slim, "Humanitarians with borders."

that "I do not listen if I hear USAID talk about humanitarian principles. What they are doing in Afghanistan completely contradicts humanitarian principles."

If the universalism of humanitarian ideals is what shields humanitarian actors from regarding themselves as political, then the practical mechanism through which this is made possible is the insistence that their advocacy flows from their role as bearing witness. Because they are present in conflict areas, and because they give victims of humanitarian crises shelter, food, and medicine, humanitarian actors argue, they represent those who cannot speak for themselves: bearing witness is in itself a key source of humanitarian actors' authority vis-à-vis diplomats and others. They are present in conflict zones and can report to others what is going on. The claim to representation is fused with an epistemic claim to authority in that humanitarian actors are able, by virtue of their presence, to report on violations of international humanitarian law, on the needs of the victims, on the logistical and political challenges of delivering relief, and so on. This fusion of a claim to moral and epistemic authority is most clearly expressed in the ideology of Médicins Sans Frontières, where advocacy is seen to flow

> directly from...experience in the field, through medical data and eyewitness accounts.... If we speak of government forces pillaging villages and burning food stocks, we do so because our medical responsibility includes asking caretakers in our feeding centres why their children are malnourished. Conceiving of fieldwork as a filter for advocacy initiatives implies that we are obliged to report what is happening when faced with the consequences. It also implies that we confront political actors with their responsibility. However, we do not propose political solutions.[24]

Note again how advocacy is seen either to be with reference to universal principles and a matter of holding states to account for their legal obligations, or it is reporting on or serving as a channel of communication from those in need to the international community. But here a tension runs through the humanitarian community: the International Committee of the Red Cross is very cautious about how it handles information gathered in conflict zones out of concern that its publication

---

[24] Marc DuBois, "Civilian protection and humanitarian advocacy: Strategies and (false?) dilemmas," *Humanitarian Exchange Magazine* no. 39 (2008), 1.

may result in a denial of future access. Médecins Sans Frontières was established precisely in opposition to the silence of the Red Cross about the behaviour of the conflicting parties during the Biafran secession. Médecins Sans Frontières thus places a premium on *témoignage*—bearing witness—as it sees other humanitarian organizations' silence about what they observe as morally untenable.

Still, while Red Cross and other humanitarian organizations would typically not publish all that they know because of a concern with access, the premium placed on witnessing and reporting forces humanitarian actors find ways to communicate to other actors what they do know. A humanitarian representative mentioned, for example, that they use a loosely organized "referral system" to get information out so that others can act on it. And a diplomat with long experience working with humanitarian organizations observed that "sensitive information collected by humanitarian actors in the field quite often ends up in the public realm. You know how this works. It is a small world, and people talk to each other."[25]

KNOWLEDGE FROM CONFLICT ZONES

Witnessing and proximity to those in need appear central not only to humanitarian actors' claims to represent others, but also to diplomats' and others' evaluation of the value of humanitarian actors it provide knowledge in the midst of a humanitarian crisis. Beyond the idea of witnessing as a source of advocacy, humanitarian actors' presence in areas where a humanitarian crisis is unfolding, in the eyes of both diplomats and humanitarians, is a central source of their authority. During the process to establish a ban against cluster munitions—modelled on the Ottawa process that resulted in the ban on anti-personnel landmines—humanitarian organizations played a central role. By most accounts they did so because of two main aspects of their operations: they possessed highly detailed technical knowledge about different types of ammunition and they prepared extensive documentation—using statistics gathered by humanitarian organizations with field presence—about the destructive effects of such ammunition.[26] A diplomat involved in the process

---

[25] Interview, foreign affairs official, 8 March 2011.

[26] John Borrie, *Unacceptable Harm: A History of How the Treaty to Ban Cluster Munitions Was Won* (Geneva: United Nations Institute for Disarmament Research, 2009).

noted, for example, that "without this type of documentation, recalcitrant states would likely not have joined the call towards the end of the process."

The same diplomat noted that humanitarian organizations were very effective in bridging the distance between the world of diplomatic negotiations and the suffering of the individuals: "When they brought individuals on the podium to talk about what they had gone through, it had an effect. It was very powerful." An NGO representative heavily involved in the coordination of humanitarian advocacy against cluster munitions similarly noted that "if diplomats were to do this without input from humanitarian organizations, it would not have worked. They don't know this stuff. They are sent out to represent." She continued to suggest that "I think one way in which we were able to stop the efforts of some governments—UK, Germany and some others—to dilute the document was that we knew the technical details so well and challenged them on technical details."[27]

This type of substantive knowledge is not only relevant to humanitarian advocacy of this type, however, but extends to the ongoing interaction between humanitarian actors and diplomats. For example, humanitarian NGOs in Norway frequently brief and interact with officials at the ministry of foreign affairs, relaying information about developments in areas where they have staff present. In Geneva—the world's humanitarian capital—all large humanitarian NGOs have permanent observers who engage the diplomatic community there. As one humanitarian representative noted, the entry point for humanitarians into diplomatic circles is intimately linked to their presence where humanitarian issues are relevant: "If we want to influence these diplomats, we *have* to bring facts from the field. They only receive UN-filtered reports that do not tell you much, so I would say that having access to the field and getting knowledge from the local scene is crucial."[28] This also holds for diplomatic circles in countries where conflicts are ongoing. A humanitarian representative argued that "in Afghanistan, diplomats don't leave the compound and they need us because we do get out there and get information." This changes the historically established image of embassy staff as having privileged access to developments in a country: in high-risk environments, the information often comes from humanitarian actors.

---

[27] Interview, official with Norwegian Peoples Aid, 16 February 2011.

[28] Interview, Norwegian Red Cross official, Oslo, Norway, 10 February 2011.

CONCLUSION: GOVERNANCE AND REPRESENTATION

I have focused on the distinct features of diplomacy and humanitarianism, and have done so by looking at the relationship that both actors have to what they (claim to) represent. But to capture the relationship between these actors, and describe its evolution over time, it is necessary to also reflect on how the tasks that these actors perform may have changed over time. Although space does not allow a discussion of it here, governance at the transnational or global level has expanded in scope and has become more ambitious over the last few decades. As an instantiation of globalization, global governance is often said to be performed by a host of actors that are supplementing, even supplanting, diplomats. There are merits in these claims: if regulatory work is increasingly done through transnational networks with participants from domestic regulatory agencies, experts, and staff of international organizations, then diplomats stand to lose their hitherto privileged position as gatekeepers between the inside and the outside.[29] If nonstate actors are becoming more actively involved in formulating and monitoring governance on health, environment, development, and finance, diplomats may be sidelined and replaced by transnational, epistemic community-like groups that share both substantive knowledge and a policy agenda. But observing that new actors are becoming more active and influential in governance efforts at the global level does not tell us anything about changes in diplomats' mode of operation and role vis-à-vis other actors. Nor does it say much about what happens if and when governance—requiring in-depth and substantive knowledge—is becoming progressively more important as the register for what diplomats do.

Drawing on interviews with diplomats and representatives of humanitarian organizations, I have described how diplomats see humanitarians as primarily contributing knowledge about the object to be governed—the character of the conflict, the health, and medical requirements of those in need, etc. Conversely, humanitarians see diplomats as contributing knowledge about the processes and mechanisms for getting states or international organizations on board with a humanitarian agenda. Indeed, both humanitarians and diplomats agree that the former brings knowledge

---

[29] Anne-Marie Slaughter, *A New World Order* (Princeton: Princeton University Press, 2004).

about governance objects that is not accessible to others, and that the latter brings procedural knowledge of how to operate to win allies and reach agreements. This is not to suggest that these descriptions should be taken at face value and that there is a functional division of labour between diplomats and humanitarians. Rather, it is to suggest that just as humanitarianism has changed considerably over the last two or three decades, so has diplomacy. The emergence of governance as the matrix for representation does not lead to the demise of diplomats, however. Because diplomatic work is constituted through the character of the relation with that which it represents—territorial units—diplomacy has a thin culture and is resilient. Being structured by criteria of evaluation that do not include substantive goals and ideals, diplomatic work may continue amid significant structural changes. But there are changes in some of the criteria of evaluation through which recognition is granted: to represent a state effectively, it is necessary to have a seat at the table. To the extent that global governance involves fragmentation of governance efforts and the increase in importance of arenas outside formal multilateral settings where all states are represented, there is a higher premium on in-depth and technical knowledge within diplomatic circles, as witnessed by the character of the efforts to ban cluster munitions and before that, anti-personnel land mines. This helps explain how diplomats strategically enrolled and used humanitarian actors in these processes.[30]

Nonetheless, diplomats engage in a practice that is not on a par with that performed by other actors whose power is said to be on the increase relative to diplomats. Diplomats are constituted as authorities by virtue of representing territorially defined, sovereign units. Their authority does not hinge on how they perform, but on the recognition of the territorial unit that the diplomat represents. So-called "new" diplomatic actors typically represent nonterritorial units, and they stand to lose their authority if they are not skilfully performing the tasks associated with their claim to authority. For diplomats, performing their assigned tasks badly does not affect their position in the sense that they are still authorized to speak and act in the name of the unit they represent, although, as Pouliot notes in his contribution, the diplomatic corps does police how diplomats should behave. For other actors, by contrast, their authority may be significantly eroded should they act in ways that contradict or undermine established standards and norms for what constitutes effectiveness, truthfulness, or generally appropriate behaviour. Thus, diplomats are *in* authority, and actors that represent nonterritorial units are

---

[30] On this, see also Ole Jacob Sending and Iver B. Neumann, "Governance to governmentality: Analyzing NGOs, states, and power," *International Studies Quarterly* 50 (2006): 651–72.

an authority. Surely, diplomats who consistently violate diplomatic protocol or fail to represent and advance the interest of a state will be removed from that position. But another person will be given that position, and the authority of the position remains similar. This is not so with actors who are *an* authority, since failing to perform in accordance with the criteria that produced the authority in the first place—whether in terms of technical knowledge or adherence to a set of principles—will undermine the authority of the person, or organization, in question.

While governance concerns acting on the world and representation concerns advancing the interests of a given constituency, they are related in a way that often favours diplomatic skills over in-depth, technical knowledge. Take the UN. A diplomat covering humanitarian issues in New York noted that discussions about humanitarian challenges and principles are quickly politicized there. Such multilateral settings privilege the skill-sets perfected by diplomats, since the ability to know all the nuances and history of specific phrases, wordings, and past resolutions is a central resource to either block or advance a particular agenda. The UN special committee on peace operations, which insiders call the C-34, is a case in point. Western governments have since long tried to give the department of peacekeeping operations a mandate to develop guidelines and strategies for the protection of civilians in areas where they operate, since this has become a central part of their mandate over the last decade. Diplomats representing governments that are opposed to the protection of civilians because of its association with the responsibility to protect have effectively blocked such a development until recently by virtue of having the diplomatic equivalent of what military strategists call "denial capability": while outnumbered and with few resources, a small group of diplomats with in-depth knowledge of past resolutions and an ability to engage in issue-linkage are able to mobilize a large number of countries (the group of 77) to block such initiatives. It is a testament to how diplomatic culture—and the attendant practices through which it is made manifest—places a premium not on substantive knowledge of the issue at hand, but the ability to use the form of diplomatic practice to one's advantage.

The unit concludes with Saleema Kauser in Chapter 12 evaluating international agreements in an empirical test, focusing on international partnerships and the resolution of conflict.

CHAPTER 12

Managing Conflict in International Strategic Alliances

by Saleema Kauser

INTRODUCTION

Collaborations across borders between firms are now so common that they are a growing subject of management research. Some firms perceive international alliances as strategic weapons (Doz & Hamel, 1998; Harrigan, 1988), while others consider them to be a superior method of investing corporate resources. In addition, competitive pressures are continuously forcing companies to partner with other firms, many of whom have different priorities, incentives, and ways of doing things. Several studies have shown that the number of alliances across borders being used by firms is increasing (Glaister & Buckley, 1994). The importance of managing successful international strategic alliances has been reflected extensively in the literature, and has primarily focused on the ex ante structuring of alliances (Parkhe, 1993). Researchers have examined the rationale for international alliances (Contractor & Lorange, 1988; Glaister & Buckley, 1994; Hagedo-orn, 1993; Harrigan, 1988; Hennart, 1988; Kogut,

Saleema Kauser, "Managing Conflict in International Strategic Alliances," *Interpartner Dynamics in Strategic Alliances*, ed. T. K. Das, pp. 187-209. Copyright © 2013 by Information Age Publishing. Reprinted with permission.

1988); partner selection and characteristics (Blodgett, 1991; Geringer, 1993); and the ownership, control, and performance relationship (Geringer & Hebert, 1989, 1991; Killing, 1983; Schaan, 1983; Tomlinson, 1970). The fundamental basis of these studies is that if the partners are not compatible, motivations of partners are not congruent, and ownership and control are not sorted out, the alliance is likely to experience difficulties and partners become dissatisfied with the outcomes.

Despite the initiatives to improve relationships between partners, international strategic alliances are plagued with problems because of potential problems associated with their management, poor perceived performance, and inflexibility (Geringer & Hebert, 1991; Parkhe, 1993). It has been estimated that between 30% and 70% of alliances fail (Bleeke & Ernst, 1991; Das & Kumar, 2009; Das & Teng, 2000; Park & Ungson, 2001). While several potential problems have been associated with their management, one main issue concerns the role of conflict in alliances and the ability of partners to deal with conflicting differences. Many researchers have emphasized the issue of managing conflict as a crucial organization process for alliance success (Ding, 1997; Geringer & Herbert, 1989, 1991; Gill & Butler, 2003; Yan & Gray, 1994). However, there is very little conceptual and empirical research available concerning the impact of partnership attributes on managing conflict (Das & Kumar, 2009; Das & Teng, 1998; Fey & Beamish, 2000).

Studies have investigated the operational aspects of international strategic alliances, including management and production control, human resources, marketing, and finance (Child & Faulkner, 1998). Researchers have found that conflict within international strategic alliances is inevitable due to the differing objectives, structures, and organizational cultures (Kauser & Shaw; 2004; Lane & Beamish, 1990). Much of this research emphasizes that while problems and disagreements are inevitable in every alliance relationship, partners can work together to develop mediating mechanisms to diffuse and settle their differences (Das & Kumar, 2009; Gulati & Singh, 1998; Kale, Singh, & Perlmutter, 2000; Kumar & Nti, 1998). One way to do this is to pay attention to relationship issues such as coordination, trust, commitment, and communication. These issues seem to be forgotten when it comes to launching alliance agreements (Das & Kumar, 2009) and have been shown to be critical in managing successful relationships (Fey & Beamish, 1999; Hambrick, Li, Xin, & Tsui, 2001; Hu & Chen, 1996; Mohr

& Spekman, 1994; Yan & Gray, 1994). There is much in the literature that emphasizes the importance of managing the alliance relationship with regards to having clearly defined goals, contributing sufficient resources, having effective communication, managing commitment, and showing forbearance among others. (Das & Kumar, 2009; Geyskens, Steenkamp, Scheer, & Kumar, 1996; Holm, Eriksson, & Johanson, 1999; Kauser & Shaw, 2004; Mohr & Spekman, 1994). However, the impact of relationship dynamics on conflict within alliances has received little attention (Das & Teng, 1998).

To understand how partners address and deal with the issue of conflict in managing international alliances, we need to emphasize the complexity involved in managing relationship dynamics between companies from different national backgrounds and their impact on managing conflict in these relationships. This chapter proposes to address this gap in the existing literature by examining the impact of partnership attributes on managing conflict within international strategic alliances, (Dang, 1977; Geringer & Hebert, 1989, 1991; Kauser & Shaw, 2004). Specifically, the study aims to investigate the relationship between conflict and the development of commitment, trust, interdependence, coordination, and communication.

CONFLICT RELATIONSHIP DYNAMICS

PARTNERSHIP ATTRIBUTES

The conceptual framework for this study is based upon the premise that international strategic alliances are inherently characterized by conflict in their daily relationships. Based on a review of the relevant literature, the relationships between the factors are shown in Figure 12.1.

The importance of partnership attributes has been reflected extensively in the literature, which has focused on commitment, coordination, interdependence, trust, and communication (Anderson & Narus, 1991; Das & Kumar, 2009; Ding, 1997; Geyskens et al., 1996; Hu & Chen, 1996; Kauser & Shaw, 2004; Lee, 2001; Madhok, 1995; Mohr & Nevin, 1990; Mohr & Spekman, 1994; Monckza, Peterson, Handfield, & Ragatz, 1998; Morgan & Hunt, 1994). Theoretical contributions (Parkhe, 1993)

Figure 12.1 Conflict and relationship dynamics.

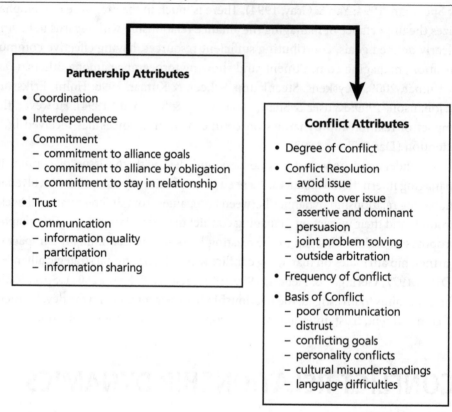

as well as empirical and case study (Mohr & Spekman, 1994; Monckza et al., 1998) research have identified these attributes as the most important factors necessary for the development of successful alliance relationships. In such relationships there exist a set of commodities that help guide the flow of information between partners, manage the depth and breadth of interaction, and capture the complex and dynamic interchange between partners. Mohr and Spekman (1994) make the assumption that the existence of partnership attributes implies that both partners acknowledge their mutual dependence and their willingness to work for the survival of the relationship and thus reduce the potential for opportunistic behavior. Hu and Chen (1996) identified four characteristics that may impact the performance of partnerships: level of commitment, control, the number of partners, and the sociocultural distance. More recently, Das and Kumar (2009) have argued that because of the buoyant nature of partnerships, misunderstandings can be handled through managing both commitment and forbearance.

Many researchers also agree that conflict between partners is strongly related to the relationship dynamics of international alliances (Anderson & Narus, 1990; Child & Faulkner, 1998; Ding, 1997; Friedman & Beguin, 1971; Killing, 1983; Lane & Beamish, 1990; Lewis, 1990). One view is that international alliances try to maintain their autonomy in an interdependent relationship, which gives rise to conflicts (Van de Ven & Walker, 1984). The drive for both autonomy and cooperation can result in the coexistence of cooperative and conflictual motives within the partnership (Aldrich, 1979; Das & Teng, 2000; Khanna, Gulati, & Nohria, 1998). Conflicts between partners can result in misunderstandings and distrust, leading to reduced cooperation and thereby deteriorating the success of the alliance (Freidman & Beguin, 1971; Kauser, 2007; Killing, 1983; Lewis, 1990; Madhok, 1995; Wright, 1979).

Habib (1983, 1987) showed that the frequency and level of conflicts between partners led to problems of commitment to goals. Others have shown that frequent disagreements in a relationship tend to cause frustration and unpleasantness and impact the relationship dynamics within strategic alliances (Anderson & Narus, 1984, 1990; Kauser, 2007; Ding, 1997). In addition, conflict may harm accomplishment of the task of the relationships. Frequent disagreements may result in complex, time-consuming decision making or in obstructive behaviors that simply block any decision making (Killing, 1983). As a result, time and resources are devoted to conflict resolution rather than activities that are productive for the alliance. Such situations may limit an alliance's ability to cope with and to respond to changes in its environment and thus to be successful in its business. Conflicts may also result in firms from cooperating and from withholding resources that may be required by the other partner to achieve its objectives (Buckley & Casson, 1988; Lane & Beamish, 1990; Nti & Kumar, 2000). Transaction cost theory advocates that conflict breaks down trust and increases the potential for opportunistic behavior, thereby resulting in economically inefficient relationships (Beamish & Banks, 1987; Buckley & Casson, 1988).

> **Proposition 1:** *International strategic alliances that exhibit coordination, interdependence, commitment, trust, and communication will display lower levels of conflict.*

There are many ways in which conflicts can arise between partners. Conflicts may arise from differences in cultural values, management styles, operational methods, and procedures, which may jeopardize the alliance (Jain, 1987). In international strategic alliances, the presence of two parent firms can lead to differences between them in terms of management style, culture, communication, and operational practices, which are conducive to conflict (Devlin & Bleackley, 1988; Ding, 1997; Glaister & Wu, 1994; Jain, 1987; Johnson, 1999; Killing, 1983; Lewis, 1990; Wright, 1979).

Wright (1979) examined 25 U.S. and Canadian joint ventures in Japan and found that conflicts between partners resulted from differences between the Japanese and the Western culture, which in turn reflected differences in management style. Glaister and Wu (1994), in their study of UK joint ventures in China, pointed out that differences in the economic systems and management systems impacted the management of the joint ventures. Cultural differences between the two countries made the actual management more difficult. These factors would appear to adversely affect the successful implementation of the joint ventures. Lewis (1990), from his investigation of 40 U.S. American and Asian alliances, observed that the potential for conflict resulted from cultural distance between alliance partners, which adversely affected the management of the alliance. Similarly, Simiar (1984) investigated the causes of failure in 29 international joint ventures in Iran and attributed the failure of ventures to conflicting goals between partners resulting from cultural misunderstandings. More recently, research has shown that the ways in which partnership relationships are managed affect conflict (Das & Kumar, 2009; Hoon-Halbauer, 1999; Hu & Chen, 1996; Johnson, Cullen, Sakano, & Bronson, 2001; Kauser, 2007; Kozan, 1997; Leung, Koch, & Lu, 2002). Essentially, the presence of conflict may monopolize the attention and the time of the management of the alliance relationship and thus is likely to block their communication, coordination, commitment, and trust. Ultimately, it may impede effective management of the alliances operations and implementation of strategy. Against this background, the following proposition was formulated:

> **Proposition 2:** *International strategic alliances that exhibit coordination, interdependence, commitment, trust, and communication will impact the basis of conflict between partnerships.*

Given that a certain amount of conflict is expected, an understanding of how such conflicts can be resolved is also important (Borys & Jemison, 1989). Research has shown that the success of international strategic alliances is very much dependent upon how partners manage daily operations and the mechanism used to resolve conflicts (Das & Kumar, 2011; Lane & Beamish, 1990; Lin & Germain, 1998; Xie, Song, & Stringfellow, 1998). Researchers have identified a range of strategies in dealing with conflict in international partnerships. In their study of Sino–foreign partnerships, Lin and Germain (1998) identified four conflict resolution mechanisms: namely, joint problem solving, compromising through negotiation, unilateral control by the dominant party, and informal and formal contracts. They found that the use of joint problem solving was positively associated with more successful partnerships. Other research has also demonstrated that partnerships are more likely to use nonassertive strategies such as joint problem solving and compromise as the most preferred strategy for managing conflict (Mohr & Spekman, 1994; Xie et al., 1998). Joint problem solving allows a mutually satisfactory solution to be reached, thereby enhancing alliance success. Partners very often attempt to persuade each other to adopt particular solutions to the conflict situation, which appears to be more constructive than the use of coercion or domination (Deutsch, 1969; Lin & Germain, 1998). Domination or coercion is seen as being the least preferred strategy, which is counterproductive and likely to strain the fabric of the strategic alliance relationship (Lin & Germain, 1998). In some strategic alliances, conflict resolution is institutionalized, and third party arbitration is recommended (Anderson & Narus, 1990). However, it has been suggested that internal resolution is more likely to lead to long-term success (Assael, 1969). Other conflict resolution techniques such as smoothing over or ignoring and avoiding the issue are somewhat at odds with the norms and values advocated in more successful strategic alliances. Such techniques do not fit in with alliances in which the problems of one party become the problems affecting both parties. Different conflict resolution strategies may also be used according to the circumstances, resulting in different outcomes (Das & Kumar, 2011; Lin & Germain, 1998). These findings suggest that managers in international partnerships are induced to use a particular conflict resolution strategy depending on the situation at hand.

Clearly, various conflict resolution strategies can be adopted in the management of international strategic alliances (Anderson & Narus, 1990; Das & Kumar, 2011;

Ding, 1997; Friedman & Beguin, 1971; Killing, 1983; Lane & Beamish, 1990; Lewis, 1990; Lin & Germain, 1998).

> **Proposition 3:** *International strategic alliances that exhibit coordination, interdependence, commitment, trust, and communication are more likely to resolve conflicts using joint problem solving.*

METHODOLOGY

The propositions were tested on a sample of 600 international agreements that took place between 1988 and 1995. This sample included strategic alliances between British companies and their U.S., European, and Japanese partners. Information concerning these alliances was gathered from *The Economist* and *Financial Times* along the lines of similar databases constructed by other researchers (Glaister & Buckley, 1994; Hergert & Morris, 1988). All companies were contacted by telephone to request their participation in the study. Questionnaires were sent out to senior managers involved in the management of alliances. A total of 287 responses (63.7%) were received. In spite of having agreed to participate in the study when contacted by telephone, 173 respondents did not complete the questionnaire, giving the following reasons for non-response: the alliance had been terminated, contract confidentiality did not allow information to be divulged, and workload; some commented that the alliance was not strategic in nature. The length of the questionnaire may also have been an issue for some companies, but the usable response rate of 114 completed questionnaires (25.3%) compares well to other studies of a similar nature (Mohr & Spekman, 1994).

MEASUREMENT OF VARIABLES

The domain of the measures used was specified and a sample of items was generated for each construct (Churchill, 1979). To ensure high content validity, all

TABLE 12.1 Reliability Scales for Relationship Dynamic Variables

RELATIONSHIP DYNAMIC ATTRIBUTES	ORIGINAL NUMBER OF SCALE ITEMS	CRONBACH'S ALPHA
Co-ordination	8	.88
Interdependence	10	.70
Commitment/Goals and Values 1	10	.93
Commitment/Goals and Values 2	5	.91
Commitment/Obligations	7	.91
Commitment/stay in relationship	6	.86
Trust 1	5	.90
Trust 2	8	.90
Information Quality	5	.89
Information Sharing	4	.72
Participation	5	.79
Total	**73**	

TABLE 12.2 Reliability Scales for Conflict

CONFLICT	ORIGINAL NUMBER OF SCALE ITEMS	CRONBACH'S ALPHA
Conflict Resolution	6	N/A
Conflict	6	.70
Total	**12**	—

measurements developed were based on a comprehensive review of the literature and detailed evaluation by the researchers. The questionnaire developed was also pretested on a number of senior managers with extensive international strategic alliance management experience. All measures were evaluated for reliability and validity using Cronbach's alpha (see Tables 12.1 & 12.2). The majority of measures demonstrated a high degree of internal consistency, with alphas ranging from 0.58 to 0.93, falling within the range of acceptability recommended by Nunnally (1978).

DEPENDENT MEASURES

A fourteen-item scale was used to measure the conflict construct. The *conflict* measure concerns the level of conflict between the partner firms and was assessed in terms of the degree and frequency of conflict, the basis of conflict (Anderson & Narus, 1990; Kogut, 1988), and how conflicts may be resolved (Mohr & Spekman, 1994) between partners.

INDEPENDENT MEASURES

Much previous research into coordination has measured this construct using either a single or two items (Mohr & Spekman, 1994; Monckza et al., 1998; Olson & Singsuwan, 1997). By contrast, this study has used eight items derived from the literature. Interdependence was measured on two dimensions—replaceability and dependency on resources (Kumar, Scheer, & Steenkamp, 1995). Following reliability, all ten measures were used for further analysis. Commitment was operationalized using an organizational commitment questionnaire, which measured the extent to which each party identifies with the goals and objectives of the alliance, is willing to exert effort on behalf of the alliance, and intends to maintain the relationship (Porter, Steers, Mowday, & Boulian, 1974). These three dimensions were assessed using 28 items, all of which remained in the analysis after reliability tests. These items have been widely used in studies of organizational behavior (Mowday, Steers, & Porter, 1979; Randall, 1990). Although many studies have recognized the importance of trust for successful collaboration, the number of measures used has been low, with many authors acknowledging that the conceptualization and operationalization of trust often does not capture the many facets of the concept (Aulakh, Kotabe, & Sahay, 1996; Mohr & Spekman, 1994; Monckza et al., 1998). This study, therefore, has developed new measures of trust using 13 different dimensions that showed very high levels of reliability. Communication attributes were measured on three dimensions—information quality, information sharing, and participation in planning and goal setting (Daft & Lengel, 1986; Huber & Daft 1987; Mohr & Spekman, 1994). Information quality in this study refers to timeliness, accuracy, adequacy, and creditability of the information exchanged (Daft & Lengel, 1986; Huber & Daft, 1987). Information sharing measures the extent of information exchange between partners (Mohr & Spekman, 1994), and participation measures the extent to which partners engage jointly in planning and goal setting (Mohr & Spekman, 1994). A total of 14 items were used in subsequent analysis.

FINDINGS

REGRESSION MODEL TESTING

To investigate the effect of partnership characteristics on the level and basis of conflicts and how conflicts may be resolved in international alliances, regression analysis was undertaken with each of the dependent variables measuring conflict. All the identified factors from the factor analysis were used as the explanatory variables (see Tables 12.1 to 12.8). The predictors and independent measures are presented in Table 12.9. Partnership characteristic factors were regressed for each measure of the dependent variables in order to identify the influence of these that might be related to each of the different aspects of conflict measured. The justification for running the regression model for each single measure of the dependent variables was to realize how much explanatory power the independent variables have for each dependent measure. Therefore, fourteen separate regression models (one for each conflict measure) were examined and reported.

The regression analysis estimates the significance of the coefficients corresponding to the set of propositions and assesses the changes in the proportion of variance explained (R^2) and the statistical significance of each of the independent variables. The regression model was defined as:

$$Y = a + \beta 1 \, X1 + \beta 2 \, X2 + \beta 3 \, X3 \dots + \beta 11 \, X16$$

where Y represents the measures of conflict (dependent measures) and a is the intercept. The intercept is the expected value of Y when the value for each X variable is zero. The X1, X2, X3 are the partnership characteristics (independent variables),

Table 12.3 predictors and Dependent variables

INDEPENDENT MEASURES	DEPENDENT MEASURES
Relationship Atributes	**Conflict Attributes**
Coordination	Degree of Conflict = Y1
Factor 1 = Coordination between partner firms = Þ1	Frequency of Conflict = Y2
Interdependence	**Conflict Resolution**
Factor 1 = Dependency on marketing capabilities = Þ2	Avoid issue = Y3
Factor 2 = Dependency on administrative support = Þ3	Smooth over issue = Y4
Factor 3 = Dependency on management skills = Þ4	Assertive and dominant = Y5
Commitment	Persuasion = Y6
Factor 1 = Commitment to alliance goals = Þ5	Joint problem solving = Y7
Factor 2 = Commitment to alliance by obligation = Þ6	Outside arbitration = Y8
Factor 3 = Commitment to stay in relationship = Þ7	**Basis of Conflict**
Trust	
Factor 1 = Trust in partner = Þ8	Poor communication = Y9
	Distrust = Y10
Communication	Conflicting goals = Y11
Factor 1 = Information quality = Þ9	Personality conflicts = Y12
Factor 12 = Participation = Þ10	Cultural misunderstanding = Y13
Factor 13 = Information sharing = Þ11	Language difficulties = Y14

and Þ1, Þ2, Þ3, are the regression coefficients for the eleven independent factors. The coefficients are the amount by which the expected value of y increases when X1 increases by a unit amount, when all the other X variables are held constant. The specific variables identified as significant predictors, the resulting standardized Beta weights, and the percentage of variance explained for each of the conflict items are presented in Table 12.9.

Table 12.4 coordination Factor Analyses Scores

VARIABLES	FACTOR 1
Teamwork with partner	.830
Exchange of ideas with partner	.818
UK firm integrated with part	.809
High level of interaction between partners	.808
Partner firm integrated with UK firm	.807
Keep partner informed about important decisions	.727
Partner activities an extension of UK firm	.570
Eigen value	4.169
Percent of variance explained	59.6
KMO	.803
Bartlett's Test of Sphericity	472.402

Table 12.5 Interdependence Factor Analysis Scores

VARIABLES	FACTOR 1	FACTOR 2	FACTOR 3
Dependency on marketing capability	.848		
Dependency on market information	.800		
Dependency on customer service	.759		
Dependency on sales/profits	.737	.834	
Dependency on administration			
Dependency on manpower resources		.823	
Dependency on financial resources			.836
Dependency on management skills			.598
Eigen value	2.558		
Percent of variance explained	31.9		
KMO	.654		
Bartlett's Test of Sphericity	246.705		

Table 12.6 commitment Factors Analysis Scores

VARIABLES	FACTOR 1	FACTOR 2	FACTOR 3
Agreement over key decisions	.825		
Agreement over goals/objectives	.773		
Agreement over future plans	.740		
Agreement over strategic direction	.731		
Agreement over roles performed	.717		
Share understanding and vision	.705		
Agreement over contractual terms	.692		
Agreement over daily operations	.590	.582	
Identify with goals/objectives			
Obligated to compromise in achieving objectives		.767	
Obligated to be patient with partner over mistakes		.759	
Obligated to listen to problems of partner		.741	
Obligated to try to overcome problems		.739	
Obligated to encourage goal achievement		.697	
Obligated to satisfy partners needs		.643	
Obligated to help build the relationship		.630	
Relationship important to achieve strategic objectives		.849	
Long-term relationship will be profitable			.771
Staying in relationship is a desire			.751
Staying in relationship is a necessity			.741
Partnership is valuable			.726
Make sacrifices to achieve long-term objectives			.506
Eigen value	11.069		
Percent of variance explained	50.3		
KMO	.992		
Bartlett's Test of Sphericity	1912.365		

Table 12.7 trust Factor Analysis Scores

VARIABLES	FACTOR 1
Partner trusted to show loyalty	.897
We can always rely on each other	.888
Partner makes effort to keep commitments	.881
Relationship marked by a high degree of harmony	.834
Partner trusted to be supportive	.806
Partner trusted to keep promises	.802
Partner trusted to be sincere	.786
Relationship open and informal	.727
We do not take advantage of each other	.727
We share work related problems	.719
Close personal ties between us	.623
Eigen value	6.937
Percent of variance explained	63.1
KMO	923
Bartlett's Test of Sphericity	952.158

To test the proposition that the amount of variation explained by the regression model is more than the variation explained by the average, the F statistic was used. The F statistic (Table 12.9) for the majority of the regression models exceeded the F critical with 93 degrees of freedom at the 0.01 level and therefore offers significant explanatory power. This means collectively the predictors explain some variation in every case. The statistical significance of the individual regression coefficients are presented in Table 12.9. These coefficients indicate the relative importance of each predictor in the prediction of each of the dependent measures of conflict.

Table 12.8 communication Factor Analysis Scores

VARIABLES	FACTOR 1	FACTOR 2	FACTOR 3
Communication adequate/inadequate	.875		
Communication complete/incomplete	.868		
Communication credible/incredible	.779		
Communication accurate/inaccurate	.760		
Communication timely/untimely	.682	.804	
Seek partners advice in decision making			
Partner seeks advice before decision making		.705	
Both keep each informed about changes		.690	
Inform partner of changing needs		.657	
Participate in goal setting		.574	
Participate in planning activities			.773
Share proprietary information			.690
Participate in regular meetings			.538
Eigen value	5.541		
Percent of variance explained	42.6		
KMO	.831		
Bartlett's Test of Sphericity	781.429		

EFFECTS OF PARTNERSHIP CHARACTERISTICS ON MANAGING CONFLICT WITHIN INTERNATIONAL STRATEGIC ALLIANCES

The results support Proposition 1, that conflict will be lower in international alliances that exhibit coordination, interdependence, commitment, trust, and communication, and it is consistent with previous findings that in order to reduce the number of disputes, partners need to work together (Fey & Beamish, 2000; Kauser & Shaw, 2004; Killing, 1983; Mohr & Spekman, 1994). In particular, the results suggest that trust and commitment in alliance relationships are a critical component in determining the level of hostility and mistrust.

Table 12.9 Regression Analysis

DEPENDENT MEASURES	Y1	Y2	Y3	Y4	Y5	Y6	Y7	Y8	Y9	Y10	Y11	Y12	Y13	Y14
Þ1	0.041	0.298	−0.010	0.186	0.370	0.144	0.051	−0.236	−0.436	−0.382	−0.042	0.011	0.104	0.014
Þ2	0.139	0.030	0.015	0.052	0.100	−0.043	−0.046	0.018	−0.033	0.037	0.070	−0.057	−0.037	−0.205
Þ3	0.115	0.087	−0.084	0.072	0.064	0.023	−0.095	−0.081	−0.080	−0.131	0.160	0.228	0.055	0.042
Þ4	−0.130	−0.034	−0.063	−0.095	−0.066	0.041	−0.103	0.057	−0.136	−0.013	0.035	−0.006	−0.004	0.130
Þ5	−0.275	−0.363	0.022	−0.269	−0.334	−0.094	−0.063	−0.190	0.295	0.203	0.389	0.257	0.016	−0.026
Þ6	−0.096	0.063	0.118	0.004	−0.122	0.001	−0.193	−0.247	0.240	0.163	0.066	0.272	0.279	0.235
Þ7	−0.125	−0.052	0.070	0.048	−0.387	0.004	−0.032	−0.029	0.176	0.171	−0.014	0.172	0.87	−0.042
Þ8	−0.553	−0.430	−0.062	−0.511	−0.375	−0.183	−0.261	0.440	−0.055	−0.112	−0.280	−0.159	0.429	−0.082
Þ9	0.057	0.019	−0.192	−0.184	−0.023	−0.218	−0.063	0.095	−0.237	0.010	0.083	−0.131	0.062	0.068
Þ10	0.134	−0.057	−0.042	−0.003	0.044	−0.120	−0.235	−0.092	−0.098	−0.125	−0.175	−0.088	0.022	−0.020
Þ11	0.140	0.021	−010	0.222	0.169	0.010	0.249	0.140	−0.089	0.170	−0.043	0.018	−0.180	0.045
Adjusted R^2	0.386	0.280	−0.040	0.665	0.265	0.035	0.502	0.065	0.111	0.082	0.033	0.053	0.356	0.029
F Statistic	0.000	0.000	0.819	0.000	0.000	0.000	0.0019	0.081	0.015	0.046	0.209	0.119	0.000	0.233

The overall findings also show support for Proposition 2. Partnership attributes are shown to be strong predictors of distrust, conflicting goals, and cultural misunderstandings within international alliances. These findings support the view that conflicts can arise over just about anything from differences in management style, culture, and communication to misunderstandings in operational practices (Devlin & Bleackley, 1988; Jain, 1987; Killing 1983). The results also indicate that international alliances avoid or smooth over the issue of resolving conflicts. This may have been due to the cultural differences between the UK firms and their partners. Peterson and Shimada (1978) found cultural differences to be the most difficult problem in managing alliances. The regression analysis further indicated that alliances less likely to share information with their partner and keep each other informed about changing needs and activities have results in greater misunderstandings.

There is also ample support for Proposition 3. In alliances where conflicts are resolved through joint problem solving, the integration of activities, commitment, trust, and communication is expected to be higher. Similarly, the findings show negative coefficients for other conflict resolution mechanisms that may be utilized such as avoiding the issue, smoothing over things, the level of arbitration, and persuasion. These findings are consistent with previous research that reports that strategic alliances are encouraged to engage in joint problem solving so that they are able to manage the uncertain environment that they are faced with (Das & Kumar, 2011; Lane & Beamish, 1990; Lin & Germain, 1998; Xie et al., 1998). Similarly, previous research has also indicated that partners very often attempt to persuade each other to adopt particular solutions to the conflict situation, which appear to be more constructive than the use of coercion or domination (Deutsch, 1969). Domination or coercion is seen as being counterproductive and likely to strain the fabric of the strategic alliance. Other conflict resolution techniques such as smoothing over or ignoring and avoiding the issue are somewhat at odds with the norms and values advocated in more successful strategic alliances. Such techniques do not fit in with alliances in which the problems of one party become the problems affecting both. More recently, Weiss and Hughes (2005) proposed that to effectively resolve conflict, companies need to devise and implement strategies around a common method that integrates conflict resolution on day-to-day basis.

In light of the above findings, managers of international alliances need to be aware of the potential existence of conflict and the need to minimize cultural misunderstandings through building trust, commitment, and communication. It is also important for managers to keep in check the level of conflict within the alliance relationship by understanding the basis of where and why conflicting situations arise. Only then can managers decide on the optimum way of minimizing conflicting situations as they arise.

DISCUSSION

The findings of this study have demonstrated that the presence of partnership attributes are associated with the level, degree, and type of conflict and that relationship dynamics play an important role in how these disputes are settled. This suggests that conflicting situations between international alliances are commonplace and not unique to any particular form of alliance relationship. They are a consequence of business relationships that extend across geographical and cultural boundaries.

The results of this study highlight three main points: first, conflict and cooperation coexist. Although relationships between different organizations require a great deal of cooperative effort, the relationship is also an arena for misunderstandings between partners, so conflicting situations are inherent characteristic in international partnerships (Child & Faulkner, 1998; Jain, 1987) because each party's relationship is characterized by competitive and joint efforts. Second, these disputes between partners can arise over just about anything, ranging from cultural misunderstandings to incompatibility in goals, capabilities, and reporting and communication processes. So conflicts can arise because members of each organization often fail to see what they have in common with their perspective partners. Partners within a strategic alliance relationship have a drive for both autonomy and cooperation, which results in the coexistence of cooperative and conflictual motives within the alliance (Aldrich, 1979). Third, the optimum way to resolve any conflicting situation is to utilize a method that will have a positive impact on developing the relationship. Given the inherent nature of conflicting situations in partnerships, attempting to resolve them through joint problem solving can help build trust, commitment, and communication.

The presence of conflict thus appears to give rise to distrust and a lack of communication and reduces the level of commitment and integration of activities in international alliances. This suggests that while conflicts are likely to result in misunderstandings and distrust, which leads to reduced cooperation and commitment, attempting to resolve them through joint problem solving helps build trust, commitment, and communication. Thus, these analyses indicate that commitment and trust play a strong part in the level of conflicts in partnerships. These strong, consistent findings for commitment and trust as a predictor of conflict for international alliances are similar to other findings (Anderson & Narus, 1990; Anderson & Weitz, 1989; Beamish, 1987; Das & Kumar, 2009; Kumar et al., 1995; Mohr & Spekman, 1994; Monckza et al., 1998; Morgan & Hunt, 1994; Noordewier, John, & Nevin, 1990).

There are a number of limitations to this study. First, given the lack of any documented official sources available on international alliances, the study relied on secondary data from press articles to identify the number of alliances for the later stage of the research. Thus there is likely to be a bias in the data as only well-known firms and alliance activities are likely to be reported in the press. However, the approach adopted is considered to be feasible, and there is a well-established precedent for researchers to compile their own database in this way (Ghemawat, Porter, & Rawlinson, 1986; Glaister & Buckley, 1994; Hergert & Morris, 1988). Second, data were collected from the perspective of the UK partners engaged in international alliances and therefore it does not capture the cooperative and conflicting nature of both partners. Thus, further research is encouraged to utilize dyadic responses from both partners in order to better understand the relationship between partnership attributes and conflict from the perspective of both firms. Third, despite the importance of these findings, knowledge concerning conflict with international alliances is at an early stage. While the concepts used in this study are highly reliable and show validity, it is not possible to capture all the complexities of the attributes studied when measuring these variables. Therefore, future research is encouraged to improve on the definitions of concepts and their operationalizations and to explore the many complexities inherent in managing international partnerships.

CONCLUSIONS AND IMPLICATIONS

The chapter has highlighted the importance of a number of partnership attributes and the presence of conflict in the management of interorganizational relationships. This study represents the first systematic collection of data assessing the relationship between partnership attributes and the management of conflict within partnerships. The findings show that conflicts are commonplace within international alliances and that, to some degree, all types of relationships are characterized by a mixture of conflict and cooperation. To minimize conflicting situations, managers in both parties should aim to identify and agree on how to coordinate and adapt the activities that are particularly critical to the relationship. This requires both parties to become closely involved in their activities. Thus, partners should be in complete agreement about the purpose of the alliance and the process by which its goals can be achieved. This will require the different functional groups of both parties to work together toward achieving goals and objectives. This will also encourage a higher level of interaction between managers as well as heighten a regular exchange of ideas between partners and thus minimize the number of conflicts.

Owing to the mutual interdependencies of the companies, conflicts may also be minimized through relying on each other for mutual support and cooperation. This means that managers must realize that each firm needs the other to provide information and resources to complete their work and so must be aware of the connections between its own activities and those of its own. In addition to helping guide mutually dependent partners to coordinate their alliance activities, managers can also assist in the development of mutual trust and commitment to the relationship. The results of this study have suggested that building trust and commitment is essential in handling both cooperative and conflicting situations.

While this study has indicated that conflicts are characteristic of international alliances that exhibit lower levels of coordination, trust, commitment, and communication, it has been readily acknowledged that disagreements are inevitable in every alliance relationship. Each firm has its own agenda and goals for the alliance, which can result in conflicting goals. Further, differences between cultures of partners can lead to cultural misunderstandings. It is suggested that partners work jointly together to develop mediating mechanisms to defuse and settle their differences. Firms can train their personnel to be sensitive to each other's problems and deal with these problems through using joint problem solving techniques.

In this way problems may be discussed to develop mutually acceptable solutions. Helping to blend in the different cultures of the partners will help to phase in the relationship between the partners.

REFERENCES

Aldrich, H. E. (1979). *Organizations and environments.* Englewood Cliffs, NJ: Prentice Hall.

Anderson, J. C., & Narus, J. A. (1984). A model of the distributor's perspective of the distribution -manufacturer firm working relationships. *Journal of Marketing.* *48*(4), 62–74.

Anderson, J. C., & Narus, J. A. (1990). A model of distributor firm and manufacturer firm working partnerships. *Journal of Marketing, 54*(1), 42–58.

Anderson, J. C., & Narus, J. A. (1991). Partnering as a focused marketing strategy. *California Management Review, 33*(3), 95–113.

Anderson, E., & Weitz, B. (1989). Determinants of continuity in conventional industrial channel dyads. *Marketing Science, 8*(4), 310–323.

Assael, H. (1969). Constructive role of organizational conflict. *Administrative Science Quarterly, 14,* 573–582.

Aulakh, P. S., Kotabe, M., & Sahay, A. (1996). Trust and performance in cross-border marketing partnerships: A behavioral approach. *Journal of International Business Studies, 27,* 1005–1032.

Beamish, P. W. (1987). Joint ventures in LDCs: Partner selection and performance. *Management International Review, 27*(1), 23–37.

Beamish, P. W., & Banks, J. C. (1987). Equity joint ventures and the theory of the multinational enterprise. *Journal of International Business Studies, 18,* 1–16.

Bleeke, J., & Ernst, D. (1991). The way to win in cross border alliances. *Harvard Business Review, 69*(6), 127–135.

Blodgett, L. L. (1991). Towards a resource-based theory of bargaining power in international joint ventures. *Journal of Global Marketing, 5*(1/2), 35–54.

Borys, B., & Jemison, D. B. (1989). Hybrid arrangements as strategic alliances: Theoretical issues in organizational combinations. *Academy of Management Review, 14*, 234–249.

Buckley, P. J., & Casson, M. C. (1988). A theory of cooperation in international business. In F. J. Contractor & P. Lorange (Eds.), *Cooperative strategies in international business* (pp. 31–53). Lexington, MA: Lexington Books.

Child, J., & Faulkner, D. (1998). *Strategies of cooperation: Managing alliances, networks and joint ventures.* Oxford, UK: Oxford University Press.

Contractor, F. J., & Lorange, P. (1988). Why should firms co-operate? The strategy and economics basis for cooperative ventures. In F. J. Contractor & P. Lorange (Eds.), *Cooperative strategies in international business* (pp. 3–20). Lexington, MA: Lexington Books.

Churchill, G. A. (1979). A paradigm for developing better measures of marketing constructs. *Journal of Marketing Research, 16*(2), 64–73.

Daft, R., & Lengel, R. (1986). Organizational information requirements, media richness and structural design. *Management Science, 32*(5), 554–571.

Dang, T. (1977). *Ownership, control and performance of the multinational corporation: A study of US wholly-owned subsidiaries and joint ventures in the Philippines and Taiwan.* Unpublished doctoral dissertation, University of California, Los Angeles, CA.

Das, T. K., & Kumar, R. (2009). Interpartner harmony in strategic alliances: Managing commitment and forbearance. *International Journal of Strategic Business Alliances, 1*, 24–52.

Das, T. K., & Kumar, R. (2011). Interpartner negotiations in alliances: A strategic framework. *Management Decision, 49*, 1235–1256.

Das, T. K., & Teng, B. (1998). Between trust and control: Developing confidence in partner cooperation in alliances. *Academy of Management Review, 23*, 491–512.

Das, T. K., & Teng, B. (2000). Instabilities of strategic alliances: An internal tensions perspective. *Organization Science, 11*, 77–101.

Deutsch, M. (1969). Conflicts: productive or destructive. *Journal of Social Issues, 25*(1), 7–41.

Devlin, G., & Bleackley, M. (1988). Strategic alliances-guidelines for success. *Long Range Planning, 21*(5), 18–23.

Ding, D. Z. (1997). Control, conflict, and performance: A study of U.S.–Chinese joint ventures. *Journal of International Marketing, 5*(3), 31–45.

Doz, Y. L., & Hamel, G. (1998). *The art of creating value through partnering.* Boston, MA: Harvard Business School Press.

Fey, C. F., & Beamish, P. W. (1999). Strategies for managing Russian international joint venture conflict. *European Management Journal, 17*(1), 99–105.

Fey, C. F., & Beamish, P. W. (2000). Joint venture conflict: The case of Russian joint ventures. *International Business Review, 9,* 139–162.

Friedman, W. G., & Beguin, J. P. (1971). *Joint international business ventures in developing countries.* New York, NY: Columbia University Press.

Geringer, J. M. (1993). Ownership and control in East-West joint ventures, In R. Culpan (Ed.), *Multinational strategic alliances* (pp. 203–218). New York, NY: International Business Press.

Geringer, J. M., & Hebert, L. (1989). Control and performance of international joint ventures. *Journal of International Business Studies, 20,* 235–254.

Geringer, J. M., & Hebert, L. (1991). Measuring performance of international joint ventures. *Journal of International Business Studies, 22,* 249–263.

Geyskens, J., Steenkamp, J. E. M., Scheer, L. K., & Kumar, N. (1996). The effects of trust and interdependence on relationship commitment: A transatlantic study. *International Journal of Research Marketing, 13,* 303–317.

Ghemawat, P., Porter, M., & Rawlinson R.A. (1986). Patterns in international coalition activity. In M. E. Porter (Ed.), *Competition in global industries* (pp. 345–366). Boston, MA: Harvard University Press.

Gill, J., & Butler, R. J. (2003). Managing instability in cross-cultural alliances. *Long Range Planning, 36,* 543–563.

Glaister, K. W., & Buckley, P. J. (1994). UK international joint ventures: An analysis of patterns of activity and distribution. *British Journal of Management, 5,* 35–51.

Glaister, K. W., & Wu, W. (1994). Management and performance of UK joint ventures in China. *Journal of Euromarketing, 4*(1), 23–43.

Gulati, R., & Singh, H. (1998). The architecture of cooperation: managing coordination costs and appropriation concerns in strategic alliances. *Administrative Science Quarterly, 43,* 781–814.

Habib, G. M. (1983). *Conflict measurement in the distribution channel of joint ventures: An empirical investigation.* Unpublished doctoral dissertation, Texas Tech University, Lubbock, TX.

Habib, G. M. (1987). Measures of manifest conflict in international joint ventures. *Academy of Management Journal, 30,* 808–816.

Hagedoorn, J. (1993). Understanding the rationale of strategic technology partnering: Inter organizational modes of cooperation and sectoral differences. *Strategic Management Journal, 14,* 371–385.

Hambrick, D., Li, J., Xin, K., & Tsui, A. (2001). Compositional gaps and downward spirals in international joint venture management groups. *Strategic Management Journal, 22,* 1033–1053.

Harrigan, K. R. (1988). Joint ventures and competitive strategy. *Strategic Management Journal, 9,* 141–158.

Hennart, J.-F. (1988). A transaction costs theory of equity joint ventures. *Strategic Management Journal, 9,* 361–374.

Hergert, M., & Morris, D. (1988). Trends in international collaborative agreements, In F. J. Contractor & P. Lorange (Eds.), *Cooperative strategies in international business* (pp. 99–109). Lexington, MA: Lexington Books.

Holm, D. B., Eriksson, K., & Johanson, J. (1999). Creating value through mutual commitment to business network relationships. *Strategic Management Journal, 20,* 467–486.

Hoon-Halbauer, S. K. (1999). Managing relationships within Sino-foreign joint ventures. *Journal of World Business, 34,* 344–371.

Hu, M., & Chen, H. (1996). An empirical analysis of factors explaining foreign joint performance in China. *Journal of Business Research, 35,* 165–173.

Huber, G., & Daft, R. (1987). The information environment of organizations. In F. M. Jablin, L. L. Putnam, K. H. Roberts, & L. W. Porter (Eds.), *Handbook of organizational communication* (pp. 130–164). Newbury Park, CA: Sage Publications.

Jain, C. S. (1987). Perspectives on international marketing strategic alliances. *Advances in International Marketing, 2,* 3–20.

Johnson, J. (1999). Multiple commitments and conflicting loyalties in international joint venture management teams. *International Journal of Organizational Analysis, 7,* 54–71.

Johnson, J., Cullen, J., Sakano, T., & Bronson, J. (2001). Drivers and outcomes of parent company intervention in IJV management: A cross-cultural comparison. *Journal of Business Research, 52,* 35–49.

Kale, P., Singh, H., & Perlmutter, H. (2000). Learning and protection of proprietary assets in strategic alliances: Building relational capital. *Strategic Management Journal, 21,* 217–237.

Kauser, S. (2007). Alliance relationship dynamics: Conflict, structure and control. *Journal of Euromarketing, 16*(3), 5–25.

Kauser, S., & Shaw, V. (2004). The influence of behavioral and organizational characteristics on the success of international strategic alliances. *International Marketing Review, 2*(1), 17–52.

Khanna, T., Gulati, R., & Nohria, N. (1998). The dynamics of learning alliances: Competition, cooperation and relative scope. *Strategic Management Journal, 19,* 193–210.

Killing, J. P. (1983). *Strategies for joint venture success,* New York, NY: Praeger.

Kogut, B. (1988). Joint ventures: Theoretical and empirical perspectives. *Strategic Management Journal, 9,* 319–332.

Kozan, M. K. (1997). Culture and conflict management: A theoretical framework. *International Journal of Conflict Management, 8,* 338–360.

Kumar, N., Scheer, L. K. & Steenkamp, J. E. M. (1995). The effects of perceived interdependence on dealer attitudes. *Journal of Marketing Research, 32*(3), 348–356.

Kumar, R., & Nti, K. O. (1998). Differential learning and interaction in alliance dynamics: A process and outcome discrepancy model. *Organization Science, 9*(3), 356–367.

Lane, H. W., & Beamish, P. W. (1990). Cross-cultural cooperative behavior in joint ventures in LDCs. *International Management Review, 30*(Special Issue), 87–102.

Lee, D. Y. (2001). Power, conflict and satisfaction in IJV supplier—Chinese distributor channels. *Journal of Business Research, 52*(2), 149–160.

Leung, K., Koch, P. T., & Lu, L. (2002). A dualistic model of harmony and its implications for conflict management in Asia. *Asia Pacific Journal of Management, 19,* 201–220.

Lewis. J. D. (1990). *Partnerships for profit: Structuring and managing strategic alliances*. New York, NY: Free Press.

Lin, X., & Germain, R. (1998). Sustaining satisfactory joint venture relationships: The role of conflict resolution strategy. *Journal of International Business Studies, 29*, 179–196.

Madhok, A. (1995). Opportunism and trust in joint venture relationships: An exploratory study and a model. *Scandinavian Journal of Management, 11*, 57–74.

Mohr, J., & Spekman, R. (1994). Characteristics of partnership success: Partnership attributes communication behavior and conflict resolution techniques. *Strategic Management Journal, 15*, 135–152.

Mohr, J., & Nevin, J. R. (1990). Communication strategies in marketing channels: A theoretical perspective. *Journal of Marketing, 54*(4), 36–51.

Monckza, R. M., Peterson, K. T., Handfield, R. B., & Ragatz, G. L. (1998). Success factors in strategic supplier alliances: The buying company perspective. *Decision Sciences, 29*, 553–576.

Morgan, R. M., & Hunt, S. D. (1994). The commitment trust theory of relationship marketing. *Journal of Marketing, 58*(3), 20–38.

Mowday, R. T., Steers, R. M., & Porter, L. W. (1979). The measurement of organizational commitment. *Journal of Vocational Behavior, 14*, 224–227.

Nti, K. O., & Kumar, R. (2000). Differential learning in alliances. In D. O. Faulkner & M. de Rond (Eds.), *Cooperative strategy: Economic, business and organizational issues* (pp. 119–150). Oxford, UK: Oxford University Press.

Nunnally, J. C. (1978). *Psychometric theory*. New York, NY: McGraw Hill.

Noordeweir, T. G., John, G., & Nevin, J. R. (1990). Performance outcomes of purchasing arrangements in industrial buyer-vendor relationships. *Journal of Marketing, 54*(4), 80–93.

Olson, L. B., & Singsuwan, K. (1997). The effect of partnership, communication, and conflict resolution behaviors on performance success of strategic alliances: American and Thai perspectives. In P. W. Beamish & J. P. Killing (Eds.), *Cooperative strategies: Asian Pacific perspectives* (pp. 245–267). San Francisco, CA: New Lexington Press.

Park, S. O., & Ungson, G. R. (2001). Interfirm rivalry and managerial complexity: A conceptual framework of alliance failure. *Organization Science, 12*, 37–53.

Parkhe, A. (1993). Messy research, methodological predispositions and theory development in international joint ventures. *Academy of Management Review, 18,* 227–268.

Peterson, R. B., & Shimada, J. Y. (1978). Sources of management problems in Japanese-American joint ventures. *Academy of Management Review, 3,* 796–804.

Porter, L. W., Steers, R. M., Mowday, R. T., & Boulian, P. V. (1974). Organizational commitment, job satisfaction and turnover among psychiatric technicians. *Journal of Applied Psychology, 59,* 603–609.

Randall, D. M. (1990). The consequences of organizational commitments: Methodological investigation. *Journal of Organizational Behavior, 11,* 361–378.

Schaan, J. C. (1983). *Parent control and joint venture success: The case of Mexico.* Unpublished doctoral dissertation, University of Western Ontario, London, Ontario, Canada.

Simiar, F. (1984). Major causes of joint venture failures in the Middle East: The case of Iran. *Management International Review, 23*(3), 58–68.

Tomlinson, J. W .C. (1970). *The joint venture process in international business: India and Pakistan.* Cambridge, MA: M.I.T. Press.

Van de Ven, A. H., & Walker, G. (1984). The dynamics of interorganizational coordination. *Administrative Science Quarterly, 29,* 598–621.

Weiss, J. & Hughes, J. (2005). Want collaboration? Accept—and actively manage—conflict. *Harvard Business Review, 83*(3), 93–101.

Wright, R. W. (1979). Joint venture problems in Japan. *Columbia Journal of World Business, 14*(1), 25–31.

Xie, J., Song, X. M., & Stringfellow, A. (1998). Interfunctional conflict, conflict resolution styles, and new product success: A four-culture comparison. *Management Science, 44*(12), S192–S206.

Yan, A., & Gray, B. (1994). Bargaining power, management control and performance in United States–China joint ventures: A comparative case study. *Academy of Management Journal, 37,* 1478–1517.-°

POST-READING QUESTIONS AND ACTIVITIES

Answer the following questions to help you fully understand the Unit 2 readings:

- Review the key elements of effective intercultural communication. Think of a situation where you have dealt with someone from another culture, while traveling, at school, or at work. What difficulties did you both encounter? How did you negotiate differently with this person? What advantages and disadvantages did each party have?

- Apply the principles-first and applications-first approaches to a work or school situation negotiation that you have encountered. Describe how each would lead to different results, timing, and satisfaction with the parties involved.

- Why is listening effectively so important in cross-cultural situations?

- How does non-verbal communication affect a party's ability to effectively decode information from parties from other cultural backgrounds?

- Develop a two- to three-page outline as a guide for people entering a negotiation with a party from another culture. What should they know, and how do they acquire that information (friends, online research, etc.)? How are the negotiations different over the telephone versus live? How does being in the other party's culture impact your approach? What advantages does it give the "home" party, and how can you counter those?

UNIT 3 OVERVIEW

NEGOTIATIONS IN BUSINESS AND ORGANIZATIONAL SETTINGS

Unit 3 analyzes one specific application of business and organizational setting negotiations. The most important negotiation that you will have in your business and organizational career will involve negotiating for a new position, with the focus on the salary and benefits but also important items such as job duties, responsibilities, and the bandwidth to make your own decisions. These three readings focus on guiding you to be more effective in your salary and job negotiations. These skills can also be applied by those who want to negotiate a better salary or different job responsibilities internally at their organizations.

Some of the key concepts in this unit include:

- How a company views the salary and job negotiation process
- Suggestions for negotiating a job change when transferring organizations
- Salary negotiation tips for a first career position negotiation—typically after college

In Chapter 13, Brian Tracy looks at salary and job negotiations from the company's perspective.

Chapter 13

Negotiate the Right Salary

by Brian Tracy

Money is a very emotional issue for most people. The way you determine what you are going to pay the chosen candidate and the benefits you are going to offer sets the stage for discussions and decisions about remuneration for the months and years ahead. You must handle this issue with care.

Here is a good rule to follow with regard to salary, bonuses, and other forms of income: "Good people are free."

Good people are *free* in that they contribute more in dollar value than you pay them in salary and bonuses. Every good person that you add to your payroll increases your bottom line. The profitability of your company is largely determined by your ability to attract and keep good people who put in more than they take out. For this reason, the amount you pay should largely be determined by the potential contribution of the employee, not some arbitrary rules in the marketplace or in your industry.

The fact is that today you have to pay talented people whatever it takes to hire them in comparison with what they could get working somewhere else. At the same time, you are buying a service for your company and you are duty bound to purchase this quantity and quality of service at the very best price. Therefore, the better prepared you are for a salary negotiation, the better deal you will make.

First, do your homework. Ask around to determine what the job is worth in the current market. Phone personnel or placement agencies and find out how much it

Brian Tracy, Selection from "Negotiate the Right Salary," *Hire and Keep the Best People: 21 Practical and Proven Techniques You Can Use Immediately*, pp. 59-63. Copyright © 2001 by Berrett-Koehler Publishers. Reprinted with permission.

would cost to hire a person with this particular level of skill. Read the want ads in the newspaper. Consider how much you are currently paying to people in similar positions.

Second, think through and determine how much you can afford to pay for someone in this position. But remember that whatever the market is paying is the *minimum* that you will have to pay as well. People may not be motivated solely by money, but money is a key consideration when it comes to taking a job. People will not accept less from one company than they can get from another for the same job.

If you are hiring someone away from another company, you will have to pay at least 10 percent more than he or she is currently receiving. Ten percent seems to be the psychological point at which people will consider moving from one company to another. This is especially true for younger workers with shallow loyalties to their current employers.

If you are unsure about how much to offer, ask the candidate, "What sort of salary or remuneration are you looking for?" or "What do you feel this position is worth?" Listen carefully to the answer. Neither agree nor disagree. Simply ask, "How did you arrive at that amount?" And listen again.

You can also ask, "How much money would you have to make to feel comfortable in this job?" Most people have two numbers in mind when they are negotiating compensation. The first is the amount that they would ideally *like* to make, which is usually far above what they've ever made before. The other, more accurate, number is the amount that they actually expect to make, the amount that they would be satisfied with. Your job is to discover the second number.

An important part of the total pay package is the range of benefits you are offering as part of the job. An attractive medical insurance package can be more valuable to a person with a family than a higher salary. Flexible work hours, a company car, or generous vacation periods can offset a lower starting wage. Be sure to emphasize these points in your negotiation.

If possible, start the person at a lower wage than she requests, but agree to increase her salary within ninety days if she does a great job. Specify that this first ninety days will be her probation or trial period.

At the end of ninety days, sit down and review the job to determine how well things are going. At that point, assuming that you both are happy, you will discuss an increase.

None of these suggestions, however, are engraved in stone. Because people and performance can be so varied and unpredictable, every recommendation in this book is subject to revision in the face of new information. For example, I hired a controller once at a salary below what she was asking, with the agreement that we would review it in ninety days. She started on a Monday, and I increased her salary on Tuesday because she was obviously so competent at her job. I never regretted it.

Don't be afraid to pay well for talented people. Remember, you always get what you pay for, especially in today's job market.

ACTION EXERCISES

Review your current salary and compensation structure to be sure that it is in alignment with the existing job market. With the valuable people you already have whom you cannot afford to lose, consider giving them an increase as an insurance policy against their being hired away. Offer them additional benefits, especially if competitors are offering them.

Be open to the possibility that you may have to offer more than you intended to get a qualified person to take the job. Your goal is to pay exactly the right amount and no more. Therefore, do your homework so that you have a clear picture of what the job pays in today's market.

In Chapter 14, Alison Konrad and Nundini Krishnan examine negotiating a job offer when changing positions.

☨ IVEY | Publishing

Chapter 14

Anjali Kumar – Negotiating a Job Offer (A)

by Alison M. Konrad and Nundini Krishnan

Nundini Krishnan wrote this case under the supervision of Alison M. Konrad solely to provide material for class discussion. The authors do not intend to illustrate either effective or ineffective handling of a managerial situation. The authors may have disguised certain names and other identifying information to protect confidentiality.

Richard Ivey School of Business Foundation prohibits any form of reproduction, storage or transmission without its written permission. Reproduction of this material is not covered under authorization by any reproduction rights organization. To order copies or request permission to reproduce materials, contact Ivey Publishing, Richard Ivey School of Business Foundation, The University of Western Ontario, London, Ontario, Canada, N6A 3K7; phone (519) 661-3208; fax (519) 661-3882; e-mail cases@ivey.uwo.ca.

Copyright © 2011, Richard Ivey School of Business Foundation   Version: 2011-12-15

After having returned home from a three-month vacation to Europe, India and Singapore, Anjali Kumar was ready to start looking for a full-time job. She had graduated from the Richard Ivey School of Business (Ivey) HBA program in April 2011, and she was interested in a marketing position. While she had enjoyed her summer job as an assistant brand manager at S.C. Johnson, she wanted

Alison Konrad and Nundini Krishnan, "Anjali Kumar- Negotiating a Job Offer (A)," pp. 1-4. Copyright © 2011 by Ivey Publishing - Richard Ivey School of Business. Reprinted with permission.

to secure a position closer to her home in Toronto. Before she had enrolled in Ivey, Kumar had spent her summer breaks working as an English teacher at a school for underprivileged children in India and as an investment advisor's assistant at one of Canada's largest wealth management firms. During her university years, she had helped other students in her role as an Ivey marketing mentor, an Ivey guru, a communications ambassador for prospective Ivey students and a University of Western Ontario (UWO) synchronized swimming coach. She knew that prospective employers would be attracted to her work experiences, extracurricular activities and her Ivey degree.

In September, Kumar began applying to online job postings and arranging informational meetings with Ivey alumni. During her job search, she saw an online posting for a marketing coordinator at Educational Exploration Tours Canada (EE), a leading international organization for educational student travel programs (see Exhibit 1). As a travel enthusiast with a long-standing passion for improving student education, Kumar was very excited about the position.

Five weeks after submitting her application, Kumar received a phone call from EE to set up a telephone interview. Later that week, a human resources (HR) representative conducted a 40-minute telephone interview with Kumar, during which she answered several behavioral questions regarding her past work experiences and extracurricular activities (see Exhibit 2). Although Kumar had prepared for the interview, she felt that her answers to a few unanticipated questions were not very strong. She hung up the phone feeling disappointed with her interview performance. She did not have high expectations for moving to the next round of interviews.

Kumar was surprised to receive a call a few days later, inviting her to a second-round interview at the EE office. A marketing manager, who would be the direct supervisor to the marketing coordinator, conducted the 45-minute interview. Similar to the telephone interview, Kumar answered behavioral questions that highlighted her strengths and experiences that were relevant to the marketing coordinator position. She left the interview feeling confident that she would be moving on to the final round of interviews.

Sure enough, Kumar was called for the final step of the EE interview process. This last stage of interviews was a two-hour process, in which she met, one at a time, with five EE employees: the marketing manager with whom she had previously met, a marketing analyst, the senior HR manager, the creative director and the VP marketing for EE. Kumar was asked a series of behavioral and technical questions about marketing analytics and advertising.

Kumar asked the interviewers her own set of questions regarding the marketing coordinator position, the culture at EE, the organization's goals for the future and her growth opportunities within the company. She was satisfied with all of the answers given by the interviewers except those related to her growth potential within the company. The HR manager, Suzy McKinlay, compared Kumar's potential growth path to a "spiral staircase," stating that EE offered many growth opportunities, but had no set path to the top of the organization.

Kumar tried to elicit a more specific response from McKinlay by asking for examples of roles that she could move toward in the future. McKinlay provided a vague answer, reiterating the abundance of opportunities within EE and the lack of a ladder-like organizational structure. Although Kumar was unclear of her growth path within EE, she knew that EE Canada had doubled its workforce in the last two years and that the international education market was growing. She was still excited about the opportunity and, after her final round of interviews, left the office with hope that she would be offered the position.

At 5:30 p.m. the next day, Kumar received a call from McKinlay, offering her the marketing coordinator position. Kumar was very happy to receive the job offer and listened carefully as McKinlay reviewed the key details of the offer, including the salary, benefits and starting date. While the benefits and three-week vacation period were very attractive, the starting salary of $37,500 was lower than what Kumar had expected. EE's salary scale was not competitive with the other four companies that would be interviewing Kumar. Because EE's offer was her first full-time job offer, Kumar felt she needed to read through the full contract and consult her mentors before making a decision. Kumar thanked McKinlay, telling her she would be in touch very soon.

After waiting all day to receive a copy of the offer, Kumar received a call at the end of the day from McKinlay, who confirmed that the offer had been emailed to her. Feeling unsatisfied with the clarity of her growth potential within the organization, Kumar took this opportunity to again approach the subject. She asked McKinlay a few more questions about growth opportunities at EE, including questions regarding future salary growth (see Exhibit 4). Unfortunately, the HR manager was unable to answer most of her questions, leaving Kumar feeling uncomfortable. McKinlay blamed EE's "spiral staircase" progression and salary structure, or lack thereof, as the reason for her vague responses.

McKinlay then asked whether the salary was an important factor in Kumar's decision because Kumar had asked some questions about it. Kumar's response clarified that the salary was only a part of the career opportunity and that she was looking to gain insight into her future career at EE.

After ending the telephone conversation, Kumar realized she had a decision to make. She could accept EE's job offer, decline it or try to negotiate better terms. EE's job offer was the first one she received, and she had no guarantee she would receive offers from the other employers who were interviewing her.

EXHIBIT 1

JOB DESCRIPTION FOR MARKETING COORDINATOR AT EDUCATIONAL EXPLORATION TOURS CANADA

Company: Educational Exploration Tours Canada
Job Description: Marketing Coordinator
Location: Toronto, ON, Canada

Synopsis
Passionate about travel and marketing? This is your chance to turn your passion for travel and natural abilities into rewards and success in a fun and energetic organization that respects, supports and rewards its team members. Why wait to earn a competitive salary, full benefits, bonuses and incentives, generous vacation time, and travel advantages? Make a smart career investment with Educational Exploration.

The Role
As a result of the continued growth of the student educational travel industry, we are expanding our Marketing Team to include a Marketing Coordinator.

We are looking for an ambitious, organized and results-driven marketing professional who will collaborate on a number of integrated marketing projects within the EE Tours Marketing Team. This person will work closely with the Marketing Manager and the creative team to create and execute unique campaigns including, but not limited to direct marketing and new season offerings. The ideal candidate has experience as a project manager, has a great entrepreneurial spirit and is an expert in multi-tasking. You are energetic, flexible, and a team player with a solid understanding of marketing concepts. Travel experience is a plus!

The Marketing Coordinator will be responsible for the development and execution of integrated marketing campaigns. Responsibilities include:

- Develop, project manage and execute Integrated Marketing Campaigns.
- Implement campaigns on all channels (direct mail, email, web).
- Report results at a campaign level and provide ad-hoc analysis.
- Coordinate maintenance of existing collateral—manage production of several booklets.
- Work closely with Marketing Manager to develop effective communication plan for key audience.
- Act as a liaison between customer service team and marketing team.
- Ensure brand consistency as per IMC and brand document.
- Support Marketing Manager on ad-hoc projects.
- Report to Marketing Manager.

Requirements
Educational Exploration Tours is most interested in individuals who possess:

- Bachelor's degree, Marketing major or BBA preferred
- 1-2 years of work experience in marketing in agency or client side
- Solid understanding of marketing concepts
- Experience in project management and demonstrated knowledge of project management tools
- Strong attention to detail and ability to multi-task
- Exceptional communication skills
- Bilingual (English/French) an asset
- Passion for travel an asset

EXHIBIT 2

BEHAVIORAL INTERVIEW QUESTIONS ASKED BY EDUCATIONAL EXPLORATION TOURS CANADA

- What do you know about Educational Exploration?
- What kind of projects did you work on at S.C. Johnson?
- How would you describe your personality?
- What have you been doing since you graduated?
- Can you tell me about some of your travel experiences?
- Tell me about a time where you did everything you could in order to make something happen.
- Tell me about a time when you had to manage several projects simultaneously and how you managed your time.
- Tell me about a time when you had to inspire a team of people.
- Tell me about a difficult decision you had to make. What was the decision-making process you used?
- Describe an analysis you worked on.
- Tell me about a time when you had to work with a difficult team member or coworker. What did you do?
- Tell me about a time when something that you recommended was implemented.
- What motivates you?
- What do you do in your spare time?

EXHIBIT 3

QUESTIONS ASKED BY ANJALI KUMAR AT THE FINAL ROUND OF JOB INTERVIEWS

- What excites you about EE?
- How long have you been with EE and why did you decide to join EE?
- Is it common for employees to do a cross-functional placement (e.g., to take on a sales position for a year to gain a diverse experience)?

- For someone coming into a marketing coordinator position, where do you see my growth opportunities within the organization?
- How much travel will be involved in this position?
- Where do you see growth opportunities for EE within the international education industry?

EXHIBIT 4

QUESTIONS ASKED BY ANJALI KUMAR AFTER THE JOB OFFER WAS EXTENDED

- In terms of the workload for a marketing coordinator, what is EE's expectation on the number of hours worked per week on average?
- In terms of progression from the marketing coordinator role, what would be the next step for me? And what would be the range for salaries for that next step?
- How long would an average employee work in a marketing coordinator position before moving on to another position?
- In terms of salary review each year, is it typical for EE employees to receive a salary raise after their first year and if yes, what would the range be for that increase?

In Chapter 15, Ryan Gower and Michael Mulvaney focus on salary negotiations—with the latter concentrating on approaching a first full-time job situation.

Chapter 15

Negotiating the Salary

by Ryan K.Gower and Michael A. Mulvaney

OVERVIEW

Very few students are afforded the luxury of negotiating a starting salary for their student internship. In fact, a significant percentage of student internships are unpaid or paid as a stipend or at a low hourly wage. At this stage in the semester, however, you have likely secured your internship placement and are rightfully thinking about the next stage in your professional career—full-time employment. Many young professionals are beginning to feel more confident in their interviewing skills, but many, due to their personality, are terrified at the prospect of negotiating their starting salary once the offer has been advanced (Divita, 1994). Although the process of salary negotiation can be uncomfortable for certain people, there are some basic steps you can follow to feel more confident in this trying stage of securing employment. And with current research showing a significant increase in starting salary for those who negotiate effectively, it is a topic soon-to-be college graduates should familiarize themselves with (Marks & Harold, 2011; O'Shea & Bush, 2002). Some analysts have even suggested that negotiating your initial starting salary could result in over $1 million dollars in additional earning over the course of your career (Rinke, 2009). Recognizing that most employers do not make

Ryan K. Gower and Michael A. Mulvaney, "Negotiating the Salary," *Making the Most of Your Internship*, pp. 215-226. Copyright © 2012 by Sagamore Publishing LLC. Reprinted with permission.

their first offer their "best" offer, there is generally some room to improve the offer if you are bold enough to begin the process. While there may be significantly less leeway in negotiating your salary when you are applying for entry- or junior-level positions, or when you don't have a great deal of experience and specialization, it is important to understand and participate in the process. Although there is significant ambiguity and stress associated with negotiating a starting salary, this chapter will outline several strategies that will help you enter negotiations more relaxed, prepared, and confident .

RECESSIONS COME AND GO

At the time of this writing, the economy is in severe depression. Unemployment is hovering just above 9% and the stock market is on a roller coaster ride. Many people have been laid off, taken on additional responsibilities without compensation, or taken a voluntary pay cut simply to hold on to their job. But the recession will not last forever, and the economy will rebound. Wise managers know that they will have difficulty holding on to valuable employees after the recession ends if they do not fairly negotiate with and compensate their employees (Porter, Conlon, & Barber, 2004).

NEGOTIATION BACKGROUND AND BASICS

The process of preparing to negotiate your salary has become significantly easier in the past decade. Traditionally, many organizations keep employee salaries a tightly held secret, fearing that exposing these figures would lead to distraction in the workplace, reduced morale, and elimination of the company's competitive advantage in the salary negotiation process (Pentilla, 2009). For this reason, some companies have even required employees to sign a nondisclosure agreement that prohibits the employee from sharing salary information with any third party. While nondisclosure agreements are most common in the private sector, public and nonprofit agencies may have salary disclosure rules as well. These rules may require full transparency of employee salaries to the general public or may restrict salary disclosure to board members or oversight committees. Regardless of the sector, it is safe to assume that most employers prefer to keep open discussion of salary ranges at a minimum for fear of creating a negative culture. Equity Theory has clearly demonstrated that when employees sense a lack of equity in their salary, the impact on their attitude and job performance can be significant (Huserman, Hatfield, & Miles, 1987).

This period of secrecy, however, is giving way to a new era of transparency. The advent of salary comparison websites such as Salary.com, SalaryExpert.com, and PayScale.com have given prospective employees access to information that has historically been hard to find, significantly complicating the salary negotiation process. These sites provide access to salary ranges for similar positions in the geographic region or salary ranges among competitors. These sites effectively answer the long asked question of job seekers: "What am I worth?" While the information on these websites has been accused of being dated, inflated, or otherwise distorted, they provide the job seeker with a loose benchmark to reduce the chances of undervaluing their services.

Now that you understand why discussion of salary is a sensitive matter, there are a few other basic facts to keep in mind as you prepare to negotiate your salary. First, most aspects related to salary negotiation are highly variable and will require you to carefully assess your needs, wants, long-term goals, personality type, and the relative strength of your capabilities. Beyond this, you must understand the unique characteristics of the hiring agency. The sector (i.e., public, private, nonprofit), size, organizational culture, and geographic location will all play a role in determining how flexible the organization can be in negotiating your salary. Understanding the dynamic interaction of these personal and organizational variables will help you establish realistic expectations. Second, salary negotiation is not about taking advantage of one party or the other, but rather it is about finding an agreeable work situation for both the employee and the employer (Huller, 2009). The needs and wants of the prospective employee and the hiring agency must be considered, and give and take should be expected. Third, salary negotiation is not always about negotiating salary, as your compensation is much more than your monthly paycheck. Entering the process understanding that everything is negotiable is extremely important. In organizations where salary ranges are highly restricted (many public and nonprofit agencies), you may still be able to negotiate on your commission structure, working hours, vacation time, office location, job title, supervisory responsibilities, travel and training budget, office equipment, benefits packages, a shorter review period, starting date, or other nonmonetary rewards such as laptops or a Blackberry.

Young professionals may wonder when the discussion of salary should take place. … With very few exceptions, you should not discuss salary with a prospective employer until the employment offer has been made (DeLuca & DeLuca, 2007). Inquiring about the salary range prior to the interview or at the conclusion of the interview may send the wrong signal to the employer, many of whom are looking for employees who believe in the "vision and the dream" (Pentilla, 2009). There may be two possible exceptions to this rule. First, while not common in the recreation, sport, and tourism fields, some employers may use a headhunter or recruiting agency to find or screen initial applicants. Such agencies are likely to inquire about your salary expectations in preliminary conversations. You need to be prepared to give a very open salary range when requested, or you may not be included in the final applicant pool. Likewise, some employers very candidly inquire about salary expectations in the very first interview. This means you should probably do some basic research about salaries before you go on your first interview. In the remainder of this chapter, we will give you some basic tools to help you prepare for effective salary negotiations.

NOTE FROM THE AUTHOR

One of the most uncomfortable interview moments of my life came during an interview with Marriott International. As the interview was concluding, the HR manager abruptly closed his folder, looked me in the eye and said, "So, Ryan. What should we pay you for this position?" I froze. I had no idea what to say. I remembered my internship coordinator told me not to talk about money during the interview, but he never told me what to say if they asked me so directly. I stammered around for a moment and finally threw out a number that was a bit higher than what I would have been willing to work for. I never heard back from Marriott International, and I've always wondered if it was because I threw out too high of a number or just wasn't the best candidate for the position.

NEGOTIATION ESSENTIALS

There are a number of excellent books on salary negotiation, and we will not pretend to encompass all the nuances and subtle tactics presented in these works in one short chapter. Instead, we will present five essential practices that will give you a solid start. At the end of the chapter, we will provide a "suggested reading" section referencing several comprehensive resources for job seekers.

NEGOTIATION ESSENTIAL #1: EMBRACE YOUR DISCOMFORT

Research suggests that a number of different variables, including personality and gender, likely influence our comfort level or willingness to engage in negotiations with a prospective employer (Divita, 1994; Wade, 2001). One of the first steps in preparing yourself for this process is to embrace and welcome the feelings of unease that you may have. Stepping out of your comfort zone will be necessary if you want to be sure you are not underselling your services. While the economy is currently in a downturn, many job seekers feel it is foolish to negotiate the offered salary. Shouldn't you accept any offer and be glad to have it? While it is true that the depressed economy and your relative lack of experience may significantly limit your ability to negotiate large increases, you will certainly not get what you do not ask for. Embrace the discomfort and commit yourself to negotiate anyway.

NEGOTIATION ESSENTIAL #2: KNOW YOUR VALUE

As we have already mentioned, there are a number of resources available to help job seekers get a general idea of what the going rate is for those in similar positions and industries. Referencing sites like Salary.com, PayScale.com, and SalaryExpert.com are a good start. Depending on the agency to which you have applied, salary information for all employees may be public information. Many park districts and other public organizations openly include this information in their annual budget. You should also boldly use any and all members of your professional network. Your peers can give insight on offers they, or their friends, have received. College professors, academic advisors, and career counselors can identify salary ranges that previous graduates have reported. Remember to keep in mind cost of living differences in the figures that your peers and professors share with you. If a friend in Naperville, Illinois, got a starting salary of $38,000 doing something similar to the job you are exploring in Colorado Springs, Colorado, your starting salary is likely to be very different. Colorado Springs is approximately 25% less expensive to live in than Naperville, meaning a comparable starting salary might be $28,000. There are a number of excellent online cost of living calculators available if you do a simple Google search.

A WORD OF CAUTION

Everyone seems to know someone who heard from someone else that a friend of theirs got a starting salary $10,000 higher than your offer. While those people may exist, they are clearly not the norm. That is why everyone is telling you about them. Be sure you maintain realistic expectations.

In the event that these resources don't provide the information you need, a more basic approach may be helpful. Exploring the basic demographic information for the community in which the organization is housed is a good starting point. Websites such as www.census.gov (look for QuickFacts or the Fact Sheet) can provide valuable information about the education and median income level in a particular community.

WHAT'S A FAIR SALARY?

Assume you have applied for and been offered an entry-level position in Champaign, Illinois. You have had no success using salary websites or your professional network to discover a benchmark to use to guide your salary expectations. Visit www.census.gov and search for "Champaign, IL"—be sure to click on the Fact Sheet. Based on what you see here, what might a reasonable starting salary for an entry-level position be in this community?

Tips:

1   Look at the economic data and see if you can find an average income for the community. Do you know the difference between median household income and median family income?

2   Look at the demographic information related to race and gender. As unfortunate as it is, how might these numbers influence your starting salary?

3   Look at the percentage of people holding a bachelor's degree or higher. How might these figures change how you determine your starting salary for an entry-level position?

NEGOTIATION ESSENTIAL #3: KNOW THE SECTORS

In the recreation, sport, and tourism industries there is a great deal of variability in the flexibility employers will have in adjusting your salary. For example, municipal and government jobs have tightly defined salary ranges. Small increases are possible, but you might more effectively negotiate nontraditional rewards or increased job responsibilities that will improve your ability to attain your longer term career goals. Likewise, nonprofit organizations typically have a small budget for payroll, but are frequently willing to accommodate requests for flextime, remote working, and cross-training for career progression and improved marketability. The private sector is highly variable depending on the size and nature of the organization. While they do not have the same pressures as public and nonprofit agencies to keep salaries equitable or low, they frequently have high demand for open positions. Let's face it. If you won't take that job working for the Chicago Cubs at $20,000 per year, hundreds of other people will. In these environments, entry-level positions frequently relate to sales, and you might be best advised to negotiate based on performance. There is a great deal of difference in commission structures, and if you are not familiar with "base plus commission," "residual commission," or "variable commission" now might be the time to do some exploration. If you are entering the sport, event, commercial recreation, or hospitality industries a change in your commission structure can significantly improve the amount of money you take home.

NEGOTIATION ESSENTIAL #4: KNOW YOUR NEEDS

By now you know there is a difference between wants and needs. In a depressed economy, this distinction is all the more important. Although this is Negotiation Essential #4, in all honesty you should not apply for, negotiate for, or accept a position until you have a firm understanding of your personal financial situation. While you may want to direct 5% of your income to savings each month, you need to cover housing, transportation, and other financial obligations. If you haven't already, now is the time to develop a comprehensive personal budget. Knowing your basic needs is fundamental to the next negotiation essential. Remember, there are areas of your personal budget that may need trimming as you transition from having financial support of family to being an independent adult. Eating out three nights a week or giving gifts to all your friends on their birthdays may not be feasible in the early stages of your career.

Microsoft has a fantastic personal budget template available at http://office.microsoft.com/en-us/templates/TC062062791033.aspx?Category-ID=CT101172321033. It likely includes some important categories that you might have forgotten otherwise.

NEGOTIATION ESSENTIAL #5: DETERMINE YOUR RANGE

Several authors and analysts suggest developing three numbers to keep in mind as you prepare to negotiate.

The "no" number. This is the salary level below which you cannot meet your basic living needs. If you have been honest and comprehensive in your approach to Negotiation Essential #4, you will know exactly what this number is. Emotions and stress could cloud your judgment, so be clear on this number from the onset. No matter how badly you need a job or like the culture of the agency, it may not be wise to accept a position that does not enable you to meet your most basic financial obligations. Remember, you don't get many opportunities to negotiate over the course of your career, and research suggests that those who are open about their issues and constraints have more success in the negotiation process (Marks & Harold, 2011). If you simply can't accept a lowball offer, be honest with the employer and explain why. What have you got to lose?

The "acceptable" number. This number might actually be a range instead of a hard dollar amount, but should represent the salary at which, based upon what you know of your value, the sector, the community, and your needs, you feel you are being compensated equitably. If the initial offer from the organization falls within this range, you may forgo negotiating salary and instead look for other perks that would enhance the quality of your working experience there.

The "wow" number. This number represents your "dream" offer and is the dollar amount that you should share when asked about your salary expectations. This number should not be a ridiculously unreasonable one and should have some basis in fact, which you can share with the employer. But recognize it for what it is—ideal, but unlikely. Research, however, does suggest that starting with a high, but supported, starting number can in fact pull up counteroffers from the organization (DeLuca & DeLuca, 2007). Be prepared to accept an offer significantly below this number.

NEGOTIATION ESSENTIAL #6: BE HONEST

In the negotiation process, honesty is critical. First, you must be honest with yourself at all times—honest about your level of experience and the value you currently bring to the organization; honest about availability of entry-level positions in your industry and the salaries they bring; honest about the constraints that the current market puts on your employment aspirations; honest about your needs, recognizing the things you want become attainable after you have proven yourself in the workplace.

You must also be honest with the would-be employer. If you have had previous employment, do not inflate your previous salary in hopes of driving up the offer from your would-be employer. A simple phone call to your current or previous employer is all it takes to verify your salary. Dishonesty will only result in a missed opportunity.

We have spent a considerable amount of time discussing the negotiation of your starting salary. It is important to note that all aspects of your employment are negotiable at the time you receive an offer. Have you considered the following:

1. Vacation time?

2. Sick leave?

3. Flextime?

4. Compressed workweek?

5. Parking?

6. Professional development? (i.e., conferences, travel, subscriptions to trade magazines)

7. Commission structure?

8. Electronic resources? (i.e., certain programs to help you be more efficient/effective on the job?)

When it comes to negotiating, everything is on the table. Take your time and be creative. The agency may be highly restricted in what they can do in terms of salary, but may be more than willing to offer other incentives to make their offer even more attractive.

SUMMARY

Salary negotiation is often seen as a distasteful process and may be fraught with dialogue and exchanges that make young professionals uneasy. There are, however, very few opportunities in your career to negotiate your salary, and even modest increases can have a significant impact on your lifetime earnings. While you must carefully prepare and always use your best judgment, salary negotiations need not be the ambiguous or awkward experience that young job seekers fear. Using the information presented in this chapter, you will be well on your way to being sure that you are being compensated fairly for the value you bring to the organization. If you are interested in learning more about this topic (and who shouldn't be?), consider reviewing the following texts:

DeLuca, M., & DeLuca, N. (2007). *Perfect phrases for negotiating salary and job offers.* New York, NY: McGraw-Hill Companies.

Dawson, R. (2006). *Secrets of power salary negotiating: Inside secrets from a master negotiator.* Pompton Plains, NJ: The Career Press, Inc.

CHAPTER [15] ESSENTIALS

- Salary negotiation often makes young professionals uncomfortable. Embrace the discomfort and press ahead.
- While cycles in the economy (and even seasonal cycles in industries) might limit the leeway companies have in negotiating with prospective employees, you will certainly never get what you don't ask for.

- Even modest increases in your entry-level salaries can have a big impact on your lifetime earnings.
- Knowing your value, knowing the industry, knowing the community, and knowing your personal limitations are all critically important if you are to negotiate successfully.

DISCUSSION QUESTIONS

1 Recognizing that the unemployment rate of college graduates is still hovering at an all-time high, what do you think a fair salary range is for someone with your level of education and background? Share this with a trusted practitioner or educator and see what they think.

2 Outside of your salary, what are other things you might negotiate with a prospective employer over? How important are these compared to your salary?

3 In the early stages of your career, there might be things you have to "give up" due to a lack of income. What are some things you have enjoyed as a college student that you might have to give up on, or scale back your consumption of, as you transition to the professional environment?

4 What is the difference between a "want" and a "need"? List your most basic needs. Use these as a baseline for your "no" number.

All Is Fair?

Sandy just completed an interview for a recreation supervisor for a municipal park and recreation department. The interview went well. Sandy connected with staff; she was confident and excited about the responsibilities associated with the position; and she liked the community.

Sandy is optimistic about her chances and was told all interviews would be completed by the end of the week with a final decision being made within the next few weeks.

Three weeks later, Sandy receives a phone call from the recreation director of the municipal park and recreation department. The director informs Sandy that she was selected as the top candidate for the position. The director offers Sandy the position at an annual salary of $41,000 with the city's standard benefits package and a municipal vehicle with gas card to use for travel to and from the various programming sites.

Sandy knows the position announcement stated the salary range would be between $40,000 and $47,000 per year and is dependent upon qualifications. Sandy has one year of part-time supervisory experience, which is near the bottom of expected qualifications listed in the position announcement ("position looking for one to three years supervisory experience"). Sandy was also not expecting the offer to include a municipal vehicle and gas card. As a result, Sandy accepts the position at the $41,000 annual salary level.

Six months later, the other recreation supervisor takes a position with another agency and leaves the department. The recreation director initiates a search process and eventually hires Barbara as the new recreation supervisor. Sandy really likes Barbara and is eager to work together as the two positions share many of the same programming responsibilities.

Shortly after Barbara begins working for the department, Sandy offers to take Barbara out to lunch to celebrate her new position. During lunch, Sandy learns that Barbara followed a very similar career path as Sandy and the two have about the same amount of work experience (i.e., about one year of previous part-time supervisory experience).

When the bill for lunch arrives, Sandy offers to pay for lunch as a way to welcome Barbara and congratulate her for securing the position. Appreciating the gesture, Barbara responds, "That is very nice of you, but Sandy you don't need to do that. A few years ago, when I was constantly pinching pennies to pay bills and rent each month I would have gladly accepted your offer. But, now that I finally got a full-time job, with benefits, a car, gas card, and more than $46,000 per year, I feel uncomfortable accepting your offer. Just you taking time out of your schedule to visit with me and welcome me to the department is more than enough. Thank you!"

While Sandy is flattered by the kind words, she is stunned to learn Barbara is earning more than $5,000 per year than she is. They both share similar responsibilities with similar amounts of previous experience. How did Barbara secure more money?

1　If you were Sandy, what would you do? Would you meet with the recreation director to discuss your concerns? If you did, what do you think would be the recreation director's response?

2　In your opinion, why did Barbara receive a salary that was near the top of the salary range? Why did Sandy receive a salary that was near the bottom of the range? What could Sandy have done to receive a higher salary?

3　Many municipal agencies are required to provide public access to compensation records of their employees. How might this information been helpful to Sandy during her job search and salary negotiation phases?

REFERENCES

Bottos, L., & Coleman, B. (2002). The new salary negotiation. *Compensation and Benefits Review, 34*, 22–28.

DeLuca, M., & DeLuca, N. (2007). *Perfect phrases for negotiating salary and job offers.* New York, NY: McGraw-Hill Companies.

Divita, S. (1994). Why be intimidated by negotiating salary? *Marketing News, 28*, 15.

Huller, K. (2009). *Negotiate, but know your value first.* Pennsylvania CPA Journal, 80,1–2.

Huseman, R., Hatfield, J., & Miles, E. (1987). A new perspective on Equity Theory: The Equity Sensitivity Construct. *Academy of Management Review, 12,* 222–234.

Marks, M., & Harold, C. (2011). Who asks and who receives in salary negotiation. *Journal of Organizational Behavior, 32,* 371–394.

O'Shea, P., & Bush, D. (2002). Negotiation for starting salary: Antecedents and outcomes among recent college graduates. *Journal of Business & Psychology, 16,* 365–382.

Pentilla, C. (2009). The salary secret is out. *Entrepreneur, 37,* 23–26.

Porter, C., Conlon, D., & Barber, A. (2004). The dynamics of salary negotiations: Effects on applicants' justice perceptions and recruitment decisions. *The International Journal of Conflict Management, 15,* 273–303.

Rinke, W. (2009). Negotiate salary; it could mean $1 million. *Sales and Service Excellence, 9,* 14.

Wade, M. (2001). Women and salary negotiation: The costs of self-advocacy. *Psychology of Women Quarterly, 25,* 65–77.

POST-READING QUESTIONS AND ACTIVITIES

Answer the following questions to help you fully understand the Unit 3 readings:

- Outline a plan to hire a person from another company for your current company or an organization that you are familiar with. How do you sell your company and the benefits of working there? How do you determine the salary offer that you will make? How do you anticipate and counter objections that the applicant may have?

- Working off of the example in Chapter 14, develop a list of questions that you would ask during an interview about a prospective company and then when an offer is made to you. Evaluate what benefits, pay structure, work situations, etc. are most valuable to you and your strategies for achieving your goals.

- Review the list of items to consider during an employment negotiation (i.e., vacation time, sick time, flextime) in Chapter 15. Which of these are most important to you, and what else is important to you? If a move to another state or country is required, what would you also want to see in the offer (housing allowance, private schools, intensive language training, trips home, etc.)?

- If you were positioning for an internal job change at your organization, with different responsibilities and an increase in pay, what techniques/strategies would you use from Chapters 13–15 to be most effective in the situation?

UNIT 4 OVERVIEW

EFFECTIVE CONFLICT RESOLUTION

Unit 4 examines effective conflict resolution in a variety of settings. We take the perspective that conflict is not something to be avoided, but rather managed, and is an integral part of any negotiation. Conflict should be anticipated, strategies developed, and issues resolved to the satisfaction of both sides.

Some of the key concepts in this unit include:

- When conflict is beneficial and when it is harmful
- Sources of organization conflict
- Five approaches to managing conflict
- Analyzing value—maximizing outcomes to develop an optimal deal when you are faced with a crisis situation in a business partnership
- Strategies for direct versus indirect confrontation
- Real approaches that have been used in past high-stress hostage siege negotiations

In Chapter 16, Geraldine Hayes discusses how conflict can foster creativity and presents five types of strategies for resolving conflict.

Chapter 16

Strategies for Managing Conflict

by Geraldine Hayes

❚❚ Getting it done" is all about daily workplace interactions. So far in Part Three we've talked about how to communicate your job expectations to your subordinates and how to give subordinates corrective feedback. Continuing our examination of tough communication challenges that you face every day, this chapter looks at conflict. Included are strategies for managing clashes between you and your boss, you and your coworkers, and you and your subordinates.

We'll first distinguish between destructive and constructive conflict; you may be surprised to learn that conflict can benefit you and your company. Then we'll peek behind the curtain to learn why conflict is always such a strong presence, especially in diverse workplaces. Finally, and probably most important to you, we'll show you five strategies for dealing with conflict and explain when each one works best.

Tensions can run high at work. As a manager, you are likely to spend up to 35 percent of your time dealing with complaints and handling disruptions in your fast-paced, diverse work environment.[1] Conflict may range from a simple disagreement over a work procedure to an argument over priorities, to a work stoppage, and even to violence. The incidence of workplace violence continues to increase at an alarming rate. Violence is the number one cause of death on the job for women,

Geraldine Hynes, "Strategies for Managing Conflict," *Get Along, Get It done, Get Ahead: Interpersonal Communication in the Diverse Workplace*, pp. 105-115. Copyright © 2015 by Business Expert Press. Reprinted with permission.

and the number two cause for men. It's a manager's duty to protect workers from violence by developing intervention efforts.

When is conflict beneficial and when is it harmful? What causes conflict, anyway? What methods can you use to resolve conflict? Is any single method best? The following discussion answers these questions.

PROS AND CONS OF WORKPLACE CONFLICT

Conflict generally is considered a negative influence that is destructive; however, it can be a positive influence if you manage it properly. Conflict forces you to analyze goals, it creates dialogue among employees, and it fosters creative solutions. It has been linked to organizational learning, and even to improved performance and productivity. Without conflict, employees and organizations would stagnate.

Conflict between diverse age groups is one example of how conflict can be positive. For the first time in U.S. history, four generations are working together. Conflict commonly is due to differences in their work style and philosophy. Older workers view "work" as a place—a location you go to at a specified time, such as 9 a.m. to 5 p.m. Younger workers tend to view "work" as something you do—anywhere, any time. They grew up in a digital world where information is always available. So it's easy for Boomers to conclude that Millennials who arrive at 9:30 a.m. are working less hard than they, who arrived at 8:30 a.m., not realizing that the younger generation may have already put in time at their home computers or smartphones while still in pajamas. To Millennials, rigid scheduling of work is unnecessary. Boomers can benefit from their younger coworkers by learning that much of today's work can be done in flextime for maximum efficiency.

Conflict may also foster creativity. It helps to overcome biases by forcing you out of your traditional ways of thinking. In this way, conflict promotes the unstructured thinking that lets you develop good, novel alternatives to difficult problems.[2]

In addition, decisions are better when there is open opposition and resistance. In one study, high-quality decisions occurred in 46 percent of the situations with strong worker resistance, but in only 19 percent of the situations where resistance was weak or nonexistent.[3]

Thus, if you are a manager who prides yourself on running a smooth ship, you may not be as effective as you think. The smooth ship may reflect suppressed conflict that could have potential benefit if allowed free play. In fact, the conflict might not be as harmful as suppressing it is.

Benefits of Conflict:
- Forces goal analysis
- Creates dialogue among employees
- Fosters creative solutions
- Stimulates organizational learning
- Improves performance and productivity
- Prevents stagnation

CAUSES OF WORKPLACE CONFLICT

When you perceive conflict in the workplace, you may assume it's due to incompatible personalities. "Why can't everyone just get along?" you plead. But once you understand that the sources of conflict are often deeper than individual personality, then you will be able to select the right communication strategy for handling it.

The underlying causes of conflict are often the organization's hierarchy, ways of doing business, and a built-in opposition between units. Research shows that conflict increases with levels of hierarchy, standardization of jobs, and the number of workers.

The distribution of the limited resources available in an organization is another source of conflict. If resources were unlimited, few conflicts would arise, but this condition seldom exists. When resources are limited, and more than one person or group wants a share, conflict and competition develop.

Diverse goals are another source of organizational conflict. For instance, clashes may occur between Quality Assurance and Production in a manufacturing company.

The goal of the quality control people is zero defects, while the goal of the production unit is filling the customers' orders on time. Conflicting goals and roles can also explain why a company's sales people routinely ignore the accounting staff's requests for expense receipts. Or why a shift foreman refuses to let his workers attend an employee development session offered by human resources. To reduce such traditional conflicts between functional units, managers should remind their people of the overarching goals, mission, and vision.

Sources of Conflict:
- The organization's hierarchy
- Ways of doing business
- Built-in opposition between units
- Highly standardized jobs
- Large number of workers
- Distribution of limited resources
- Diverse goals

STRATEGIES FOR MANAGING CONFLICT

Once you have pinpointed the sources of workplace conflict, you are ready to manage the conflict. This section offers strategies for managing conflict up the ladder of power and authority, across the ladder with peers, and down the ladder with subordinates. While reviewing these strategies, keep in mind that different conflict situations call for different strategies, so effective communication means that you match the strategy to the situation.

MANAGING CONFLICT WITH THE BOSS: AVOID

You might think that the best way to handle conflict with your boss is to avoid it. The avoidance or withdrawal strategy combines a low concern for production with a low concern for people. If you use this style a lot, you see conflict as useless. Rather than undergo the tension and frustration of conflict, you use avoidance simply to remove yourself from conflict situations, either physically or psychologically. You dislike tension, don't take sides in a disagreement among others, and feel little commitment to any decisions reached. This conflict management style is the second most popular among U.S. managers.

Avoidance doesn't need to be dramatic. You can avoid by ignoring a hurtful comment or quickly changing the subject when conversation begins to threaten. Another way to avoid is to place the responsibility for an issue back on your boss. A third way to withdraw is to use a simple response of "I'm looking into the matter," with the hopes that the boss will forget the issue.

The avoidance strategy is frequently used in large bureaucracies that have too many policies. Rather than tackling the conflict, you simply blame it on "policy." If you lack self-confidence in your communication abilities, you may hope the problem just disappears. However, following the dictum, "never complain, never explain," usually doesn't work in the long run. In fact, withdrawal has been negatively associated with knowledge of the boss's feelings and attitudes; open, upward communication; perceived helpfulness of the subordinate; and strength of the planning relationship. Thus, avoiding conflict with the boss doesn't usually make things better in critical managerial areas.[4]

MANAGING CONFLICT WITH THE BOSS AND WITH PEERS: ACCOMMODATE

The second type of conflict resolution is accommodating. You try to deal with conflict by giving in, hoping to make everyone happy. When using this approach, you emphasize maintaining relationships with bosses and coworkers, and you de-emphasize achieving productive goals. Since you are aiming for others' acceptance, you often give in to their desires in areas that conflict with your own. You use this style if you believe confrontation is destructive.

Typical attempts to accommodate may include such things as calling for a coffee break at a tense moment, breaking tension by cracking a joke, saying "you're right" when they're not, or engaging in some ritual show of togetherness such as an office birthday party. Since these efforts are likely to reduce feelings of conflict, they are better than simple avoidance. But handling conflict by giving in will probably have short-range effects. Just because someone does not experience a hostile or negative feeling does not mean the real cause of the conflict is resolved. In fact, accommodating is a camouflage approach that can break down at any time and create barriers to progress. Research has found that managers in low- or medium-performing organizations accommodate to reduce conflict more often than managers in high-performing organizations do.

In addition, accommodating hurts open communication with the boss and with participation in goal setting. Think of your latest performance review with your boss. Did you give in to the judgments of your work quality without discussion or pushback? If so, did the boss think you had accepted the judgments as fair and true? How did you feel afterward—motivated to work harder? Probably not.

Managing Conflict with Bosses and with Peers: Compromise

Compromise, the third strategy for conflict resolution up and across the ladder, assumes that half a loaf is better than none. Since compromise provides some gain for both sides rather than a unilateral victory or loss, you might judge this approach to be better than the other strategies just discussed.

Compromise is used when one of two conditions exists: (1) neither person thinks he/she can force their way on the other person or (2) one or both people believes winning may not be worth the cost in money, time, or energy. Compromise is often highly related to negotiating, which is a legitimate conflict resolution strategy in today's workplace. Compromising may make both parties think they won, but they may also both feel like losers. A negative overtone may develop in the working relationship, and any sense of trust may break down. While both people probably entered the negotiations with a cooperative attitude, a sense of competition may be the final outcome.

A second concern with compromise is that the person with the most information has the better position, usually the person who has a better network. This power of information may restrict open communication, often resulting in a lop-sided compromise. A third factor is the principle of the least-interested party: The party that has the least interest in the outcome is the more powerful person in the negotiations. As a result, a coworker who has little concern about your welfare or the team's welfare may have the most influence in a compromise.

MANAGING CONFLICT WITH SUBORDINATES: FORCE

The previous sections described traditional ways to approach conflict upward, that is, between you and your boss, and horizontally, between you and your peers at the same level of power. But what about conflict down the ladder, when you are experiencing conflict with your subordinates?

You use force when you need to meet production goals at all costs, without concern for the needs or acceptance of your subordinates or team.

Losing is destructive because you think it reduces status, seems weak, and fosters a poor image. You must win no matter what, because winning gives you a sense of excitement and achievement. Not surprisingly, forcing is the number one conflict resolution strategy that U.S. managers use.

The forcing strategy will probably cause later conflicts, however. To see the negative effect this style may have, just think about the language managers use to describe conflict: beat the opposition, battle, fight, conquer, coerce, smash, nuke. Such language and imagery can result in long-lasting, emotional wounds.

While force can resolve immediate disputes, the long-term effects will probably include a loss of productivity. Forcing in conflict situations is negatively associated with adequacy of planning, helpfulness of the supervision, and participation in goal setting. The major result of forcing is that your employees are reluctant to carry out orders because they think that the ultimate resolution of the conflict will put them on the losing side of a win–lose position.

Interestingly, while little doubt exists that forcing has limited use, managers consider forcing to be their favorite backup strategy for dealing with conflict. Immediate compliance is misperceived as a long-term solution in these cases.

Managing Conflict with Anyone: Collaborate.

So far, it may seem that no totally acceptable, productive strategy exists to manage conflict. I've discussed everything in terms of loss. Fortunately, this is not the case. Collaborating, the fifth strategy, is a win–win strategy for conflict. This complex and highly effective style requires skillful, strategic managerial communication, but it reaps a big dividend; thus, the remainder of this chapter centers on this strategy. Let's first describe the win–win strategy and then examine specific ways to use it.

The key to this strategy is that it follows a mutual problem-solving approach rather than a combative one. In contrast to managers who use accommodating, avoiding, compromising, or forcing, managers who collaborate assume that a high-quality, mutually acceptable solution is possible. Everyone directs energies toward defeating the problem and not each other.

Here are the five steps in the collaboration process:

1   *Define the problem.* The problem definition must be specific. A statement of the problem in a conflict situation is usually much more difficult than it seems, and most people jump to solutions before they clearly define the problem. Because of this, our inclination is to state the problem as a solution rather than as a goal, which results in ambiguous communication. The outcome may be increased conflict. One helpful strategy is to write out the problem statement clearly, so everyone can see it and agree on it. Or you can agree on a problem stated as a question. State goals in the form of group goals rather than your own goals.

2   *Analyze the problem.* Again, most people want to skip this step. After all, they may argue, they live with the problem. What is the point of spending more time wallowing in it? The answer is that by exploring the depths of the problem, by looking at its history, causes, effects, and extent, you can later come up with a solution that addresses more than symptoms, one that is more than a bandage. The analysis will address the root cause of the problem, thus improving the chances of being successful.

3   *Brainstorm alternatives.* Everyone involved in the conflict should offer potential solutions. One idea may stimulate other ideas. The more you

communicate in an open, trusting environment, the greater the potential for finding effective solutions. Trust, of course, evaporates when an idea is criticized during a brainstorming session. As soon as someone says, "That's a terrible idea. It'll never work," who would be willing to take the risk of coming up with another idea? Make sure that you don't judge ideas prematurely.

4   *Develop criteria for a good solution.* These criteria, or standards, may already be in place and available. Other times, your boss will tell you what a good solution must look like. Occasionally, you and/or your team are allowed to develop your own criteria. The most common criteria for a good solution are:

- It must be cheap.

- It must be easy to do.

- It must call for using resources already on hand.

- It must be legal.

- It must be in line with the company's mission or values.

5   *Evaluate the brainstormed alternatives using the criteria.* This is really the easiest step. By this time, you have reached agreement on the problem, and everyone has had a say about possible solutions. The best solution will appear naturally because it is the brainstormed alternative that matches your list of criteria.

Steps in the Collaboration Process:
1   Define the problem
2   Analyze the problem
3   Brainstorm solutions
4   Develop criteria for a good solution
5   Find the best match

You might be asking, if collaborating is the best all-around strategy for resolving conflict, why don't we do it more often? The simple answer is that this process calls for two prerequisites: time and ability. You can't count on reaching consensus on a solution right away. Hearing everyone out takes time and patience, commodities that are rare in today's workplace. Secondly, the people have to know how to collaborate; they must be familiar with, and be willing to follow, the five steps described above.

Once I had a graduate student who managed the third shift in a manufacturing company. After attending my evening class from 6:00 to 9:00 p.m., Rob would head off to work from 11:00 p.m. to 7:00 a.m. Before class one evening, Rob told me that two of his subordinates had been locked in conflict for some time over a tools issue, and so he had tried using the collaborative strategy that I had taught in class. "How did it go?" I asked eagerly. Rob reported, "It didn't work." He had put his employees into the break room and said, "Come out when you two have reached an agreement." After an hour, they had returned to the line, saying they'd worked it out, but Rob said they hadn't used the process he had learned in class. When I asked what they had used, he told me, "Seniority." The worker who had been on the job longer got his way.

This example demonstrates the importance of training people on the steps in the collaboration strategy for conflict resolution. It's based on how we think when we are trying to rationally solve a problem, but participants must know and stick to the steps in the process for it to work.

SUMMARY

To help you "get it done," this chapter focuses on strategies for managing conflict. Conflict is inevitable in the workplace, and it's even more powerful a factor when the workforce is diverse. You will be able to successfully deal with conflict by following the steps described here: read the situation to identify the source of the conflict, recognize whether the conflict is constructive or destructive, select the right strategy out of the toolbox, and then apply it. Table 16.1 will help you choose the right conflict resolution strategy.

Table 16.1 When to Use Each Conflict Resolution Strategy

CONFLICT RESOLUTION STRATEGY	WHEN IT WORKS BEST	RESULT
Avoiding	• There's little chance you'll get your way • The potential damage of addressing the conflict outweighs the benefits of resolution • People need a chance to cool down • Others are in a better position to resolve the conflict • The problem will go away by itself	I lose You lose
Accommodating	• Preserving harmony is important • Personal antagonism is the major source of conflict • The issue itself is unsolvable • You care more about the relationship than getting your way	I lose You win
Compromising	• Two opponents are equal in power • Temporary settlements on complex issues are needed • Opponents do not share goals • Forcing or problem solving won't work	I half win, half lose You half win, half lose
Forcing	• Quick, decisive action is needed, as in a crisis • A rule has to be enforced • You know you're right • You must protect yourself	I win You lose
Collaborating	• Both sets of concerns are too important to be compromised • It is important to work through hard feelings • Commitment to the resolution is important • A permanent solution is desired	I win You win

NOTES

1 L.A. Erbert (2014). "Antagonistic and Non-Antagonistic Dialectical Contradictions in Organizational Conflict," *International Journal of Business Communication* 51, no. 2, pp. 138–58.

2 L. Putnam, S. Wilson (1988). "Argumentation and Bargaining Strategies as Discriminators of Integrative and Distributive Outcomes," in *Managing Conflict: An Interdisciplinary Approach,* ed. A. Rahim (New York, NY: Praeger Publishers), pp. 121–141.

3 R. Hoffman, E. Harburg, N.R.F. Meier (1962). "Differences and Disagreements as Factors in Creative Problem-Solving," *Journal of Abnormal and Social Psychology* 64, no. 2, pp. 206–24.

4 W.A. Donohue, M.E. Diez, R.B. Stahl (1983). "New Directions in Negotiations Research," in *Communication Yearbook* 7, ed. R.N. Bostrom (Beverly Hills, CA: Sage Publications), pp. 249–79.

In Chapter 17, Martin Davidson discusses
the causes of conflict in organizations.

Chapter 17

Managing Conflict in Organizations

by Martin Davidson

M anagers often behave as though serious interpersonal confrontations are the result of personality defects. They label people who are frequently involved in conflicts "troublemakers" or "bad apples" and attempt to transfer or dismiss them as a way of resolving conflict. While some individuals seem to have a propensity for making trouble and appear to be cantankerous under even the best of circumstances, "sour dispositions" actually account for a small minority of the organizational conflicts that typically emerge.

This proposition is supported by research on performance appraisals. It has been shown that managers generally attribute poor performance to personal deficiencies in workers, such as laziness, lack of skill, or lack of motivation. However, when workers are asked the causes of their poor performance, they generally explain it in terms of problems in their environment, such as insufficient supplies or unco-operative coworkers.[1] While some face-saving is obviously involved here, this line of research suggests that managers need to guard against the reflexive tendency to assume that bad behaviors imply bad people. In fact, aggressive or harsh behaviors sometimes observed in interpersonal confrontations often reflect the frustrations of

---

[1] Robert L. Heneman, David B. Greenberger, and Chigozie Anonyuo, "Attributions and exchanges: The effects of interpersonal factors on the diagnosis of employee performance," *Academy of Management Journal* 32(2) (1989): 466–476.

Martin N. Davidson, "Managing Conflict in Organizations," pp. 1-8. Copyright © 2001 by Darden Business Publishing. Reprinted with permission.

people who have good intentions but are unskilled in handling intense, emotional experiences.

THE CAUSES OF CONFLICT

An alternative to the personality-defect theory of conflict is a "multiple sources" model of conflict that proposes three fundamental causes of conflict in organizations—*identity-related differences, role incompatibility,* and *environmental stress.*[2]

Identity-related differences. Individuals bring different personal backgrounds, experiences, and cultural values when they enter organizations. Different socialization processes, levels of education, and so forth, shape their experiences and values. As a result, their interpretations of events and their expectations about relationships with others in the organization will vary considerably. Conflicts caused by incongruent personal values *that stem from* these social identities are among the most difficult to resolve because they evoke values we hold deeply.

Such a conflict occurred in a major industrial company between a 63-year-old white U.S. executive vice president and a 35-year-old Chinese member of the corporate legal department, who was exiled in 1989 following Tiananmen Square. They disagreed vehemently over whether the company should accept a very attractive offer from the Chinese government to build a manufacturing facility outside of Beijing. The vice president felt the company had a responsibility to its stockholders to pursue every legal opportunity to increase profits. Moreover, though the human rights issues in China troubled her, she believed that economic engagement was the most effective way to bring pressure to bear on oppressive governments. In contrast, the lawyer felt that collaborating with the Chinese government in any way was tantamount to condoning its morally repugnant disregard for human rights.

Note that in this example, both parties are expressing values flowing from their respective identities. The vice president values success in her work and takes seriously her obligation to her stockholders and to the U.S. economic system. This is a kind of professionalism and conscientiousness that is encouraged in her culture. Moreover, she is a product of a culture in which economic prosperity has repeatedly resolved

---

[2] Based on the work of Louis R. Pondy, "Organizational Conflict: Concepts and Models," *Administrative Science Quarterly,* 12(2) (1967): 295–320.

social injustices (e.g., lifting immigrant populations from poverty and discrimination to wealth and membership in the U.S. system of governance). Therefore, she would be deeply convinced that expanding into China was the right thing to do.

The lawyer, in contrast, has had the experience of living in a culture in which many of its members are struggling to create personal freedom. She has had a direct and powerful experience of engaging in that struggle. To be willing to do business with the oppressive Chinese government is not only to condone the government's behavior, but it also betrays the people with whom she fought to change that behavior, many of whom gave their lives in the struggle.

Neither of these individuals is unambiguously right or wrong in her stance. What is noteworthy is that the identity-related experience of each has placed them in a difficult conflict.

Role Incompatibility. The complexity inherent in most organizations tends to produce conflict between members whose tasks are interdependent but whose roles are incompatible.[3] This type of conflict is exemplified by the ubiquitous goal conflicts between line and staff, production and sales, marketing, and R and D. Each unit has different responsibilities in the organization, and as a result each places different priorities on organizational goals (e.g., customer satisfaction, product quality, production efficiency, and compliance with government regulations). It is also typical of firms whose multiple product lines compete for scarce resources.

During the early days at Apple Computer, the Apple II division accounted for a large part of the company's revenue. It viewed the newly created Macintosh division as an unwise speculative venture. The natural rivalry was made worse when a champion of the Macintosh referred to the Apple II team as "the dull and boring product division." Since this type of conflict stems from the fundamental incompatibility of the job responsibilities of the disputants, it can often be resolved only through the mediation of a common superior.

Role incompatibility conflicts may overlap with those arising from identity differences. The personal differences members bring to an organization generally remain dormant until they are triggered by an organizational catalyst, like interdependent task responsibilities. And one reason members often perceive that their assigned roles are incompatible is that they are operating from different bases of

---

[3] Robert L. Kahn, Donald M. Wolfe, Robert P. Quinn, J. Diedrick Snoek, and Robert A. Rosenthal, *Organizational Stress: Studies in Role Conflict and Ambiguity* (New York: John Wiley, 1964).

information. They communicate with different sets of people, are tied into different reporting systems, and receive instructions from different bosses.

Environmental Stress. Another major source of conflict is environmentally induced stress. Conflicts stemming from identity differences and role incompatibilities are greatly exacerbated by a stressful environment. When an organization is forced to operate on an austere budget, its members are more likely to become embroiled in disputes over domain claims and resource requests. Scarcity tends to lower trust, increase ethnocentrism, and reduce participation in decision making. These are ideal conditions for incubating interpersonal conflict. When a large hospital announced a major downsizing, the threat to employees' security was so severe that it disrupted long-time, close working relationships. Work team effectiveness diminished, people met less frequently at informal coffee breaks, and car pools disbanded because of the increased tension.

Uncertainty in the environment also fosters conflict. When individuals find it difficult to predict what is going to happen to them from month to month, they become very anxious and prone to conflict. This type of "frustration conflict" often stems from rapid, repeated change. If task assignments, management philosophy, accounting procedures, and lines of authority are changed frequently, members find it difficult to cope with the resulting stress, and sharp, bitter conflicts can easily erupt over seemingly trivial problems. This type of conflict is generally intense, but it dissipates quickly once a change becomes routinized, and individuals' stress levels are lowered. When a chemical manufacturing firm announced it was bringing a new production facility online, suboptimal communication of the specifics of the project left employees wondering and worrying about whom would be transferred to work in the new facility and how work shifts would be assigned. People were concerned about the disruption of personal and family routines, and some even considered leaving the company to avoid the turmoil of the transition. Also, employees were constantly "jockeying" for position to get the most favorable assignments should they be transferred to the new facility.

CONFLICT RESPONSE ALTERNATIVES

Responses to interpersonal conflicts, whatever their causes, tend to fall into five categories: forcing, accommodating, avoiding, compromising, and collaborating.

Figure 17.1—Two-Dimensional Model of Conflict

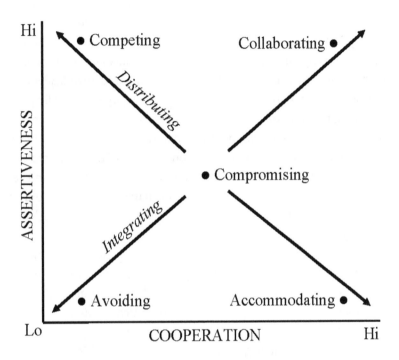

These responses can be organized along two dimensions, as shown in Figure 17.1.[4] These five approaches to conflict reflect different degrees of cooperativeness and assertiveness. A cooperative response is intended to satisfy the needs of the interacting person, whereas an assertive response focuses on the needs of the focal person. The cooperativeness dimension reflects the importance of the relationship, whereas the assertiveness dimension reflects the importance of the issue.

The *competing approach* (assertive, uncooperative) is an attempt to satisfy one's own needs at the expense of the other individual's. This can be done by using formal authority, physical threats, manipulation ploys, or by ignoring the claims of the other party. When using a competing approach, one may use the authority of one's office ("I'm the boss, so we'll do it my way"), one may intimidate, or one may use manipulation or feigned ignorance to achieve one's goals in the interaction. For example,

---

[4] Thomas L. Ruble and Kenneth W. Thomas, "Support for a Two-Dimensional Model of Conflict Behavior," *Organizational Behavior & Human Performance,* 16(1) (1976): 142–155.

a leader might appear to be democratic by proposing that conflicting proposals be referred to a committee for further investigation. However, the leader ensures that the composition of the committee reflects her or his interests and preferences, so that what appears to be a selection based on merit is effectively predetermined. The repeated use of this conflict-management approach can breed hostility and resentment. While observers may intellectually admire authoritarian or manipulative leaders because they appear to accomplish a great deal, their management styles generally produce a backlash in the long run as people become unwilling to accept the emotional costs.

The *accommodating approach* (cooperative, unassertive) satisfies the other party's concerns while neglecting one's own. A common example of accommodation is the case of a board of directors of a failing firm that neglects its interests and responsibilities in favor of accommodating the wishes of management. Accommodation emphasizes preserving positive and friendly relations over protecting one's personal rights and privileges.

The *avoiding approach* (uncooperative, unassertive) neglects the interests of both parties by sidestepping the conflict or postponing a solution. The manager who never gets around to delivering negative feedback and appraisals to her subordinates exemplifies the avoidant approach to conflict. Really tough problems tend not to be addressed, and this can cause frustration in relationships. Interestingly, in workgroups led by avoidant managers, people sense a leadership vacuum and try to fill the void, often creating considerable confusion and animosity in the process.

The *compromising response* is intermediate between assertiveness and cooperativeness. A compromise is an attempt to obtain partial satisfaction for both parties, in the sense that both receive the proverbial "half loaf." To accommodate this, both parties are asked to make sacrifices to obtain a common gain. This approach has considerable practical appeal to managers, because by definition, each party gets some portion of what he or she wants.

The *collaborating approach,* (cooperative, assertive) is an attempt to address fully the concerns of both parties. It is often referred to as the "problem-solving" mode. In this mode, the intent is to find solutions to the conflict that are satisfactory to both parties rather than to find fault or assign blame. In this way, both parties can feel that they have "won."

The diagonals in Figure 17.1 labeled *"distributive"* and *"integrative"* characterize approaches to conflict. Distributive approaches occur when a person approaches the conflict as managing the proportion of satisfaction of each person in the

Table 17.1—Conditions that Favor Each of the Five Conflict Approaches

	PERCEIVED ISSUE COMPLEXITY	TIME PRESSURE	MANAGEMENT OF OTHER'S FEELING	ATTENTION TO LEARNING IN THE SITUATION
Collaborating	High	Low	High	High
Competing	Low	High	Low	Low
Compromising	High	High	High	Moderate
Accommodating	Low	Moderate	High	High
Avoiding	Low	Low	High	Low

dispute—in essence, she or he approaches the conflict as a zero-sum game. In contrast, integrative approaches seek to increase the pie, to work out "win-win" solutions. From this perspective, you can think of collaboration as a "win-win" outcome; avoiding a "lose-lose" outcome; and the compromising, accommodating, and forcing approaches as win-lose outcomes.

CHOOSING THE RIGHT RESPONSE TO A CONFLICT SITUATION

At first glance, it is tempting to assume a skillful manager would always approach conflict collaboratively. After all, who wouldn't always want win-win situations? However, conflict-relevant phrases like "let sleeping dogs lie" and "win at all cost" emerge in our vernacular for good reason. Managing conflict skillfully means using the appropriate responses at the appropriate times. What constitutes the appropriate response depends upon the situation as well as the people involved.

Choosing approaches that fit the situation best. Table 17.1 lists several dimensions of a conflict situation and identifies the conditions under which each conflict approach could be used to greatest effect. These dimensions are extracted from reports by 28 chief executives who identified situations in which they felt that each of the conflict approaches would be appropriate.

Perceived issue complexity is an assessment of how intricate the issues driving the conflict are. If the issues are very complex, collaboration or compromising would seem more appropriate. When the issues are simpler, competing, accommodating, and avoiding approaches can be more effective. For example, when a conflict has identity-related factors as a cause, responding competitively or with avoidance can escalate the conflict. Identity-related factors are both deeply held and often complex, involving personality, culture, and past history. Such conflicts are better dealt with using integrative approaches such as compromise and collaboration. When the issue is simpler, such as difference of opinion of where to position the furniture in the reception lobby, the other approaches may work easily.

Time pressure can also constrain approaches to a conflict situation. Competing and compromising approaches are more prevalent in situations in which time pressure is high and some course of action must be decided. For example, chief executives identified emergency decisions (e.g., cost-cutting) as situations in which a conflict may need to be decided by fiat, a competitive approach. In contrast, when time pressure is moderate to low, approaches such as collaboration or even avoidance may be more appropriate. Collaboration requires consensus building and creativity and can take time. For avoidance to be a feasible approach, the issues at hand must be less pressing. Otherwise, avoidance could be disastrous.

Attention to *managing the other party's feelings* can also determine the best approach in a given situation. When there is little care for how the other responds, competing approaches often ensue. However, whenever there is concern for the feelings of the other party, any of the other four approaches may be appropriate. For example, avoidance can be useful as a means of suppressing angry or frustrating emotions and is often used for just that reason. Accommodation works in similar ways, suppressing hostile feelings by giving the other what she or he wants. Collaboration "cools out the mark" in a different way—by respecting the other's position and feelings and working to create a solution that would appease the other party. Moreover, collaboration is also effective in working through feelings that have previously hampered positive relations between the parties. In sum, all of these examples represent high levels of attention to feelings in the conflict.

Finally, when you want to learn from the conflict interaction, some approaches seem to be more appropriate than others. Chief executives identify collaboration as the best way to learn in the midst of conflict. Perspectives are shared and diverse approaches are coordinated which leads to high levels of learning. Similarly, learning can occur in accommodating approaches because part of the stance in accommodation is to listen to and learn from the other party. Also, accommodation can create potential learning labs for the other, especially when the other party is a subordinate. By accommodating in this situation, you create an opportunity to succeed or fail, and learning can come for the subordinate because they won, own, and are committed to the decision. Learning tends to be minimal in competing and avoiding situations, an overall pattern that is correlated with attention to and concern for the other party.

The appendix lists several situations and their optimal conflict approaches.

OTHER CONSIDERATIONS IN MANAGING CONFLICT EFFECTIVELY

Understand the cause of the conflict. Just as identifying and analyzing case facts is a critical first step of in determining how to respond to a managerial situation, it is also critical to understand the cause of a conflict situation before trying to manage it. Knowing that a person is angry not because he is "just a hostile person," but because he is trying to negotiate interdepartmental conflict helps the manager determine what the right approach to conflict should be both for the individual and the organization.

Understand your preferred style of dealing with conflict. In the real world, people vary in the degree to which they are comfortable in engaging conflict. Comfort levels are determined by personality, culture, past experience, and a variety of other factors. Thus, a manager may not be able to turn on the collaborative switch so easily. Researchers have developed a number of inventories specifically for the purpose of helping managers determine what their preferred style of conflict management is.[5] As is true with the Myers-Briggs inventory, managers are not doomed to use only one approach. Rather, everyone can learn different approaches even if they are not initially the most comfortable.

---

[5] For example, popular measures include the Thomas-Kilmann Conflict Mode Inventory, or the Blake and Mouton Managerial Grid. Explore websites such as http://www.teleometrics.com/smi02.htm to get a sense of what such tools might look like.

APPENDIX

Collaborating	To find an integrative solution when both sets of concerns are too important to be compromised
	When your objective is to learn
	To work through feelings that have interfered with a relationship
	To merge insights from people with different perspectives
	To gain commitment by incorporating concerns into a consensus
Competing	On important issues where unpopular actions need implementing—e.g., cost-cutting, enforcing unpopular rules, or discipline
	When quick, decisive action is vital—e.g., in emergencies
	Against people who take advantage of noncompetitive behavior
Compromising	To achieve temporary settlements to complex issues
	To arrive at expedient solutions under time pressure
	When opponents with equal power are highly committed to mutually exclusive goals
	As a backup when collaboration or competition is unsuccessful
Accommodating	When issues are more important to others than they are to you—to satisfy others and maintain cooperation
	To allow subordinates to develop by learning from mistakes
	When harmony and stability are especially important
	When you find you are wrong—to allow a better position to be heard, to learn, and to show your reasonableness
Avoiding	When an issue is trivial or more important issues are pressing
	To let people cool down and regain perspective
	When you perceive no chance of satisfying your concerns
	When others can resolve the conflict more effectively

In Chapter 18, Deepak Malhotra presents the idea of salvaging situations that have gone wrong in business settings.

Chapter 18

Partners, Not Opponents

Caught in the Crossfire

by Deepak Malhotra

Not so long ago, a successful entrepreneur who was a student of mine ("Sam") found himself at the tragic end of a true reversal of fortune. It had all started out so well. A year earlier he had received a call from one of the largest retailers in the United States, asking whether he would be interested in earning some extra revenue. There was no catch. The retailer had decided to switch suppliers for one unique type of apparel, and the new supplier was an overseas Asian company. The retailer had never worked with this Asian company before and reached out to my student for help. Sam already had a good business relationship with the retailer, and although he did not know the Asian company either, he was very familiar with the manufacturing landscape where the company was located. The retailer wanted Sam's company to act as an intermediary between them and this Asian company. For almost no work at all other than coordinating the purchase and sale of product, he would get a percentage of each transaction that took place. If all went well, Sam's company stood to make over a million dollars each year—a sizable amount of money for him.

The celebrations did not last long. Just a few months into the relationship, Sam received a letter from a US manufacturer. The letter claimed that in making this

Deepak Malhotra, "Partners, Not Opponents: Caught in the Crossfire," *Negotiating the Impossible: How to Break Deadlocks and Resolve Ugly Conflicts (Without Money or Muscle)*, pp. 171-179. Copyright © 2016 by Berrett-Koehler Publishers. Reprinted with permission.

apparel, the Asian company had violated the US manufacturer's patent. Given the nature of the relationship between the parties, the US manufacturer was suing the retailer, the Asian company, and Sam. The US manufacturer was open to settling out of court, but was demanding a huge settlement. Legally, the retailer was in a very safe position and had no incentive to negotiate. For practical reasons, the Asian company could not easily be made to pay through litigation. This left only my student squarely in the crosshairs. And the US manufacturer was going to come at Sam with everything they had—because this wasn't just about patent infringement. The US manufacturer had been the original supplier of this apparel to the retailer until the Asian company had come into the picture and undercut them on price. They were not happy.

Sam did not want to pay millions in a settlement, but he also did not want to go through a legal battle. He decided to reach out to his allies in this mess, in the hope that one or both of them would be willing to chip in money to help settle the matter. The retailer was very sympathetic and felt bad that Sam had been dragged into this, but while they offered to vouch for him in legal proceedings, they were unwilling to offer any money. The Asian company argued that there was no patent infringement so there was no reason for them to offer money, an easy thing for them to say given they were outside the reach of the law. He was on his own. He asked his lawyers to reach out to the US manufacturer and explain that although he was clearly innocent in this matter, he was willing to settle for a few hundred thousand dollars, a goodwill gesture aimed at helping everyone avoid court. It did not work. They went to court.

After seven months and $400,000 in legal fees, the court ruled in favor of the US manufacturer. Sam was asked to pay almost $2 million, which was more than four times as much as he'd made in the deal before it had come to a halt due to the lawsuit. His only options now were to pay the money, to appeal the decision, or to try again to settle out of court. Paying up would be extremely costly. An out-of-court settlement would be even harder now than it had been last time, given the US manufacturer's legal victory. The lawyers believed an appeal made the most sense, but they did not pretend his chances were good. Which route to take? You've already lost once in court, the other side has the leverage, you are facing a multi-million-dollar loss, none of your allies are coming to your aid, and the party on the other side of the dispute seems out for blood. What now?

WITHOUT MONEY OR MUSCLE

As Sam tells the story, he was sitting around one day when the thought came to him: *What would my negotiations professor advise?* It did not take long to come up with an answer. *Look for the value-maximizing outcome.* In other words, given the interests, constraints, and alternatives of all the parties, what approach or outcome would create the most amount of total value in this situation? *Before worrying too much about how you will get there, first figure out what the optimal deal would be.* So he started to map out the negotiation space and think this through.

In the very beginning, the **retailer's** relationship with each of the three parties had been as follows:

	RELATIONSHIP WITH RETAILER	PRODUCT TO SELL	BEST PARTNER FOR RETAILER
US Manufacturer	Good	Expensive	YES
Asian Company	None	Cheap	No
Student	Good	None	No

After the Asian company undercut the US manufacturer with the help of my student, the situation changed:

	RELATIONSHIP WITH RETAILER	PRODUCT TO SELL	BEST PARTNER FOR RETAILER
US Manufacturer	Good	Expensive	No
Asian Company	None	Cheap	No
Student	Good	None	No
Asian Company + Student	Good	Cheap	YES

Once the Asian company's patent infringement was revealed, and after the US manufacturer sued the other three parties, things changed again. The US manufacturer's relationship with the retailer was now bad, and the Asian company's product was no longer viable for sale in the United States.

	RELATIONSHIP WITH RETAILER	PRODUCT TO SELL	BEST PARTNER FOR RETAILER
US Manufacturer	Bad	Expensive	No
Asian Company	Bad	None	No
Student	Great	None	No
Asian Company + Student	Unclear	None	No

The value maximizing outcome was starting to come into focus. The US manufacturer had the power to squeeze money out of Sam, but there was an even bigger pot of money that was now missing from the entire equation: no one was capable of selling any product to the retailer. The lawsuit could yield a few million dollars for the US manufacturer, but many more millions in value were being destroyed because no one had the necessary combination of assets: a good relationship with the retailer *plus* a product to sell. But there was one possible entity that could bring both assets to the table: it would be a *partnership between the US manufacturer and Sam.* Might this work?

Sam called up the CEO of the US manufacturing firm and told him that he was getting on a plane to come and see him. "I have an idea I'd like to share with you. If I can't convince you in 20 minutes, I will fly right back." The CEO agreed to meet. On the way to the meeting, my student also called up his contacts at the retailer to share the broad outlines of what he planned to propose. They gave him the go-ahead to try to structure such an arrangement.

In the CEO's office, Sam explained his analysis and the idea. The retailer would never buy directly from a company that had sued it, but the manufacturer's patented product was a good one and there was no substitute supplier. Sam had a good relationship with the retailer, not to mention the retailer felt they owed him for putting him through the terrible ordeal. Sam could be the intermediary between the manufacturer and the retailer. The manufacturer would have to make a few concessions to the retailer to smooth things over, but a deal was possible. The two sides crunched some numbers, haggled a bit, and then came to the following agreement: (a) Sam would pay the manufacturer a few hundred thousand dollars upfront, partly to reimburse the manufacturer's legal costs; (b) Sam would become the exclusive intermediary between the manufacturer and the retailer—this would be worth a couple million dollars to his company in the coming years; (c) Sam would become the exclusive distributor for the US manufacturer for overseas sales—another valuable win for him.

All three parties signed off, and the reversal of fortune had been reversed once more.

PARTNERS, NOT OPPONENTS

When someone sues you, how are you likely to view them? Most people would see that person as an enemy, or at least as an adversary. This is understandable, but potentially dangerous, because we tend to think and act differently based on how we view the person on the other side of the table. We typically have lower tolerance, less hope, and a reduced willingness to engage constructively with our enemies. And this tendency can be costly—to us and to them.

In the martial arts dojo where I practiced, it was not uncommon during class to hear students ask questions such as: What if your opponent is bigger? What if your opponent grabs you like this? What if your opponent . . . ?

Such statements always invited a caveat by our instructor. "They are partners, not opponents," he would correct his students any time they used the word "opponent" to describe the person they were practicing with in class. "Remember that the people you are sparring with are there to help you learn. How will you learn from them if you think of them as opponents?" Often, he would take it a step further: "Even the person who attacks you on the street is your partner. How will you remember to stay calm, or attempt to resolve the situation without fighting, if you think of him as an opponent?"

The same is true in deadlocks and in ugly conflicts. As my student's experience illustrates, it can be dangerous to see others one-dimensionally, and especially to label them as an opponent or enemy. If you pigeon-hole someone based on their prior behavior, you may miss opportunities that emerge when the game changes. In this case, the US manufacturer started out a stranger, turned into an adversary, and ended up an ally. The Asian company went from being a strategic asset to a legal liability in a matter of months. The biggest obstacle to solving Sam's problem may have been the inability—at first—to see that situations change and that people can outgrow their labels.

Labels might provide an efficient means of describing someone ("she's my competitor"), but they are necessarily incomplete and limiting. It is always best to remember that the people you are dealing with are not competitors, allies, enemies, or friends—they are just *people* who, like you, have interests, constraints, alternatives, and perspectives (ICAP). As a negotiator, your job is to understand these factors and to address the situation accordingly. In my negotiating, I still find it useful to retain the label *partner* for everyone (whether they are acting like a "friend" or "foe"), because it reminds me to have empathy, to be open to the possibility of collaboration in even the most difficult relationships, and to shed assumptions about what is or is not possible.

> *See the other side as your partner, not your opponent, regardless of the type or degree of conflict. It is hard to empathize or collaborate with "opponents."*

LOOK FOR WAYS TO CREATE VALUE

In the world of business, negotiators often talk about "creating value." It is a reminder that there may be ways to improve the deal for everyone, or at least to improve it for some people without hurting others. Deal makers should obviously try to improve agreements and create more value. After all, would you rather be arguing over how to share $100 or $200? It is easier to find a solution, not to mention more profitable, when there is more to gain from reaching a deal, or more to lose from no deal.

The same principle holds in all negotiations—that is to say, in all areas of human interaction. Negotiators should be in the business of creating value whether they are bargaining over deal terms, facing deadlock, or addressing an ugly conflict. In relatively simple situations it is easy to see what is necessary to create value. For example, in the NFL or NHL, you create value when you end a strike or lockout because only by playing games can you bring money into the system (from viewers, advertisers, etc.) that you can share. To achieve this, you need to solve some difficult problems, such as agreeing on revenue split, but now you have clarity on the direction in which you should move.

It's not so easy when the situation is complex: when there are many parties, many divergent interests, competing intuitions about the right strategy, or a lack of clarity or consensus on what the goal should even be. For example, it was not obvious what Sam should have been even trying to accomplish. Minimize the cost of settlement? Find a way to win in court? Appeal to the manufacturer's goodwill? Leave it to the lawyers? Find a way to pressure the Asian company?

In such situations, an effective way to clarify objectives and choose between options is to ask: *What would be the value-maximizing solution?* Focusing on this principle immediately helped shift the student's attention to the idea that it might be possible to make everyone better off, and that it was unwise to start off assuming the conflict was a zero-sum situation. Thinking in terms of value creation also helped to increase the set of visible options. For example, creating a business relationship with the person who is suing you is not intuitive, unless you are dispassionately looking to create value in every situation. Here again, we see the value of regarding all other parties as *partners, not opponents*, in the process. When you see them as your partner, you are more likely to identify and implement value-creating solutions to the problem.

> *Start by asking: What would be the value-maximizing outcome? Are there ways to create value?*

FIRST, IMAGINE THE IMPOSSIBLE

One of the reasons people fail to focus on unlocking value is because the situation seems impossible. They are already so sure there is no *good* solution that they fail to consider the possibility of a *great* one. This type of thinking can sometimes be changed. One of my executive students was the president of his family business. His father, who owned 90% of the business, was still heavily involved, although he had officially retired. After years of conflict over matters big and small, the son had decided to talk with his father about how to move forward given the bad and worsening situation. The father was constantly overriding the son's decisions and getting involved in matters where he did not have enough information. He was also making it difficult for the son to get out of his shadow and be seen as a legitimate president in the eyes of employees and customers. The conversation was likely to be ugly. It had come to the point where the son felt he would have to leave the business or ask his father to step away, and no matter what, he expected there to be anger, resentment, and potentially, a worsening of the conflict. He was dreading it. He was unsure how to start the conversation, which issues to bring up, or what outcome he even preferred.

When I heard his story and his prediction of disaster, my first question was this: Is there any possibility that both of you will walk away from the conversation *happier* than you had been before talking? He was quiet. He then told me he had never even considered the possibility. I said to him, "Imagine a world in which both of you are glad that the conversation happened. And now paint me a picture. What would that world look like?" And then the conversation changed. He started talking about how his father might be feeling as he thought about his retirement after decades of building a business. He spoke with regret about how little time they spent together outside of work because neither of them wanted another fight. He wondered whether his father was also longing to have this conversation. He was still not sure what the right solution would be, but he was much more confident that he would be able to go in with an open mind and have a potentially value-creating conversation. I do not know how this particular story ended, but before he left the executive program to go back to his business, the student told me that he was looking forward to seeing and talking with his father.

The same approach can also help when you are facing intransigence. In business deals, for example, when the other side says something cannot be done, or that they are unable to accept our request, I might say to them as I did to my student, "Imagine a world in which you were able to say 'yes.' And paint me a picture. What would that world look like?" This helps shift the conversation from what cannot be done to why it cannot be done. There are times, especially when an agreement seems unlikely, when even the people saying no have not carefully thought through exactly what would allow them to accept what is currently unacceptable. Of course, sometimes this conversation still leads to a dead end. But other times, they bring up concerns or obstacles that we are actually able to address in ways they would not have anticipated. At the very least, we get clarity on what needs to change if we want to revisit the possibility of a deal in the future.

Ask people to imagine a world in which the seemingly impossible actually happens. Then ask them to paint you a picture of what that world looks like.

By seeing the other side as a partner rather than an opponent, by focusing on the principle of value creation, and by pushing others to challenge their own assumptions about what is possible, you increase the possibility of breaking deadlock and resolving ugly conflict. Of course, you might still need to knock down barriers, manage the process, help the other side sell the deal, and so on, but you will have a better understanding of where you are going and the steps you need to take.

I end this section with some thoughts on what many would consider to be the ugliest of situations—those that are rife with long-standing mistrust, deep hostility, and a protracted history of grievances. We will consider some of the reasons why extremely divergent perspectives can persist, sometimes for generations, and how we might change our approach and perspective when dealing with seemingly intractable conflicts.

In Chapter 19, Kristen Behfar, et al., focus on strategies for direct and indirect confrontations, with applications in business and intercultural settings, which dovetails with our discussion of cross-cultural negotiations in Unit 2.

Chapter 19

Confronting Directly and Indirectly: Are You Attuned to Notice?

by Kristin J. Behfar, Allison Elias, and Jeanne Brett

Confrontations are not always angry fights; sometimes they happen when there is a need to deliver bad news, or to say no to what another person is asking of you. Many managers ask questions such as "What is the right way to say no to a boss?" "To challenge or oppose someone else's opinion?" "To deliver criticism to a colleague?" The answer to these questions depends to an extent on the context. And one important element of context is whether the parties are from direct- or indirect-confrontation cultures. Though some people might be familiar with cultural differences and norms for confrontation, the difference between direct and indirect confrontation often takes managers by surprise. The challenge in cross-cultural confrontation is being attuned to pick up on and appropriately interpret expressions of confrontation in a way that allows you to respond effectively.

Before turning to the business world, consider this experience one of our colleagues had in the classroom:

> I was teaching an undergraduate class where the learning objective was to promote awareness about how national culture impacts personal values. I asked an exchange student from

Kristin J. Behfar, Allison Elias, and Jeanne Brett, "Confronting Directly and Indirectly: Are You Attuned to Notice?" pp. 1-6. Copyright © 2015 by Darden Business Publishing. Reprinted with permission.

Japan if he would be willing to bring to class an artifact from home, and explain to his classmates how it represented an important Japanese cultural value. The student said that was "interesting," that he would consider it, asked for time to think about it. In the next class, he gave me a long list of reasons why he was worried about his ability to do this assignment: his English was not good enough, he needed to study for exams, and the other students already know a lot about Japan. These reasons seemed puzzling to me because his English was perfect, exams were six weeks away, and no one in the class knew a thing about Japanese culture. I wondered, is he experiencing a confidence problem? What is he worried about? Then I realized—he was not "worried." He was very clearly telling me "no."

This example illustrates how opposition is expressed in cultures similar to Japan's, wherein indirect, not direct, confrontation is normative. After initially being puzzled, the professor recognized the indirect cues the student was sending via noncommittal statements, delayed response time, and excuses. If you were the professor, and wanted this student to do the presentation—how would you respond? We will return to how the professor responded later.

In a business setting, this type of indirect confrontation may puzzle Western managers.[1] If the behavior is interpreted as intentional evasion, it may be viewed as deceptive. If the student in the above example had been an employee, shouldn't he have just said no and explained why? A quick "no" is more understandable, respectful, and efficient to most Western managers than a noncommittal response. Shouldn't problems and conflict be addressed directly and resolved efficiently? Although direct confrontation may be the pervasive approach to conflict in Western culture, people in some other cultures (including the student in the example above) engage in indirect confrontation. This document provides a guide for understanding how to recognize and respond to direct versus indirect approaches for engaging in confrontation. Such understanding is important for managers because missteps

---

[1] Jeffrey Sanchez-Burks, Fiona Lee, Incheol Choi, Richard Nisbett, Shuming Zhao, and Jasook Koo, "Conversing Across Cultures: East–West Communication Styles in Work and Nonwork Contexts," *Journal of Personality and Social Psychology* 85, no. 2 (2003): 363–72.

can undermine interpersonal and intergroup relationships by causing misunderstandings that seriously damage relationships with global business partners.

DISTINGUISHING BETWEEN DIRECT AND INDIRECT CONFRONTATION: WHAT IS THE DIFFERENCE?

Direct communication is hard to miss: the words, actions, and intended meaning all match. Direct communication is characteristic[2] of Western managers, who come from more individualistic cultures where people are accustomed to promoting their self-interest in interpersonal settings and to focusing more on the task than relationships in work settings.[3] In these cultures, individuals tend to be action oriented and solution minded when confronting one another. They are likely to propose specific alternative solutions and debate the merits of those solutions to themselves and to the other party.[4] The process typically goes like this: one party states the problem ("you have missed the deadline"), explains why it is a problem ("you are creating delays in the manufacturing line"), and tells the other person what will happen if he or she does not respond favorably ("we need this information by 3:00 p.m. today or you will be held responsible"). Inferential skills are seldom required to interpret the problem or understand the expectations of the speaker. Responses to a direct confrontation also tend to be an explicit, open acceptance or rejection of responsibility for the problem: "Yes, we missed the deadline and it is not our fault. The lawyer is still doing due diligence on the contractor. You will have to be patient."

---

[2] We are describing central tendencies of a culture rather than the explicit behavior of individuals from that culture. There will be variance in behavior within a culture.

[3] Nancy R. Buchan, Rachel T. Croson, and Eric J. Johnson, "When Do Fair Beliefs Influence Bargaining Behavior? Experimental Bargaining in Japan and the United States," *Journal of Consumer Research* 31, no. 1 (2004): 181–190; Jeffrey Sanchez-Burks, "Protestant Relational Ideology and (In)Attention to Relational Cues in Work Settings," *Journal of Personality and Social Psychology* 83, no. 4 (2002): 919.

[4] Jeanne Brett, Kristin Behfar, and Jeffrey Sanchez-Burks, "Managing Cross-Cultural Conflicts: A Close Look at the Implication of Direct Versus Indirect Confrontation," in *Handbook of Research in Conflict Management*, ed. Neal Ashkanasy, Oluremi B. Ayoko, and Karen Jehn (United Kingdom: Edward Edgar Publishing, 2014).

If the claimant is not willing to accept the rejection of his claim, negotiations may ensue. Parties then may try to convince each other of their perspective on the facts, threaten to use power, and—most successfully—identify and address the interests underlying the claim and its rejections.[5] If they are unable to reach agreement in negotiation, then they may involve a third party. But involving a superior in managerial disputes is usually a last resort because norms in Western culture hold that effective managers should be able to resolve conflict themselves.[6]

For East Asian managers accustomed to indirect confrontation, the direct Western approach of explicitly acknowledging the problem, making a claim, and proposing a solution causes both parties to lose face. *Face* in indirect-confrontation cultures is a person's social reputation (i.e., what others think of him or her). When confronting directly, therefore, the claimant loses face because he or she took a socially incorrect direct approach, and the respondent also loses face, because the claim is an accusation of failing to follow through on his or her social responsibilities. Direct confrontation can be deeply offensive to those who are not accustomed to it, because it appears disrespectful and causes loss of face.

In contrast, indirect confrontation communicates both the problem and the solution more subtly—but no less clearly—to parties familiar with indirect confrontation.[7] The purpose of indirect confrontation is to address substantive issues while maintaining both parties' face.[8] Although no one wants to be shamed or embarrassed, Westerners' sense of self-worth is less dependent on reputation and the social approval of others than East Asians' (Leung & Cohen, 2011).[9] Westerners tend to view claims as violations of individual rights (and therefore have the freedom to act and respond), not as a loss of face. This has two implications: Westerners are less likely to interpret the other person's direct claim as totally legitimate, and are very likely to advocate for their own self-interest in response. With indirect

[5] William L. Ury, Jeanne M. Brett, and Stephen B. Goldberg, *Getting Disputes Resolved*, 2nd ed. (San Francisco, CA: Jossey-Bass, 1993).

[6] Brett, Behfar, and Sanchez-Burks.

[7] Nalini Ambady, Jasook Koo, Fiona Lee, and Robert Rosenthal, "More Than Words: Linguistic and Nonlinguistic Politeness in Two Cultures," *Journal of Personality and Social Psychology* 70, no. 5 (1996): 996–1011.

[8] P. Christopher Earley, *Face, Harmony, and Social Structure: An Analysis of Organizational Behavior Across Cultures* (New York: Oxford University Press, 1997); John G. Oetzel and Stella Ting-Toomey, "Face Concerns in Interpersonal Conflict," *Communication Research* 30, no. 6 (2003): 599–624.

[9] Angela Leung and Dov Cohen, "Within- and Between-Culture Variation: Individual Difference and the Cultural Logics of Honor, Face, and Dignity Cultures," *Journal of Personality and Social Psychology* 100, no. 3 (2011): 509.

communication, confrontation is not as explicit. Indirect confrontation will typically unfold when one party calls attention to a problem by signaling or cuing the existence of the problem. This is not done by explicitly naming the problem. Rather, subtle cues pointing out the problem are conveyed, often by telling a story of an experience that has a lesson embedded, using metaphor or imagery, asking more questions, providing noncommittal responses, delaying, postponing, or stalling. The indirectly confronted party is left to infer not just the nature and scope of the problem but also the most suitable response.

For example, an American who was negotiating in China told us: "We'd be having an in-depth conversation about pricing, and all of a sudden they would start asking me about my summer vacation plans. That is when I knew I was pushing too hard." By not saying no directly, the indirectly confronting party withholds blame and responsibility, trusting that the confronted party will respond appropriately. Or it may be the confronting party who gets creative. As one manager put it, "I knew that delays and stall tactics by some East Asian team members signaled that they did not have approval from their home departments to do the work I was giving them. It was up to me to notice the problem and do some digging around to figure out how to secure that approval for them." Thus, the confronted party gains latitude to respond in a way that the confronting party may not have considered. Most importantly, withholding blame allows all concerned to save face. The solution appears as a goodwill gesture. In indirect-confrontation cultures, it is not an uncommon practice for disputing parties to involve a third party (mostly one which has more power or status) to intervene in anticipation of a confrontational situation, even before there has been any confrontation between the parties. This value for harmony is closely held in collective and hierarchical cultures.[10]

---

[10] Dean Tjosvold and Haifa Sun, "Social Face in Conflict: Effects of Affronts to Person and Position in China," *Group Dynamics: Theory, Research, and Practice* 4 (2000): 259–71.

STRATEGIES FOR MANAGERS TO USE IN INDIRECT AND DIRECT CONFRONTATION

The question, then, is: Once you recognize that you are being confronted directly or indirectly, how should you respond?

Returning to our opening example about the Japanese student telling our colleague no, we see that the student indirectly confronted the professor by using noncommittal statements (e.g., "that's interesting" and "I will consider it"), by delaying the final response, and by expressions of worry. It is highly likely that the professor's request itself, which put the student in a position to impart knowledge to his peers, was very uncomfortable for someone new to the American classroom. Once the professor recognized this, a culturally attuned response was easier to formulate. The professor acknowledged that studying for exams was indeed important, and complimented the student's diligence in preparing for exams. Then she told the student about a previous class wherein a student from France had brought in one of her favorite homemade meals to share with the class, and how she had told everyone about the recipe having been handed down from her grandmother, how the ingredients were grown on her family's land, and how stories of her heritage had been passed from generation to generation while in the kitchen preparing this dish together. The professor shared that it had been one of the highlights of the term for the American students and had sparked conversations and friendships among the students as they came to understand one another better.

The message of the story was that the assignment was meant to share culture among students and to connect them with one another—not to force one person to demonstrate superior knowledge of a particular culture. The next day, the Japanese student came to class prepared to give the presentation, and opened with the story the professor had told him the previous day, saying he hoped his presentation would accomplish the same result for both the other students in the class and for himself. Had the professor been more direct, by repeating the request, telling him not to worry, or that his decision was disappointing, it is likely the student would have withdrawn—or, if he had complied, been extremely uncomfortable.

Understanding the difference between direct and indirect confrontation is valuable for managing conflict in business relationships that carry pronounced financial and relational consequences. Consider another example that demonstrates the advantages of being adept at both direct and indirect confrontation.

An American entrepreneur had a contract with a Chinese computer-parts manufacturer to produce patent-pending components for computer hard drives. He made clear to the Chinese plant manager that he wanted access to the plant limited to employees because of the insecure state of his intellectual property. On one of his impromptu visits to the factory, however, the entrepreneur found the plant manager giving a German engineer a tour of the facilities! The plant manager cordially introduced the entrepreneur to the visiting German engineer, explaining that additional plant facilities were under construction, and the German engineer's company was a potential customer. The plant manager seemed unfazed by the encounter, which upset the entrepreneur.

Although the German engineer left immediately after the tour, the entrepreneur was unsure of how much the German had learned about his patent-pending product. How long had he been walking around the plant? Was this a return visit? Had other competing engineers toured the plant in search of new factory space, becoming aware of the product? How should he deal with this situation?

The entrepreneur could have taken a direct approach berating the Chinese plant manager, accusing him of violating trust, asking specifically who else had been at the plant, and amplifying the requirement for privacy. The entrepreneur might have demanded installation of cameras, the presence of his own employee at all times, or access to review visitor logs. Instead, he decided to take a more culturally attuned approach.

The entrepreneur invited several senior members of the plant operations team, including the plant manager, to dinner. During dinner, he asked them casually about the construction progress of the new facility, hoping to gather more information about external visitors. Attuned to the entrepreneur's indirect cues of discomfort and concern, the Chinese plant manager responded by telling a story:

Centuries ago, two generals learned the art of war from the same master, a master who instructed all of his students not to reveal some of his specific teachings until needed on the battlefield. The two generals, who were still young and untested, were invited by the emperor to visit the palace for several days. Although the emperor did not disclose his motivations to the generals, he was choosing who should lead the largest group of skilled warriors against potential invaders. He spent time with both generals alone, asking them in particular about the specific teachings.

One was eager to impress the emperor with his knowledge, elaborating on all of the master's teachings. The other general told the emperor that he trusted his master's wisdom and wanted to preserve some of the teachings for use on the battlefield. The emperor called the two generals together with their master, announcing that he had chosen the second general to lead. He was impressed with the second general's respect for authority as well as his trustworthy nature. According to the emperor, building trust in relationships was more important than acquiring greater status.

Had the entrepreneur gone with his first inclination to demand information from the Chinese plant manager and insist that no more external guests enter the factory where his product was being produced, he might have irreparably destroyed the trust and relationship he so critically depended on with that Chinese manager—and in doing so, lost future opportunities to use this and potentially other nearby Chinese plants to manufacture his product. Instead, he engaged in a culturally sensitive indirect confrontation, which led the Chinese manager to acknowledge the entrepreneur's concerns and reassure him of the safety of his intellectual property.

Confrontation is a pressure point in cross-cultural business settings because both the content and the delivery can aggravate the conflict. Many Western managers are extremely uncomfortable with the entrepreneur's actions in the hard-drive manufacturing example. Western cultural norms emphasize control and verification (i.e., rights and power); managers from Western cultural backgrounds perceive the security of an important patent that hinges on a manufacturer's understanding of the entrepreneur's expectations as a huge risk. Was the story about the two generals enough of an assurance? The entrepreneur couldn't know for sure. What he did know was that there was a major risk in using direct confrontation in this situation: the Chinese plant manager would lose face in being blamed for the violation of privacy, and as a result, his motivation to protect the entrepreneur's intellectual property would not be high. The effective global manager needs to be able to weigh the pros and cons of direct and indirect confrontation before choosing a strategic approach.

It is not easy to keep one's culturally comfortable style of confrontation at bay when confronted with another approach. Cultural conditioning is deeply ingrained as a result of years of experience and socialization. Moving fluently between direct and indirect confrontation requires focus and control. But managers such as the entrepreneur in the manufacturing story are using that fluency to their advantage when doing business in a global environment. **Figure 19.1** outlines some strategies for managers to use in response to indirect and direct confrontation.

Figure 19.1. Formulating a response to direct versus indirect confrontation.

	STRATEGIES FOR WESTERN MANAGERS TO USE WITH INDIRECT CONFRONTATION	STRATEGIES FOR EAST ASIAN MANAGERS TO USE WITH DIRECT CONFRONTATION
Recognize it's a problem	You are being told a story or a metaphor. Think: Why this story? Why this metaphor? Consider what is being conveyed and why.	Understand that behaviors—such as direct questioning, challenging assumptions, offering solutions, expecting you to take responsibility—that are offensive to you but are not necessarily intended to be personal (particularly because this is a business setting)—are completely normal behavior on the part of the counterparty.
	Listen for "that might be difficult" or just a noncommittal "yes" suggesting that your approach is not optimal.	
	You may be able to ask some questions of knowledgeable advisers: Why do you think the protagonist did this? What was he expected to do? What was he trying to accomplish?	Try not to be offended; try not to be defensive; try to be as direct as possible in responding.
Address the problem	Ask a hypothetical question about what would be an appropriate way to approach a similar problem. Listen to the response and resist interrupting. Paraphrase, or try coming back with a story of your own that you think may capture the crux of the problem.	Try to understand the interests underlying the problem. Focus the conversation on "why," not "what."
		Instead of saying "that would be difficult," try to explain *why* responding as requested would be difficult; reveal your interests by explaining why acting as requested would be difficult.
	Suggest how you would like to address the problem. Ask for feedback. Listen for "that might be difficult" or just a noncommittal "yes" suggesting that your approach is not optimal.	Don't give up and go to the boss right away.
		Work together to generate alternative approaches that meet common interests.

Figure 19.1. (*continued*)

| *Address the problem* | Take your situation to a cultural mentor outside of the organization to check your understanding of the situation and ask for ideas for how best to respond. (Remedy implies solution rather than process.) | If you need a superior's authorization, consider going to the boss together with the counterparty and explaining what you want to do together and why. |
| | If this is a Western company, ask the counterparty to hold off involving a superior. Explain that so involving the superior may have negative implications for you and for the counterparty. | You are not required to make all strategic concessions, but you need to be willing to meet your counterparty halfway if you are to build a good working relationship going forward. |

Source: Created by case writers.

When global managers acquire this facility in switching confrontation approaches, they will be able to more effectively navigate the potential and avoidable misunderstandings in cross-cultural business.

In Chapter 20, Paul Wilkinson looks at the high-stress negotiation process of hostage-taking sieges over the past 50 years from a historical perspective, including a well-publicized historical case in Eastern Europe.

Chapter 20

Hostage-Taking, Sieges and Problems of Response

by Paul Wilkinson

Hostage-taking is a characteristic tactic in the repertoire of modern terrorism.[1] By exercising a terrible threat against the lives of their victims, the terrorist hostage-takers seek to exert a degree of psychological pressure to obtain changes of policy or major concessions, such as huge ransom payments, the release of fellow terrorists from gaol or the broadcasting or publication of their grievances and demands. The vast majority of kidnappings are carried out by common criminals to gain ransoms. In Latin America this has become a major industry with huge profits to be made.[2] It is estimated that in Colombia alone there are several thousand such kidnappings annually.

Since the late 1960s politically motivated terrorists in many parts of the world have taken to using kidnap and ransom as a means of financing their activities. They have also targeted the symbols of their 'enemy' national government, for example by kidnapping diplomats, seizing embassies and other diplomatic premises, and by hijacking the civilian airliners of national 'flag' airlines, a particularly dramatic form of hostage-taking that always brings wide international media coverage.

It is easy to see why hostage-taking has enjoyed a growing popularity in recent years as a terrorist tactic. It is extremely cheap and requires only small numbers of hostage-takers armed with standard, widely available weaponry. Above all, it is one of the very few terrorist tactics with a track record of success in forcing

Paul Wilkinson, "Hostage-Taking, Sieges and Problems of Response," *Terrorism Versus Democracy: The Liberal State Response*, pp. 103-121, 231-233. Copyright © 2006 by Taylor & Francis Group. Reprinted with permission.

governments into major concessions, such as the release of large numbers of imprisoned terrorists and even, in some instances, changes in government policy.

Roberta Wohlstetter has argued that it was Raul and Fidel Castro who pioneered the modern wave of political kidnappings that 'used foreign nationals ... as pawns in a domestic struggle for power'. And she points out that: 'They violated not only internal rules of political order, but also the meagre international rules that lend stability to relations among states.'[3] It is clear that the sensational publicity gained from the rash of kidnaps of US citizens in the American and Canadian press considerably aided Castro in his campaign to intimidate the United States into withholding assistance to the Batista regime. (By late June 1958, the Castro guerrillas had kidnapped at least 47 US citizens, including 30 servicemen. Castro even used the US captives as a weapon to make the United States force the Cuban air force to cease the bombing of the rebel zone in Sierra Cristal.[4] Raul Castro told the United States that the guerrillas would hold the US captives in the bombing zone. In the late 1960s and early 1970s the political kidnapping of foreigners (especially Americans) in Latin America, southeast Asia and the Middle East reached epidemic proportions. Between 1968 and April 1983 diplomats from 113 countries were victims of international terrorism.[5] Among them were 23 ambassadors from 13 different countries who were assassinated, including the US ambassadors to Lebanon, Cyprus, Sudan, Guatemala and Afghanistan, and the Turkish ambassadors to Australia, France, Spain, Austria and Yugoslavia.

During 1979–80 a new scourge developed: the terrorist fashion of seizing whole embassies and their staffs and occupants. This is still a fairly easy operation for well-armed terrorists in countries where the security forces are too ill-trained, ill-equipped and ill-prepared to protect embassies adequately. In the notorious case of the seizure of the US Embassy in Tehran by about 400 Iranian students on 4 November 1979, the Iranian regime totally failed to carry out its obligation under international law.[6] The Islamic revolutionary authorities made no attempt to assist the US mission staff. They provided no police or military protection for the US personnel or property; they made no attempt to return the embassy to US control by expelling the students. On the contrary, they compounded their offences against the international law of diplomacy by 'adopting' the siege as their own, not only by giving the official blessing of the Ayatollah Khomeini but also by manipulating the hostage crisis to inflict maximum international embarrassment and humiliation on the United States. This was the first time in recent history that any state has so flagrantly defied the norms and conventions of diplomatic relations.[7] To most ordinary Americans, the hatred and abuse hurled at them by the screaming mobs paraded before their embassy in Tehran seemed quite incomprehensible. The feeling of helplessness and frustration provoked by these scenes, displayed on US television screens week after week, undoubtedly did much to undermine the domestic support and credibility of the Carter administration, and the reaction against it inevitably helped Ronald Reagan, with his more hard-nosed and assertive stance, to win his overwhelming election victory.

However, the Americans were by no means alone among the major democracies in experiencing the feelings of frustration and helplessness in the face of terrorist hostage situations. The whole world was stunned by the terrorist attack on the Munich Olympics in 1972.[8] The risks of terrorist attack on the Olympic Games had been underestimated. The Olympic Village was particularly vulnerable, and lacked adequate perimeter security.

On 5 August, eight terrorists climbed the perimeter fence and headed for the Israeli accommodation block. Two athletes were shot dead and nine others taken hostage. The terrorists demanded the release of 200 imprisoned Palestinians.

Expert advice from Israeli officials was ignored, and the task of rescuing the hostages was placed in the hands of the Bavarian police. The response team was ill-prepared, ill-equipped and outnumbered. The Israeli hostages were killed in the tragically bungled rescue attempt. It was this disastrous hostage crisis that led the United States and other Western governments to make an urgent review of policies and resources for combating terrorism, including hostage-taking.

The case for reviewing the response to hostage crises currently is every bit as strong as it was in the 1970s. The University of St Andrews–RAND Corporation international terrorism chronology data show that in the early 1990s there was a 33.5 per cent rise in incidents of kidnappings of foreigners worldwide. The US Department of State's *Patterns of Global Terrorism* statistics for the mid-1990s indicate that between 14 and 15 percent of all international terrorist incidents worldwide fall into the category of kidnappings or barricade and hostage situations. We should also bear in mind that these statistics exclude politically motivated hostage-taking by fellow nationals within the same state. They also exclude the use of mass hostage-taking by regimes and factions as a weapon in the period preceding full-scale international or internal war, or during such conflicts. The growth of this phenomenon, which flagrantly breaches the humanitarian laws of war, should be a cause of major concern to all democratic governments. Mass hostage-taking was used by Saddam Hussein in his notorious 'human shield' tactic,[9] a crude attempt to coerce the coalition allies into backing off from military action to liberate Kuwait from Iraqi occupation. A similar tactic was used by Serb militants in an attempt to intimidate soldiers in the UN Protection Force (UNPROFOR) in Bosnia and to dissuade the NATO allies from taking any forceful action against further aggression by Serb forces.[10] Also, in the mid 1990s, the Chechen militants employed the weapon of mass hostage-taking against the Russians, with lethal and dramatic effect. We will examine the key aspects of these events later in this chapter, as they have major implications not only for the fragile emerging democracies of the former soviet bloc but also for the governments of Western democracies as a reminder of the folly of abandoning their expertise, resources and mechanisms for hostage crisis management, or of allowing them to fall into disrepair.

BARRICADE AND HOSTAGE SIEGES

The politically motivated barricade and siege situation presents the democratic government and its security forces with very different problems and dilemmas from those confronted when the kidnap victims or hostages are held in an unknown location, perhaps in remote and inhospitable terrain or in the urban jungle of a huge city. In a barricade and hostage situation the government and security forces have a key advantage: the terrorists themselves become hostages and a part of the deal they seek will be a safe exit. This can be used as a powerful lever in police siege tactics. Also, a siege provides the authorities with *time* and an opportunity for a planned security agency response, which, if skilfully implemented, may offer a chance of rescuing the hostages without surrendering major concessions to the hostage-takers. Few other terrorist tactics offer a similar opportunity to the security forces: it is true that in some incidents a bomb will be preceded by a warning, but frequently the warning time is so brief and the information on the location of the bomb is so vague that there is no chance for the police to be able to evacuate the area.

Democratic governments are faced with the most adverse circumstances of all when the hostage incident involving their nationals is in a foreign country where the government and a high proportion of the general population are hostile. The seizure of the US diplomatic mission in Tehran was just such a case. The Iranian regime brazenly adopted the hostage-taking and defied all calls from the United States and the international community for the release of the diplomats. President Carter, frustrated by the failure of diplomatic and economic pressures to bring the release of the hostages, embarked on a military rescue operation, Operation Rice Bowl, in April 1980.[11] It was a tragic failure, leading to the deaths of eight American military personnel, but even if it had been better coordinated and equipped, the odds were stacked against its success. The Reagan administration experienced similar frustration when TWA Flight 847 was hijacked by Hezbollah terrorists who then proceeded to turn it into a hostage situation by moving passengers to unknown locations in the sprawling suburbs of Beirut.[12] The domestic demand for the release of the TWA Flight 847 hostages placed such pressure on the US government that it led them to press their Israeli allies to release over 700 prisoners demanded by the hostage-takers, thus conceding an enormous political and psychological victory to the terrorists and demonstrating the potential of hostage-taking as a high-yield weapon against even the most militarily powerful democracy, where public opinion insists on paying almost any price for saving the lives of fellow citizens. Similarly, Western governments were forced to rule out the idea of sending elite commando forces into Lebanon to rescue Terry Waite, John McCarthy, Brian Keenan, Terry Anderson and the other Western hostages held for much longer periods, mostly by Hezbollah.[13] The terrorists, however, took no chances and constantly moved their captives from one secret hideout to another in order to confuse Western intelligence services and forestall a rescue attempt. The ultimate release of the Western hostages was due to a combination of propitious circumstances: the Israelis were interested in striking a deal with Hezbollah in order to discover the whereabouts of missing Israeli servicemen; the Iranian regime, which sponsored Hezbollah and could exert considerable influence upon its leadership, decided that the hostage crisis in Lebanon had become an obstacle to their efforts to improve their economic links and to meet the crippling costs of their war of attrition with Iraq; Syria, the dominant military power in the Lebanon, wished to gain credit for being seen to help facilitate the freeing of the Western hostages in order to improve its diplomatic position in the Middle East; and, last but not least, the UN provided a patient and skilful negotiator, Mr Giandomenico Picco, who played a vital role in brokering the deal that led to the hostages' rescue.[14]

In dealing with barricade and hostage situations, however, the United States, Britain and other Western democracies began to develop an increasingly effective law enforcement response. Initially, police hostage tactics were developed mainly in confronting sieges where the hostage-takers were criminal gangs or mentally disturbed persons in domestic siege situations. Frank Bolz of the New York Police Department pioneered many of the police techniques of hostage negotiation that were later acquired by the Metropolitan Police in Britain and other law enforcement agencies in the United States and elsewhere. By studying the complex psychology of the siege situation, and by thorough debriefing and reassessment after each incident, the police began to perfect tactics and techniques that would maximise their chances of success.

A famous hostage-taking incident in Stockholm in 1973, involving bank robbers who took four hostages during a bank raid. It gave its name to the psychological bonding process between captor and captive: the Stockholm Syndrome.[15] During the siege, one of the female hostages formed a deep emotional bond with one of the gunmen, and she refused to cooperate with those who wanted to liberate her. Forming such a bond is believed to have saved the lives of many hostages, and it has been claimed that it explains why, during the 1977 siege at Lima, the life of one of the Peruvian hostages, the Minister of Agriculture, was saved.[16] However, it would be a great mistake to see the Stockholm Syndrome as an automatic or inevitable process. So much depends on the personalities of the individuals involved. Moreover, in many hostage-taking incidents the terrorists appear to have gone to considerable lengths to prevent any bonds of personal attachment with their captives, by changing guards frequently and ensuring that hostages are regularly abused, beaten and subjected to constant humiliation.

In the 1970s and early 1980s, however, there were some dramatic successes for the security forces in siege situations, which began to indicate that in 'close quarters' hostage situations, at least, the balance of advantage was swinging in the direction of the authorities. For example, in December 1975, the Metropolitan Police had to deal with a gang of four IRA terrorists who had taken refuge in a flat in Balcombe Street and had taken the occupants, Mr and Mrs Matthews, hostage.[17] The police played a softly-softly waiting game. They kept talking to the terrorists but did not give in to their demands. The Home Office called in the SAS but kept their availability a secret. Electronic surveillance equipment was installed to enable the police to monitor the conversations between hostages and terrorist. The police waited until the sixth day, when they judged that the terrorists were getting hungry and their resolve was weakening. A key factor in persuading the terrorists to surrender peacefully may well have been the deliberate leaking of the news through a broadcast bulletin that the SAS were at the scene.

The strategy of patience does not always result in a peaceful surrender by the terrorists. For example, the Dutch were compelled to use a marine rescue force to rescue passengers held hostage on a hijacked train south of Groningen in May 1977, and 105 children and six teachers held hostage in a simultaneous operation by Moluccan terrorists at a primary school in Bovensmilde.[18] In the Dutch cases, again, the value of concealed microphones in gathering precise information on the position of the hostages and the terrorists and the value of thoroughly planning the entire rescue operation were clearly demonstrated. In the storming of the train by the marines, 53 hostages were freed, two hostages died and six terrorists were killed. Considering the great difficulties involved in mounting such a rescue, it was a remarkable achievement.

A dramatic illustration of Britain's growing expertise in handling siege situations came in 1980, when six anti-Khomeini terrorists seized the Iranian Embassy in London, with 26 hostages.[19] Initially, the police employed the strategy of patience. There followed five days of negotiation, during which five hostages, including pregnant women, were released. The terrorists were delighted when the British authorities granted the concession of permitting their political message to be read on the BBC World Service. But the terrorist leader became more aggressive on the sixth day because not all the demands had been met. The terrorists killed one hostage and threatened to kill another every 40 minutes until their demands had been granted. As soon as it became clear that the terrorists had started to murder the hostages, the decision was taken by the Cabinet Crisis Committee to send in the SAS to end the siege and rescue the remaining hostages. The SAS executed the rescue with impressive speed and efficiency. All the remaining hostages were rescued, and only one of the hostage-takers survived. There is little doubt that this display of highly professional military force used against terrorists acted as a stimulus to other states to develop their own hostage-rescue capabilities and as a considerable deterrent to similar embassy takeovers by terrorists not only in London but also in other major cities. It is true that there was a confrontation with the police involving the Libyan 'People's Bureau' (the Libyan regime's designation for an embassy) in 1984, but this was not triggered by hostage-taking but by the killing of WPC Yvonne Fletcher, on duty in St James's Square, by a gunman inside the Libyan People's Bureau.[20]

It would be a major mistake, however, to assume that the deployment of military force in a rescue operation is invariably the correct or most effective ultimate solution to a siege situation. There have been some highly successful resolutions by negotiation leading to the hostages being released unharmed. For example, this was the outcome of one of the most internationally complex sieges in the history of terrorism in Latin America: the seizure of the Dominican Embassy in Bogotá in February 1980 by 18 M19 terrorists.[21] There was a diplomatic reception on at the time and 80 hostages were taken, including 18 ambassadors. The hostage-takers threatened to kill all their captives if the police stormed the embassy. They demanded: the release of over 300 prisoners from gaol in Colombia, including 200 suspected M19 terrorists captured from the previous year; the payment of a ransom of $50 million; safe passage for themselves out of the country; and the publication of their manifesto by all the countries represented among the hostages. The terrorists appeared prepared to hold out for as long as was necessary to get their demands, and observers were impressed by the planning and organisation that had gone into the mass hostage-taking. The siege lasted 61 days and was ended not by force but by negotiation. The basis of the deal was that the Colombian government would set up a panel of ten leading lawyers to process trials for the imprisoned M19 members. The Inter-American Human Rights Commission of the Organization of American States (OAS) was brought in to monitor the trials. Safe exit to Cuba was arranged for the hostage-takers, and the Castro regime offered them asylum. In return the hostages were released. The government refused to pay the ransom demanded, but did permit the private business community to pay a ransom of $2.5 million. Some might argue that the concessions granted to the terrorists were too large a price to pay for the lives of the hostages. Against this one has to weigh the fact that the terrorists were known to be well armed and ruthless and that their key demands were refused. A major complication for the Colombian government was the fact that it was difficult to get agreement from all the countries involved in the incident. In view of the circumstances, the compromises can be fully justified as a means of avoiding large-scale loss of life while at the same time minimising as far as possible the gains of the hostage-takers.

Premature or clumsy use of military force to end a siege situation can be particularly dangerous where the law enforcement agencies are dealing with religious or political fanatics with a tight control of the mindsets of their followers and with some adherents and sympathisers at large in the community. The case of the siege at the Branch Davidian cult's compound at Waco, Texas, in 1993 offers a dramatic illustration of the problems involved.[22] The 51-day siege was triggered when the Alcohol, Tobacco and Firearms Unit entered the compound. There was an effort to negotiate, but it appears that serious mistakes were made; insufficient use was made of the expertise that does exist on extreme religious cults, and on the Branch Davidian cult and its leader, David Koresh, in particular. There was no proper plan for ending the siege with the use of force. Eighty people, including 25 children, died when the authorities sought to end the siege, most of them from asphyxiation in the fire that, arson investigators claim, had been started by cult members. The Federal Bureau of Investigation (FBI) took rapid steps to learn from this tragic experience, and the formation of the Critical Incident Response Group (CIRG) was an attempt to bring together the very best skills in hostage negotiation, the most sophisticated technical resources and the most highly trained rescue team to deal with future sieges. These enhancements of the FBI's capability to respond to sieges have been partially effective: more lives have been saved in hostage situations. But we do not overlook the unfortunate longer-term effect of an event such as Waco on the overall levels of violent extremism. For many in the militia movement and other organisations of the American extreme right, Waco provides yet another stick with which to beat the federal government. It is worth noting that testimony given at the trial of Timothy McVeigh, convicted for his part in the Oklahoma bombing, suggested that one of his motivations for the bomb attack was his desire for revenge against the federal law enforcement authorities for their role at Waco.[23]

MASS HOSTAGE-TAKINGS BY CHECHEN MILITANTS

Russia, like America, also experienced problems of domestic terrorism and hostage-taking in the 1990s, but the scale was much greater and the political impact of the hostage crises in 1995 and 1996 on Russian policy was far more dramatic than that of any hostage crisis in Western countries. Perhaps the most dramatic and effective of the mass hostage-takings by Chechen militants against Russian targets came in June 1995, when a group of Chechens under the leadership of Shamil Basayev carried out a cross-border raid into the Russian town of Budennovsk.[24] Having tried unsuccessfully to seize the police station, they seized a hospital and around 2,000 hostages, including children and pregnant women. The scale of this was unprecedented. Russian troops and police surrounded the hospital, and in their initial assault 37 army personnel and police were killed. Many civilians were caught in the crossfire and pleaded with Russian troops to stop firing. The Chechen gunmen were heavily outnumbered but fought with fanatical determination and stuck to their key demands: an end to Russian military operations in Chechnya and negotiations to discuss the withdrawal of forces. In response to this unprecedented hostage crisis, the Russian prime minister, Viktor Chernomyrdin, offered huge concessions. He announced in a TV broadcast: 'I am asking you to let the hostages go. Here, before millions of people watching us on television. I am officially making an order to halt military actions in Chechnya and start negotiations.'[25] Negotiators did sign an agreement the following month, but continuing clashes led to failure of the pact.

A highly dangerous precedent had been set. Hostage-taking of civilians, explicitly prohibited under the Geneva Conventions, had been carried out on a massive scale and had been rewarded by a massive policy change by the Russian government. Many observers share the view that Chechen demands for autonomy are fully justified on both political and moral grounds, especially in the light of the appalling treatment they received during the communist period. But by making dramatic changes in policy to obtain the release of hostages the Russian leaders were sending the message that mass hostage-taking works, and were storing up trouble for the future.[26]

It was therefore no great surprise when in January 1996 a group of militant Chechens, this time led by Salman Raduyev (the son-in-law of Dzhokhar Dudayev, leader of the Chechen independence movement), seized over 2,000 hostages, including pregnant women, newborn infants and children when they occupied a hospital at Kizlyar in neighbouring Dagestan.[27] Raduyev threatened to avenge every Chechen death with 15 Russian deaths. It was a carbon copy of the mass hostage-taking at the hospital at Budennovsk six months previously. What is surprising is that the Russian authorities, their intelligence services, police, military and security advisers appear to have been totally unprepared for this attack. The

Chechen fighters were able to carry out their mission without any opposition, despite the fact that they had traversed two major emplacements of Russian soldiers to enter Kizlyar. President Yeltsin's fury at this humiliating turn of events was understandable. At a cabinet meeting confrontation shown on television, President Yeltsin shouted at the Defence Minister, Pavel Grachev:

> What are you Generals up to? Why have you learned no lessons from previous events? We have been dealt with another blow. We had information in advance that the rebels were coming, but no action was taken. What have you Generals been doing?[28]

Despite Yeltsin's promise to take the 'most resolute action' to restore law and order, the initial reaction of the officials in Dagestan seeking to save the hostages' lives was to strike a deal with the Chechens almost identical to the bargain struck in the Budennovsk hostage crisis in June 1995. The Chechens freed over 2,000 hostages in return for a guarantee of safe exit across the Chechen border. They took over 150 hostages from Kizlyar, including children, in a convoy of buses heading for the Chechen border. But the convoy was halted when its exit was blocked by the blowing up of a bridge by the Russian army at the village of Pervomayskaya. There was a tense stand-off between the Chechen fighters and the Russians: Russian troops surrounded the convoy while the Chechens threatened to kill their hostages if the Russian troops failed to guarantee safe passage. On the night of 15 January, Russian troops stormed the village of Pervomayskaya, using artillery and helicopter gunships to end the mass hostage crisis. The village was virtually destroyed and there were heavy casualties. Inevitably a large number of hostages were killed in the ferocious Russian assault.[29] It become almost inevitable that the Russian authorities would use force to end the crisis even at a heavy cost in lives, because they had been so heavily criticised for allowing a second mass hostage-taking in seven months and for their weakness and confusion in responding to the crisis. Russian television reported that the decision to attack had been taken after the Chechens shot six Siberian policemen among the hostages, but the Chechens denied that they had killed any hostages and claimed they were willing to negotiate.

It is clear that the tragic mass hostage crises of June 1995 and January 1996 did serious damage to the reputation of President Yeltsin and the Russian government, and of security forces as a whole. However, it was the reputation of Mr Viktor Chernomyrdin that suffered most directly, because his televised order to halt Russian military action in direct response to the hostage seizure was seen as having set a dangerous precedent.

An additional and potentially dangerous consequence of major confrontations between hostage-takers and the security forces of the government they oppose is that they sometimes provoke further terrorist actions by sympathisers acting in support of their rebel colleagues. Where there is a network of sympathisers in an ethnic diaspora, these sympathetic or supportive actions may well occur. The Chechens have a diaspora of small communities not only in the Middle East but also as far afield as the United States. During the second major Chechen hostage-taking in January 1996, a group of sympathisers seized a Turkish ferry at the port of Trabzon and threatened to blow it up with all its 118 Russian passengers aboard when it reached the Bosphorus unless the Russian forces halted their attacks on the Chechen militants holding the hostages at Pervomayskaya.[30] The Chechens released the ferry passengers and the incident ended peacefully, but the Russians criticised the Turkish authorities for their leniency to the gunmen. However, it would have been foolish of the Russians to alienate the Turks. The Turks feel some affinity with, and some sympathy for the Chechens, but they have no wish to see an escalation of terrorism in the area. In view of the volatile ethnic relations between the Russians and other ethnic groups in the Caucasus, it makes good sense for the Russian authorities to seek improved cooperation with neighbouring states to help prevent any other embryonic terrorist campaigns from emerging. And, after all, the outcome of the Turkish handling of the ferry hijacking was successful in preventing bloodshed. All the hostages were freed without loss of life. This is a stark contrast to the heavy-handed Russian tactics, which resulted in the virtual destruction of the village of Pervomayskaya, and the deaths of many of the hostages the troops were supposed to be rescuing. If the prime aim of the assault at Pervomayskaya had genuinely been to free the hostages, a surgical rescue operation by a special forces commando unit, using highly accurate man-portable weapons should have been used. In reality, the main aim of the Russian authorities seems to have been to win the grudging approval of the right-wing Duma by a crushing display of military force against rebels. However, this could not disguise the underlying political reality. The two tragically botched mass hostage crises had played a part in wearying the Russian public of the Chechen conflict. There was a serious upsurge of fighting between Russian troops and Chechens in Grozny in August 1996. Then General Lebed, given responsibility for solving the Chechen crisis, managed to obtain a ceasefire agreement just in time to prevent another Russian bombardment of Grozny at the end of August.[31] On 29 December 1996 Russian combat troops withdrew from Chechnya,[32] effectively handing over control to the rebel government. However, in 1999 Russia invaded Chechnya again, following apartment bombings in Moscow for which Chechens were blamed.

The Chechen militants continued to plan further mass hostage takings in their increasingly desperate struggle against the Russians. On 23 October 2002 one of the Chechen terrorist leaders, Barayev, led a group of 40 terrorists in a mass hostage-taking in a Moscow theatre during the performance of a musical show set in the Second World War and seized 1,000 people. The terrorists were heavily armed, and the women terrorists had explosives strapped to their bodies and threatened to blow up the theatre unless Russia withdrew its troops from Chechnya. The Russian authorities were faced with an apparently impossible task: how could they free the hostages without the Chechens blowing up the theatre? They had at their disposal special forces units with some experience of confronting Chechen terrorists, but the traditional hostage rescue technique of launching a coordinated multiple-entry-point attack on the hostage-takers, using to the full the advantages of surprise and speed, was unavailable. The Chechens manned every entry point and would have been able to detonate their bombs and blow up the theatre, probably killing all the hostages. It was clear to the authorities and to the hostages that Barayev's terrorist group were all prepared to die for their cause. It was the worst mass hostage situation any modern government had ever been faced with.

The Russians decided to use gas to knock out the hostage-takers and rescue the hostages. Government scientists in many countries had been searching for years to find a gas powerful enough to knock out terrorists almost instantaneously without causing death, thus enabling them to save hostages without any loss of life. The Russians clearly believed they had found this elixir and infiltrated the gas through the ventilation system.[33] It was certainly very potent: the Russian soldiers had waited an hour before entering the theatre and shot dead all the terrorists, including their leader, Barayev. At first the Russians thought they had mounted a completely successful rescue operation. They soon discovered that a large number of hostages had died in their theatre seats. Many of the 129 hostages who died choked to death when their heads lolled back and they stopped being able to breathe. The soldiers had held back over an hour before intervening and even then were not properly briefed on the kind of swift medical intervention needed to revive the hostages who had been more seriously affected by the mystery gas. Hostages were taken out onto the street and laid on their backs. When hostages were at last taken to hospitals in Moscow, the medical staff had no idea how to revive them because they had not been told what kind of gas had been used to end the siege. We will never know how many of the 129 hostages who died could have been resuscitated if these elementary mistakes had not been made. However, the Russian authorities hailed the outcome as a great success for the security forces. It is true that they saved over 800 lives, but at enormous cost.

In the longer term, the Moscow theatre siege of October 2002 is likely to intensify research in the West to discover an effective knockout gas to end mass hostage situations. Western scientists were puzzled as to the nature of the gas used by the Russians, but the most informed guess is that it is a derivative developed from fentanyl, an opiate well known in the medical profession. The fact that the gas caused a less than a 20 per cent level of fatalities shows it was not as powerful as the well-known derivative carfentanil and was designed to mitigate the chances of those exposed to the gas dying through cessation of respiration and the ensuing cardiac arrest. It is also to be hoped that scientists in Russia, America and Western Europe can combine efforts and share knowledge in order to perfect a knockout gas capable of ending all kinds of siege situations and saving large numbers of innocent lives.

For the Chechen militants, the Moscow theatre siege was clearly a major defeat. Yet this did not deter them from making another major attempt to blackmail the Russian government through a spectacular mass hostage-taking. In September 2004 a Chechen terrorist gang seized an entire school of children and parents at Beslan in North Ossetia at the start of the new school term. A total of 331 hostages, including dozens of children, died when devices planted in the school by the terrorists started to explode and the security forces stormed the school. Many of the children were killed when they tried to escape from the building. Those who watched TV pictures of the siege were struck by the apparent chaos of the security forces' response. There was no effective cordon to seal off the area around the school. Parents appeared to be rushing past the security forces and into the school grounds without any effort being made to stop them. But the mistakes were not confined to the incompetent action of the security forces. According to Alexander Torshin, leader of the federal inquiry appointed by Moscow, the Russian Interior Minister had sent telegrams, based on intelligence, to the regional police in North Ossetia, ordering them to strengthen protection of all educational facilities on 1 September, but the order was ignored. Mr Alexander Torshin's report contradicts the earlier report by a prosecutor exonerating the security forces. Once again the Chechen terrorists had shown utter ruthlessness in their tactics, again seizing a soft target. The cruelty shown towards the children and parents at Beslan was fully in keeping with the previous Chechen hostage-taking when they had been willing to put the lives of pregnant mothers and babies at risk by seizing control of a hospital. Sadly the Russian authorities' handling of the situation at Beslan showed no improvement over their performance in the mass-hostage situations in 1995 and 1996.

THE MASS HOSTAGE CRISIS AT LIMA

On 17 December 1996 14 terrorists belonging to the MRTA seized the Japanese ambassador's residence in Lima during a diplomatic reception. They took 500 hostages, including high-ranking members of the Peruvian government, diplomats and Japanese businessmen, in addition to the Japanese ambassador and members of his staff. Eight US officials were among the hostages held when the ambassador's residence was seized, but they were released after five days – an indication that, for once, the US government was not the terrorists' target.

The MRTA is a Marxist revolutionary group that was formed in 1983, inspired by the example of Castro's Cuba, bitterly anti-American, and aiming to destabilise and topple the Peruvian government.[34] Unlike Sendero Luminoso, it has primarily used the methods of urban guerrilla warfare and cultivated close links with other Marxist revolutionary groups in the region. It takes its name from Tupac Amaru II, executed by the Spanish after leading the 1780 Indian revolt. In the 1980s most MRTA attacks appear to have been aimed at property. But since 1992 they have killed policemen, soldiers and civilians, including a Peruvian businessman who refused to pay a large ransom after they kidnapped him in Lima.[35]

The demands of the MRTA in the Lima siege were for the release of over 300 of their gaoled comrades, an improvement in prison conditions and changes in Peru's economic policies to curtail the involvement of Japanese and other foreign business interests. Their key demand was for the release of their imprisoned comrades. The terrorist movement wanted them to be flown to a jungle hideout where they could then have used them to rebuild their movement, which had been seriously depleted by the action of the Peruvian security forces. They could then continue their struggle.

The Lima siege came as a major shock to President Fujimori and his colleagues. They clearly believed that the MRTA, a smaller and weaker movement than the Sendero Luminoso, had been virtually wiped out by the security forces' capture of key leaders. (It is always dangerous to underestimate the tenacity of 'old' groups and the appeal of well-tried tactics.) President Fujimori was understandably adamant in his refusal to give in to the MRTA's demands. Since 1982 terrorism has cost Peru at least 27,000 lives and an estimated $23 billion. Any release of prisoners under duress would have threatened the stability and survival of the Peruvian economic and political system. After all, Fujimori had won 64 per cent of the vote in the 1995 general election. MRTA had no democratic mandate and is a criminal organisation.

The international community as a whole had a clear interest in backing President Fujimori in his firm stance against the blackmail of the hostage-takers. There is no shadow of doubt that taking diplomats and civilians hostage is a serious violation of international law.[36] The international community could never condone or encourage such crimes. It is therefore not surprising that the Peruvian president received backing from the G7 countries (US, UK, France, Germany, Japan, Canada and Italy) for its firm refusal to give in to the terrorists' key demands. In a significant change of policy the Japanese government gave its support, albeit reluctantly, to this firm policy. (In the 1970 and 1980s Japanese governments facing demands from JRA hostage-takers or hijackers followed an unusually conciliatory policy, meeting ransom demands in order to secure the release of hostages.)[37] In the Lima crisis the Japanese authorities were for the first time made forcibly aware that they had become a key target in the eyes of certain foreign terrorist groups. Moreover, despite its distaste for the use of force, Japan has increasingly come to recognise that appeasement sends dangerous signals to others who might be tempted to use terrorism to attack Japanese targets and who might damage the economic interests of both Japan and its key economic partners.

The Peruvian president wisely played for time by opting for a strategy of patience.[38] Periodic attempts were made to negotiate the safe release of the remaining hostages (reduced to 72 by the end of the siege), but the hostage-takers stuck firmly to their key demand for the release of prisoners. At one stage the Peruvian authorities hoped that they could persuade the terrorists to release their hostages in return for a safe exit to Cuba, which President Fujimori had negotiated. The hostage-takers turned this down and reaffirmed their main demand.

After 126 days, after a long and thorough planning, and frustrated by the lack of any breakthrough in the efforts to gain the release of hostages by peaceful means, President Fujimori decided to send in a military rescue team.[39] It was a brilliant success. Tunnels were constructed beneath the ambassador's residence. Explosive charges were placed in the tunnels and detonated when some of the terrorists were playing football above, and the rescue troops stormed the building. Their careful training and planning, using a mock-up of the building, paid off handsomely. Seventy-one of the 72 hostages were freed and 14 MRTA terrorists, including their leader, were killed. The contribution of advice from elite hostage-rescue units from friendly countries is evident in the outcome. This in no way detracts from the outstanding success of the Peruvian authorities' handling of the situation.

There has been much discussion of the fact that the Japanese government was not consulted before the rescue troops were sent in. While it is true that the Japanese government technically held legal jurisdiction over the territory of the Japanese ambassador's residence, one must take account of the following factors:

- Under the Vienna Convention on Diplomatic Relations the host state (in this case Peru) has a clear responsibility for taking measures to protect the embassy and its staff.

- The Peruvian security forces were the only available force on the ground in the correct location and were fully equipped to undertake a rescue role.

- It was the Peruvian authorities who had most at stake, even more than the Japanese, in a successful outcome. The government had been engaged in a long and bitter war of attrition with terrorists on a scale scarcely imaginable in Japanese experience. From the perspective of President Fujimori the hostage crisis was a threat to his whole policy of the eradication of terrorism and hence a threat to the stability and survival of Peru's economy and political system.

- It was essential to achieve total surprise against the terrorists. Had there been wider international consultation on a rescue plan, details might have been leaked and the whole rescue plan jeopardised.

KIDNAPPINGS IN IRAQ AND GAZA 2004–05

Between spring 2004 and spring 2005 there were over 260 kidnappings of foreigners in Iraq. Criminal gangs took advantage of the endemic instability and lack of basic law and order to kidnap for ransom. Criminal gangs that seized foreigners often sold them on to the extremist groups such as Zarqawi's Al Qaeda in Iraq, which wanted to use hostage-taking as a political weapon in order to terrorise foreigners into leaving the country, both to show their supporters that they could inflict blows on the 'enemy' and also, above all, to blackmail foreign governments into withdrawing their troops and civilian contractors from Iraq.

One might have thought that it would be difficult to add any cruel refinements to the kidnapping tactics so fully deployed in other conflict situations (for example in Colombia, Lebanon and the Philippines), but the political terrorists in Iraq exceeded even the cruellest of those recent hostage-taking events. In order to maximise the fear and suffering of their victims' families and communities, and the victims themselves, they issued video images of the hostages dressed in Guantanamo-style orange jumpsuits pleading for their lives and then carried out their threats to kill them by beheading the hostages and showing pictures of the beheadings being carried out.

A terrorist murder that caused great outrage in the UK and internationally was the beheading of a British hostage named Ken Bigley, a civilian contractor, by the Tawhid and Jihad Group, led by Zarqawi, leader of Al Qaeda in Iraq.

One of the kidnappings that caused particular outrage not only internationally but in Iraq itself was the abduction of Mrs Margaret Hassan. Margaret Hassan had joint British, Irish and Iraqi citizenship, was married to an Iraqi and had a record of years of dedicated humanitarian aid to Iraqi people through Care International, a respected humanitarian nongovernmental organisation (NGO). In spite of numerous passionate pleas for her release from Iraqis, from Muslim organisations and from the governments of Britain, Ireland and all EU member states, and from the UN, the terrorists refused to release her and then killed her. The readiness of Al Qaeda and its affiliated extremist groups to seize aid workers indicates another worrying trend and makes it difficult for humanitarian NGOs to deploy staff to the very troubled areas where their skills and commitment are so needed.

Another widely reported hostage-taking occurred in Gaza in December 2005 where Ms Kate Burton was employed as a human rights worker for the Al Mezan Centre for Human Rights. Ms Burton was accompanied by her parents when she was seized, and all three were held hostage by a terrorist group calling itself the Mujaheddin Brigades, Jerusalem Branch, a previously unknown group. It is truly ironic that Kate Burton is a passionate supporter of the Palestinian cause.

Fortunately the combined pressure of the Palestinian Authority, the militant Palestinian groups, including Hamas and the al-Aqsa Martyrs Brigade, resulted in the release of Ms Burton and her parents. It was clear from Ms Burton's interviews with the press after her release that she wanted to continue with her humanitarian work, but felt understandably angry and betrayed by the militant group that inflicted such an ordeal, albeit brief, on her and her parents.

Meanwhile the German authorities faced another complication from a hostage-taking, that of Ms Ostoff, an archaeologist working in Iraq. She was released, it is alleged, by the payment of a considerable ransom, yet she stated her intention to stay on working in Iraq, clearly placing herself in danger of a replay of the hostage-taking. This prospect has clearly caused some alarm in Germany and more widely. It may be that this is yet another argument for resisting the payment of ransoms, a practice that we know from experience gives massive encouragement to terrorists to take further hostages.

CONCLUSION

Terrorist hostage-taking presents democratic governments and law enforcement agencies with acute dilemmas. The tactic of mass hostage-taking has now been sometimes used—as in Spain and Fiji—to overthrow elected governments. Fragile, ethnically divided democracies are particularly at risk. Because of the high value we place on each individual life there is a natural urge to concede to terrorist demands in order to save the lives of hostages. But suppose that by so readily giving in to terrorist blackmail we encourage more hostage-taking, putting more lives at risk? Very often terrorists' demands include the release of large numbers of their imprisoned comrades. Would it be morally right to agree to release a large number of terrorists back into circulation when they will then be able to cause more deaths through their campaigns of violence? Sometimes, terrorists demand changes in policy or in the law: is it morally right to make such changes to appease the terrorists and in so doing ignore the will of the legislature, the courts and the democratic process? Governments, unlike families and private business organisations, have responsibilities to the whole of society. In a hostage crisis involving one of their embassies abroad they have a duty not only to the unfortunate victims of this particular incident but also to the staff in other embassies that could be the targets of such incidents and to those who in the future might be at higher risk if potential hostage-takers can see that the government has caved in to ransom demands on previous occasions. If the US government had not upheld the 'no ransom' policy in respect of its diplomats during the 1970s it would have been faced with a tidal wave of hostage-taking of diplomatic and consular staff.[40]

Another problem faced by governments dealing with politically motivated hostage-takers or terrorists motivated by religious fanatics is that in some cases the demands of the perpetrators are *expressive* rather than *instrumental*: that is to say, the hostage-taker may simply be giving vent to hate, anger or desire of vengeance rather than aiming to achieve clearly defined tactical goals. Expressive terrorists are particularly difficult to deal with: if their hatred or desire of vengeance if strong enough there is nothing the authorities can do other than try to reach the hostages before they are murdered. In some cases the terrorists may also want to make the ultimate statement of fanatical belief by taking their own lives as well as the lives of the hostages.

A recurrent theme of the hostage crises examined in this chapter has been the importance of careful planning and coordination and high-quality intelligence, as well as expertise in hostage-negotiation, crisis management and tactical response for a successful outcome. The expertise and training required for these tasks cannot be achieved overnight. Therefore it would be the height of folly to allow these specialisms to be abandoned in the name of economy or to become badly run down and out of date. They should be part of the law enforcement and security resources of every democratic country. A crucial requirement is the availability of expert hostage-negotiators and a specialist back-up staff of interpreters, terrorism experts and psychologists, vital in helping crisis managers facing hostage situations with terrorists, many of whom are highly trained and experienced in dealing with the authorities. It is not a job for amateurs, and it is deeply regrettable that many countries have failed to take the business of the selection and training of negotiators seriously. The necessary skills take time to acquire, but states with highly experienced police-negotiator teams are generally willing to provide training facilities for friendly countries. This form of training is not vastly expensive, and it is in the international interest that it should be made available even to the poorest countries, if necessary by making the training courses part of an aid programme.

In most cases it will probably be desirable to use trained police negotiators. The authorities should always be suspicious of private individuals recommending themselves for the job, or external organisations offering their 'good offices' to negotiate. In many cases the real motives behind such offers have much to do with self-publicity or furthering a political agenda rather than a satisfactory and speedy resolution to the hostage crisis.

The negotiator should be selected with great care. He/she must be firm and tough, while also being skilled at building up some rapport with the terrorists and using all available bargaining chips to coax concessions out of them, and to play for time. A good negotiator needs considerable courage, coolness and determination to stand up to the bullying and often brutal aggression of the hostage-takers, and to cope with the considerable stress involved. The job calls for enormous patience and a high degree of intelligence to spot clues to the terrorists' intentions, motives, interpersonal relations and likely tactics and behaviour.

It is also vital for the crisis managers to understand fully the limits of the negotiator's role, and to use the negotiator skilfully. The negotiator is not a decision-maker. He must refer hostage-takers' requests to a higher authority while at the same time building up a working relationship with the terrorists' negotiator and using persuasion and force of personality to get the hostage-takers to release their captives unharmed. The upsurge of hostage-taking of aid workers and other civilians in Iraq, the Gaza Strip and elsewhere in 2004–05 underlines the need for expertise in both hostage negotiation *and* hostage rescue.

As we saw in the case of the Russian hostage crises of 1995–96 the absence of appropriate expertise, training and planning was a crucial factor leading to tragic failures in response. The history of modern terrorism shows that highly trained hostage-rescue commandos and tactical response teams have just as vital a role as highly trained hostage negotiators. It is true that many dangerous hostage situations have been ended without a shot being fired. But, as was clearly demonstrated in the Balcombe Street siege, often the mere knowledge that a highly trained elite armed force could be unleashed against them can have a salutary effect on persuading hostage-takers to release the hostages peacefully. For all these reasons, in my view, urgent attention should be paid to enhancing cooperation among the G8 countries (US, UK, France, Germany, Japan, Canada, Italy and Russia) to improve the training, expertise and planning capabilities of those states that are lagging behind in this field.

But the central lesson for democratic governments on the problems of response to hostage-taking is that prevention is far better than cure. It they wait until a hostage-taking crisis is upon them, they are already too late to avoid a great deal of disruption, damage and the inevitable high risks of decision-making in these agonising circumstances. An effective, proactive counter-terrorism policy, founded upon the highest possible quality of counter-terrorism intelligence, national security coordination and international cooperation, offers the best chance of avoiding such events, or at any rate significantly reducing the chances of their occurrence.

NOTES

1 On hostage taking generally see: Richard Clutterbuck, *Kidnap and Ransom: The Response* (London: Faber, 1978); C. C. Aston, 'Political Hostage-taking in Western Europe: A Statistical Analysis', in L. Z. Freedman and Y. Alexander (eds), *Perspectives on Terrorism* (Wilmington DE, Scholarly Resources 1983); M. S. Miron and A. P. Goldstein, *Hostage* (New York: Pergamon Press, 1979); C. C. Aston, *Governments to Ransom: The Emergency of Political Hostage-taking as a Form of Crisis* (Westport CT: Greenwood Press, 1982); R. D. Crelinsten and D. Szabo, *Hostage Taking* (Lexington MA: Lexington Books, 1979); B. M. Jenkins, J. Johnson and D. Ronfeldt, 'Numbered Lives: Some Statistical Observations from Seventy-seven International Hostage Episodes', *Conflict*, 1: 1 (1978); and C. Moorehead, *Fortune's Hostages: Kidnapping in the World Today* (London: Hamish Hamilton, 1980).

2 See Richard Clutterbuck, *Terrorism in an Unstable World* (London: Routledge, 1994), pp. 172–6.

3 Roberta Wohlstetter, 'Kidnapping to Win Friends and Influence People', *Survey*, 20: 4 (93), p. 2.

4 Ibid.

5   The most authoritative analysis of the earlier phase of diplomatic kidnappings is provided in Edler Baumann, *The Diplomatic Kidnappings* (The Hague: Martinus Nijhoff, 1973). For the later phase see Andrew Selth, *Against Every Human Law: The Terrorist Threat to Diplomacy* (Rushcutters Bay NSW: Australian National University Press, 1988).

6   See: Alfred P. Rubin, 'The Hostage Incident: the United States and Iran', in G. W. Keeton and G. Schwarzenberger (eds), *The Yearbook of World Affairs* (London: Stevens, 1982), pp. 213–40; Francis A. Boyle, 'The United National Charter and the Iranian Hostage Crisis', in H. H Han (ed.), *Terrorism, Political Violence and World Order* (Lanham MD: University Press of America, 1983), pp. 537–58; and Gary Sick, *All Fell Down: America's Tragic Encounter with Iran* (New York: Random House, 1985).

7   See Selth, *Against Every Human Law.*

8   See Aston, *Governments to Ransom.*

9   See Tim Lewis and Josie Brookes, *The Human Shield* (Lichfield: Leomansley Press, 1991).

10 See 'Hope for Hostages: Reaction Force Plans', *The Independent,* 31 May 1995, p. 2 on the problems facing UN peacekeeping troops held hostage by the Bosnian Serbs.

11 For a vivid personal memoir of the failed rescue mission by its leader, see Charlie A. Beckwith and Donald Knox, *Delta Force* (London: Collins/Fontana, 1984).

12 Much of the pressure stemmed from the mass media coverage: see Alex P. Schmid 'Terrorism and the Media', *Terrorism and Political Violence,* 1: 4, pp. 539–65.

13 See: Terry Waite, *Taken on Trust* (Sevenoaks: Hodder & Stoughton, 1993); Brian Keenan, *An Evil Cradling* (London: Hutchinson, 1992); and Terry Anderson, *Den of Lions; Memoirs of Seven Years in Captivity* (Sevenoaks: Hodder & Stoughton, 1994).

14 On the Western governments' handling of the crisis and the key role of Mr Giandomenico Picco, see Magnus Ranstorp, *Hizb'allah in Lebanon: The Politics of the Western Hostage Crisis* (Basingstoke: Macmillan, 1997).

15 For analysis of the Stockholm syndrome see: F. M. Ochberg, 'What is Happening to the Hostages in Tehran?', *Psychiatric Annals,* 10, pp. 186–9; and T. Strentz, 'The Stockholm Syndrome', in D. A. Soskis and F. M. Ochberg (eds), *Victims of Terrorism* (Boulder CO: Westview Press, 1982).

16 See reports on ending of the siege in the *New York Times*, *Washington Post* and *International Herald Tribune*, 23–25 April 1997.

17 For an account of the lessons learned from the Balcombe Street siege, see Clutterbuck, *Kidnap and Ransom*, Chapter 11.

18 See: Valentine Herman and Rob van der Laan Bouma, 'Nationalists Without a Nation: South Moluccan Terrorism in the Netherlands', in J. Lodge (ed.), *Terrorism: A Challenge to the State* (Oxford: Martin Robertson, 1981), pp. 119–46; and Robert Hauben, 'Hostage-Taking: The Dutch Experience', in L. Z. Freedman and Y. Alexander (eds), *Perspectives on Terrorism* (Wilmington DE: Scholarly Resources, 1982).

19 See: Chris Kramer and Sim Harris, *Hostage* (London: John Care Books, 1982); and *Sunday Times* Insight Team, *Siege* (London: Hamlyn, 1980).

20 See George Henderson, 'Murder in the Square', *Middle East International*, 4 May 1984, pp. 4–5.

21 For an analysis of this episode see William F. Slater, 'Terrorist Kidnappings in Colombia', in Brian M. Jenkins (ed.), *Terrorism and Personal Protection* (Boston MA: Butterworth Publishers, 1985), pp. 116–19.

22 See James D. Tabor, *Why Waco? Cults and the Battle for Religious Freedom in America* (Berkeley CA: University of California Press, 1995).

23 See 'Oklahoma Bomb was Revenge for Waco Cult Deaths', *The Times*, 8 February 1997.

24 See Diane Curran, Fiona Hill and Elena Kostrit-Syna, *The Search for Peace in Chechnya: A Sourcebook* (Cambridge MA: Harvard University, Department of Government, 1997), pp. 10–11; also a report by Carlotta Gali and Carey Scott, 'Carnage in Hostage Hospital', *Sunday Times*, 18 June 1995, p. 15.

25 See 'Russia Offers Halt to Chechen War if Hostages are Freed', *The Times*, 19 June 1995.

26 On the criticisms of President Yeltsin's Chechen policy at the G7 summit at Halifax, Nova Scotia, see Martin Fletcher, 'Yeltsin Defends Attack on World Terrorism Center', *The Times*.

27 See: Alan Philips and Robert Fox, 'Chechens Seize 2000 Hostages', *Daily Telegraph*, 10 January 1996; and James Meel and David Hearst, 'Nobody Gets out Alive', *The Guardian*, 10 January 1996.

28 Quoted in Philips and Fox, 'Chechen Seize 2000 Hostages'.

29 See Thomas de Waal and Carlotta Call, 'Villagers See Tanks Blast Their Homes into Rubble, *The Times*, 10 January 1996.

30 The seizure of the ferry lasted four days. The armed Chechen sympathisers, who had been holding 170 hostages, surrendered peacefully to Turkish security forces on 19 January 1996.

31 See: Aledsandr Lebed, 'How I made Peace with the Chechens', *The Times*, 10 October 1996; and Richard Beeston, 'Chechen Success Boosts Lebed's Poll Popularity', *The Times*, 30 December 1996.

32 See Richard Beeston, 'Troop Withdrawal Seals Moscow's Chechnya Debacle', *The Times*, 30 December 1996.

33 BBC's *Horizon* TV programme carried out a detailed investigation of the Moscow theatre siege and gathered valuable expert opinions from scientists in a number of countries on the mystery of the gas used by the Russians.

34 For commentary on the MRTA, see Mary Powers, 'Latin American Diehard Rebels Press on Despite Cold War Thaw', Reuters, 1 January 1992, and 'Death of Americans Underscores Risks of Drug War', Reuters, 22 January 1992.

35 See *Patterns of Global Terrorism*, US Department of State, annual report, 1993. Articles on Reuters news website.

36 See, for example, UN Convention Against the Taking of Hostages (1978) and the UN Convention on the Prevention of Punishment of Crimes against Internationally Protected Persons, Including Diplomatic Agents (1973).

37 See Taiji Miyaoke, 'Terrorist Crisis Management in Japan: Historical Development and Changing Response', *Terrorism and Political Violence*, 10: 2 (summer 1998).

38 On the strategic options during the Lima hostage crisis, see Paul Wilkinson, 'Beleaguered in Lima', *Times Higher Educational Supplement*, 21 February 1997.

39 See reports on the ending of the siege in the *New York Times*, *Washington Post* and *International Herald Tribune*, 23–25 April 1997.

40 The position of employees of corporations is somewhat different, however. For a clear analysis of the pros and cons of allowing corporations to pay ransoms for the release of hostages, see Brian Jenkins, *Should Corporations Be Prevented from Paying Ransom?* (Santa Monica CA: RAND Corporation, 1974).

POST-READING QUESTIONS AND ACTIVITIES

Answer the following questions to help you fully understand the Unit 4 readings:

- Think of a recent negotiation situation that you dealt with in an organizational or school situation that involved conflict.
  - Was it beneficial or harmful?
  - How was it resolved, and how could you have handled it differently?

- Examine the five strategies for handling conflict. Which do you tend to use more often, and why?
  - Would another approach be more useful in certain situations, and why?

- Examine one of the hostage situations discussed in Chapter 20, or select one of your own.
  - Critique how it was resolved and particularly the planning and coordination procedures of the team trying to save the hostages

- In three to four pages, analyze a negotiation you have participated in or are familiar with.
  - Describe the situation, assess the strategies used and their effectiveness, and make recommendations for handling a similar situation in the future. This can be from a business, school, political, or sports situation.

CPSIA information can be obtained
at www.ICGtesting.com
Printed in the USA
BVHW08s0844210818
524959BV00002B/19/P